IT'S ALL OVER NOW

MANDY SMITH

with

Andy Coulson and Ingrid Millar

BLAKE

Published by Blake Publishing Ltd,
98-100 Great North Road, London N2 0NL, England

First published in Great Britain in 1993

ISBN 1 85782 0444

British Library Cataloguing-in-Publication Data:
A catalogue record for this book is available from
the British Library.

Typeset by BMD Graphics, Hemel Hempstead

Printed in Finland by WSOY

1 3 5 7 9 10 8 6 4 2

Dedication

This book is dedicated to every woman and girl who has
suffered abuse – sexual, emotional and psychological – at
the hands of a man.

To my dearest Pat (Reggie), Mum, Nic (Cola),
Aunt Pauline, Dr Dalton and the dear Lord God above,
and to Andy Coulson, Ingrid Millar, 'Pud' Kelvin
MacKenzie, Stuart Higgins and thanks to
the *Sun* newspaper.

"That which does not kill us makes us stronger . . ."

FRIEDRICH NIETZSCHE

Contents

CHAPTER ONE

The Early Years

I never knew my father. He'd gone by the time I was three.

My earliest memories are all of Mum. I don't really remember Dad being around at all. She was very sick. She was so ill all the time. She was virtually bedridden from the time I was five. Nobody really knew what was wrong with her – least of all Mum, but she suffered from violent allergies that would, quite literally leave her gasping for breath, fighting for her life. She could eat very little and, even to me, at five, she seemed so tiny and frail, so pale and lovely and delicate, lying there in the bed.

Countless doctors attended to her but none of them could find a cure for this incapacitating illness. There were plenty of scares, though, naturally, none of them were meant to reach my ears. However, I can clearly recall one cold, bleak night, listening at the keyhole to hushed voices behind Mum's bedroom door.

The doctor was saying, 'I'm sorry, Patsy, there is nothing more we can do for you.'

There was talk, too, of strange diseases with names I never understood, like multiple sclerosis and chronic asthma and all sorts of words that put the fear of death into me.

Many, many times I thought Mum might die. I used to pray to God every night before I went to bed: 'Please God, forgive me for fighting with Nicola and making a hole in my socks and please, please, please make Mum better. I promise I will be good for the rest of my life if you can just manage that for me.' And in the morning when I awoke, the first thought that entered my head was always the same: 'I hope Mum's all right today.'

She was so brave. She never moaned or complained. She just accepted that she was unwell and refused to let it get her down. She wasn't bitter or depressed – at least, she never showed it to us.

Sometimes, though, I would go into her room quietly when she was asleep and would find her lying there with a hankie in her hand, all wet. Once there were tears on her cheeks, not yet

1

dried. That broke my heart. Mum had so much pain but she kept it to herself.

I also knew that not everyone cared about her, not in the way that I did. Not everyone really believed she was so ill. When they couldn't find out the cause of her illness, some doctors said it wasn't real, as if she was making it up, as if it was all in Mum's head. I hated them for that. They didn't see her like I did, lying there day after day, hardly able to move or even to breathe sometimes. That was real, all right.

There were times when, young as I was, I used to feel that no one really understood. It was just Mum, Nic and me against the world.

Mum's bedroom was her sanctuary – and mine. It was comforting, in a way, to walk in and know that she would always be there, so pale against the white sheets, with her hair spread out over the pillow. I would slip in beside her and curl up against her, feeling her warmth. Sometimes we would say nothing and just lie there. I would listen to her breathing and feel her heart beating against my cheek. Sometimes I would count the beats of her heart and think how much I loved her. Mum was all we had.

I never wanted to burden her with anything. It wouldn't have been fair. What could Mum do about me having a fight with the boy next door, or me ripping my best dress climbing over the fence down the road? I guess I tried to protect her from any pain or nuisance as far back as I can remember. I was desperate never to upset her for fear it would make her condition worse. I wanted to look after her. She was the most important, lovely person in the world.

Nicola was two years older than me and, really, between us, we had to do everything ourselves. We started going to school on our own when I was five. That wasn't a great problem for us. We had never known anything different, so we settled into it, as kids do. Anyway, life was different then. Kids could do things like play on the streets and go to school on their own. It was safer. It was an age of innocence. It never entered anyone's head that there might be some demented stranger waiting round the corner to pounce on unsuspecting children. There was no massive unemployment, no street violence or brutality. At least, I was never aware of any where we lived.

We'd walk down the road to the bus stop every morning and a coach would pick us up to take us to school. I used to feel so sad about that sometimes. I'd see the other kids being dropped off and picked up from school by their parents and wished I could be like that too. Sometimes I felt like crying because I wanted Mum to be standing there at the school gates, waiting for me. But I got over that. I'd meet up with Nicola in the playground, we would team up to go home together and it would be all right. At least there were two of us.

I didn't feel sorry for myself. I just felt sorry for Mum. She was the one who was helpless and alone all day long.

Sports days and prizegivings were lonely occasions, though, and I used to dread them coming around because I'd have no one there to watch me. I remember one end-of-year prizegiving – I suppose I was five or six years old – looking round the audience and everyone I knew was sitting there with their mum and dad next to them and I was on my own. Loneliness is a horrible, empty feeling. You feel different to everyone else. I got a big lump in my throat and the tears were piling up behind my eyes. Then I thought of Mum back at home in her sick bed and my tears were for her, not me.

School outings were the worst. The other kids would all take their parents and it would be more like a family outing than a school trip. They'd all be skipping along, holding their mums' hands and laughing. Their mums would buy them a cold drink and an ice cream. Their mums would tell them things about what we saw. If I wanted a drink, I had to ask the teacher if I could go to the toilet and get some water from the tap.

I had no one to ask questions except the teachers and they would either give a lecture on the subject or tell me to save the questions for later, back in the classroom. They didn't mean to be unkind but they were teachers, after all.

At times like that I used to feel as though I was standing outside life, looking in, with my nose pressed up against a wall of glass. I could look, but I couldn't get in, couldn't be like them. I couldn't get inside the glass where every little girl had a dad and a healthy happy mum.

That sense of aloneness used to give me a real, physical pain in my chest. It was like having a hole where my heart should have been.

3

I wanted my mum there with me, just to hold my hand but it was impossible, so I'd take the day off and spend it at home with her instead.

I guess I developed a kind of resilience even at that age. I learned never to expect much from other people. Love and warmth came from your mum but if she couldn't be with you, then you just had to get on with things on your own. And it wasn't as if I was totally on my own. It was the same for Nicola too.

However, there was one outing that I really begged Mum to try to come on. It was to the Victoria and Albert Museum in London. I desperately wanted to go because I was fascinated by historical dress and I knew they had some wonderful Victorian costumes on display. I wanted Mum to see them with me. I pleaded and pleaded and, in the end, she said OK, she'd try to come.

The night before the trip, I said a special prayer, promising God I would be good forever and nice to Nicola and the horrible kids next door and even the grumpy old man down the road who used to swear at us for riding our bikes through his allotment – anything – just so long as Mum was able to come with me on this trip.

The next morning I was up at first light. The anticipation was like Christmas coming. I'd hardly been able to sleep a wink all night. I was almost scared to go into Mum's room for fear that she'd have woken up unwell but there she was, up and dressed and ready herself. She said, 'I promised I wouldn't let you down, Mandy, and I won't.'

I was so pleased and excited. I wanted to show her off to all the other children in the class. Nobody had a mum as great as mine. I was so proud of her and they'd never even seen her. Finally, we set off on our great adventure, just the two of us. I felt ten feet tall walking down the road with that rarest of all treats – my hand in Mum's.

First we had to take a tube to Kensington where the V&A was. I was as excited at the thought of going on the underground as anything else. I clutched Mum's hand like it was the most precious thing in the world, which of course, to me, it was.

Mum was all right until we got into the tube station. I was so thrilled that, for the first time since she'd become ill I'd actually

4

got her with me, I didn't notice at first that she was having a bad turn. She was trying desperately to control it but as we went down the escalator to the platform, she suddenly started to shiver uncontrollably.

Then she collapsed and fell to her knees on the escalator. I felt a sudden surge of panic in my throat but I grabbed hold of her and held her up. I was saying, 'It's all right Mum, you're going to be all right.'

We got to the bottom and she sat down on a bench with her head between her knees. Gradually the dizziness cleared and she sat there looking at me, saying, 'I'm so sorry, Mandy.'

Suddenly, the stupid trip wasn't important any more. I just wanted to get Mum back home where she would be safe in bed. I put my arms round her and told her it really, really didn't matter. The one thing I didn't want her to feel was sorry that she had let me down. She hadn't. She never did. So we blew out the school trip and went home. It was sad but not for me. It was sad for Mum who could never join in things with the children she loved. All I wanted in life was to look after her, make sure she never came to any harm and never had to force herself into a situation like that again. I was seven at the time.

Nobody else understood. If it wasn't the doctors or even Mum's own family thinking that her illness was all in her head, then it was the neighbours thinking we were all mad – or bad – whichever was the worse. They simply didn't like us. We didn't fit in. Mum wasn't physically able to go and sit in someone else's living room drinking tea and bitching about the folk in the next street, like the rest of them. Not that she would have anyway; she simply wasn't that kind of person.

So she became an obvious target. Behind her back, they called her names and gossiped about her. She was a very pretty young woman, on her own with two little kids. She was a threat to all the married women on the estate. They all thought she fancied their husbands.

The truth was that they all fancied her and, naturally, that caused a lot of resentment locally.

Mum refused to retaliate. She knew what was being said about her – totally without justification – but she wouldn't rise to the bait, even if she had had the energy to do so.

After what happened with Dad, she got used to going it

alone. She knew that, when the chips were down, it was up to her. She couldn't turn to the neighbours for help with the shopping or repairs around the house. She knew she couldn't lean on anyone else, so she kept herself to herself. What was wrong with that?

There were some *real* women of dubious morals down the street, other single mums, who had men coming and going at all times of the day and night but no one ever called them a tart. They stuck together. Mum was out on a limb. She held to her own principles and shut them out – just Mum, Nic and me against the world.

Even our religion set us apart. Mum had been brought up in the Catholic faith and always had a strong belief in God. Despite her illness, she always had faith that basic human goodness would see us through. She brought us up to be religious and to have faith in a greater power.

She had insisted that we attend a convent school and, prior to her illness, had always made sure we went to church and Sunday school on a regular basis. After she became ill, of course, we couldn't go to church on Sunday any more because Mum couldn't get out of the house. That was a most convenient situation for the neighbourhood gossips. They all thought we were complete hypocrites who didn't care.

Being the target for all this local vitriol could have hurt Nic and me very much, but Mum knew what they were saying and she would tell us, 'Never mind them. We know what we are. Just mind your own.'

So, in a way, Nic and I assumed responsibility for the family unit. It fell to us to do the cleaning, the shopping and the cooking – easy stuff like spaghetti on toast, fish fingers and beans, sometimes chips. Believe me, it was no great hardship. Perhaps if we had been boys we'd have resented the domesticity that was foisted upon us so early but for two girls it was fun, like being grown-ups. We enjoyed playing mum, playing nurse, playing big people – for real.

It had its dangerous moments, however. When I was seven, we had a near catastrophe, when I was cooking sausages one night and the grill caught fire. There I was in my pinny, gaily turning over the bangers one minute and in the next, when I turned my back, the cooker became a replica of the Towering Inferno.

Luckily, I had the good sense to dial 999 instead of pouring water on the blaze or trying to suffocate it with a wodge of kitchen roll. I guess even then I had a kind of inbuilt survival guide.

The Fire Brigade arrived within minutes and some very patient, and probably very perturbed firemen, seeing that they had to caution a seven-year-old, explained that some fat on the grill had caught fire and ignited the cooker. I was not so much shocked as deeply fed-up. It took me ages to clean the kitchen.

Mum would try to cook sometimes but as soon as the food was on the table she'd have to go back up to bed, feeling faint and sick. The slightest thing would set her off, such as strong smells or eating anything at all. She lived on eggs and lentil soup.

Sometimes, for apparently no reason, she'd suddenly come over faint, her temperature would shoot through the roof and she would collapse, breathing very fast. It was incredibly distressing at first but in the way that children do, we very quickly adjusted to things. Although, initially, we thought that Mum was going to die, we soon realised that if we could get her to bed, in a quiet place with all the windows open, she would fall asleep and wake up better again later. She just had to lie down and rest for a few hours and it would pass – until the next time.

If she needed anything, she would bang on the bedroom floor with a slipper and I'd go up to see what she wanted. I never resented having to trek up and down the stairs to get her a drink of water or anything else. I loved the sound of that thump on the floorboards. It meant she was alive.

From the age of seven years old, I did virtually all the housework. Quite simply, I had to, otherwise it wouldn't get done. Nicola was dead messy and left things everywhere. Mess simply did not bother her but I couldn't stand it. I had a huge thing about cleaning and being tidy.

It might not be a mansion, but our maisonette was a palace compared to the options, so Mum used to say. She had never forgotten how, after Dad walked out, leaving her with a mountain of bills, we'd had notice to quit from our rented flat.

She'd walked the streets for days, banging on doors, tapping up friends for a floor for us to sleep on, until she found this place and she wouldn't have anyone knock it.

Morant Place was on a new council estate. It was clean and respectable. So, maybe it wasn't Cheyne Walk but it was a whole lot better than a hostel for the homeless.

Until she became too ill to do it herself, she'd always been immensely houseproud, so I stepped into the breach – Mandy Smith, Mini-housewife of the Year, aged seven. I'd dust and polish every room from top to bottom each week, even inside the drawers and cupboards. Nothing missed my eagle eye. I had a big thing about the balcony. I thought having a balcony was the bees' knees. I'd go out there and gaze up into the sky over north London and dream my huge dreams about one day having my own aeroplane and taking off on adventures to another country – like Spain. The balcony was my safe haven, where I could tuck myself away in my dream world.

Later, it was to be my safe haven to sneak off to for a sly ciggie where Mum couldn't find me. One way or another, it never lost its allure for me. I would sweep it religiously every day, so that it wouldn't look dusty – not the easiest of tasks, given the dirt in the London air. I would even scrub it down once a week; Old Mother Riley would have been proud of me.

I also had a major fetish about sunlight. The windows had to be sparkling. I'd do the insides of the panes myself and get a window cleaner to come and do the outsides. Personally, I was up for doing the outsides too, but one day Mum caught me hanging out of the bedroom window practically holding on by my teeth, trying to wash the far corners with a sopping duster on a stick, so she put the kibosh on that.

I suppose it was a bit odd, two little girls running the Smith home and one of them with an obsession of the first order about housewifery, but it didn't really bother us. It was what we were used to.

Sometimes I'd see other families and wish we could be like them, with a dad and a healthy mum but, gradually, I stopped wanting a dad; he really didn't figure in our lives. I just wished Mum was better. Apart from that the three of us got on fine on our own.

We did have the odd disaster though. Once a friend of Mum's popped round to visit and brought a friend of hers with her – a man we didn't know. Mum couldn't cope with smoke fumes in the house, so they went out on to the balcony to have a ciggie.

8

Meanwhile, I walked into the living room and thought it was pretty draughty so I closed the French doors to the balcony. The man didn't notice they were shut and, after he had smoked his cig, he turned round abruptly and walked straight through them. There was this huge crash and shattered glass everywhere.

I was sitting about six feet away, watching television when shards of glass came flying at me and the noise was horrendous, like a clap of thunder right over my head. I screamed and screamed, an instant childish reaction – and then screamed even more as I saw this bloodied, wounded figure fall to the floor at my feet. Nicola rushed in and took charge, trying to stem the flow of blood from a gaping wound in the man's head while I frantically dialled for an ambulance. Poor Mum thought the world had caved in but she couldn't get downstairs. I had to rush up and tell her what had happened. The poor chap ended up in hospital where he received several stitches and developed a firm resolution never to visit the booby-trapped Smith household ever again.

After Mum got over the shock, she said, as cool as you like, 'Right, sack the window cleaner. At least if they're dirty no one's going to walk through the damn things.' She must have been fairly unhappy about someone being virtually decapitated in our home, not to mention the cost of repairing the French doors and having a howling gale blasting through the entire house until they were boarded up but she still managed to laugh. It's always been the Smith family's saving grace – the ability to have a giggle even when disaster is staring us in the face.

You laugh more easily when you're flat on your back, both literally and metaphorically. That was a lesson I learnt early from Mum. I can recommend it to anyone.

Laughs apart, it really wasn't easy for her, lying there in her sick bed, watching life – with its many and varied catastrophes when Nic and I were around – pass her by while she was powerless to do anything about it.

Money, too, was always a major worry. Mum received only £47 a week in benefits to live on. After the rent was paid there was only £30 for the bills and to feed and clothe us all. Yet I never felt we went short. We never went hungry and we were always dressed nicely. Mum always made sure we looked smart. She refused to have people look at us as if we were paupers.

She taught me the value of having respect for the way you look and the clothes you wear.

We always had a nice present at Christmas. When I was ten I got a bike. At eleven, I had a pair of roller skates. I loved them to bits and never took them off. I even used to wear them to go upstairs to bed. I would go clattering up the stairs, sounding like a herd of elephants and making enough noise to waken the dead, but Mum never complained even when she was poorly. As long as we were happy, she was happy. She thought that the sight of me in my nightdress, with my roller skates welded to my feet, was hilarious.

There were sad moments, though, when I realised that we really were not, and probably never would be, the picture-postcard, perfect happy family. The saddest thing for us was on Christmas Day when Mum couldn't eat a proper Christmas dinner. I used to long for us all to be able to sit down round a table groaning with roast turkey and all the trimmings and just feast ourselves on food and Happy Families but it never happened. Dad would always manage to visit us at some point during the day. I don't remember the atmosphere being strained. Both he and Mum wanted it to be a special day for Nic and me, so there were never any arguments – nor any overt antipathy between them.

I wasn't aware of it being sad in any way, but Dad obviously was. Christmas was when he felt the loss of his family more than at any other time. Sometimes he would bring us a present, sometimes a card with a fiver in it. There was usually a tear in his eye when he left. He knew that, by walking away from us all those years before, he had shut himself out. He would never really be part of our family. We didn't need him. We'd learnt to survive on our own. It may sound hard but by then I already really didn't miss him. What you sow in life, you later reap. He'd left. He'd lost us. It was his choice.

I suppose we missed his presence in some ways – most probably the discipline, because dads are supposed to be the ones with authority in the family. I was always a bit of a rebel when it came to facing up to authority. If Dad had been around to implement that kind of respect while we were young, things might have been different.

As it was, I used to get up to some terrible tricks. I was

particularly keen on dancing for a while and really fancied myself as a bit of an Olivia Newton John, shimmying down with John Travolta in *Grease*. I was mad on tap-dancing in particular and used to practise regularly in a pair of clumpy shoes on the wooden dining table – until the day, quite out of the blue, Dad unexpectedly walked in and caught me!

I also flirted with a bit of smoking when I was around nine. My cousin Kim and I would go out on the balcony for a sneaky fag while Mum was upstairs in bed. Mum's bedroom window was right over us, so Kim would keep a lookout while I had a puff.

There was no discipline about when we went to bed. Well, for a start there was no one to put us to bed and I was one of those hideously hyper little kids, always on the move, into everything, the sort every mother dreads. I used to get a second wind, a sort of burst of manic energy, around nine at night so I'd never be in bed much before eleven o'clock, even when I was seven or eight. Yet despite all the naughtiness and all the things we missed out on from a so-called 'normal' childhood, they were happy, halcyon days.

There were lots of kids on the estate and we all played together in the courtyard or down at the dump. That was our favourite. Lots of dust and grime, piles of discarded household rubbish and the odd, abandoned settee made for a brilliant kids' base. We'd escape down there, far away from prying adult eyes and just lark around in gangs.

We had to share the dump with a colony of cats who seemed to breed on a daily basis. We were forever finding stray wild kittens, really scraggy, flea-ridden little things. I'd take them home to show poor Mum, who'd be horrified. There she was, allergic to everything and this horrible daughter would bring back scraggy moggies and dump them on her bed. Just what the doctor didn't order! I'd feed them in the kitchen on all the leftover scraps or, more likely, my own dinner, hug and cuddle them for a bit, then take them back to fend for themselves after a bit of five-star treatment.

I was definitely mischievious but I don't think I was very naughty, not compared to some of the other local kids. Plenty of them were seriously into shoplifting from a very young age. I almost fell into it too but my good Catholic schooling and the thought of how horrified Mum would be if she knew, held me back.

I did succumb to the odd foray, of course, just to fall in line with the rest of the gang and not lose face as a wimp. I used to go into the corner shop, buy two Blackjack chews for a penny and pocket a handful at the same time. However, I was a coward at heart. A liberal dose of Catholic guilt was too high a price to pay for a jawful of black toffee so that was about the extent of my pilfering, while the other kids were venturing into Kray-style knocking-off. The man in the shop knew I was at it but he never said anything.

I stopped forever, though, when I got into serious shoplifting – just the once. Neighbours took us into the West End for a treat – a big day out – and I promptly ruined it all by stealing a little eraser that slipped over the end of a pencil. I felt so guilty afterwards that I threw it away down by the garages. That, and a few Hail Marys, put me to rights.

There's no doubt that my Roman Catholic upbringing had a huge effect on me. From stealing to sex, it left its mark – and its scars. I felt I could never do anything bad. The nuns at school and the priests in church had indoctrinated me that if I ever put a foot out of line, hellfire and brimstone would be waiting round the next corner. Personally, I always felt I would rather walk through that, in bare feet if necessary, rather than live with the guilt.

The strict moral code was to stand me in good stead when it came to my next sin – sex.

Apart from my addiction to housework and my lasting love affair with dressing up, I'd been a proper little tomboy as a young girl. I was the first one to shin up the highest tree. I was the little bruiser in the middle of the scrum when the boys had a kickabout. When it came to larking around, I was well and truly one of the lads, probably the most laddish of them all but, imperceptibly, and I can't put my finger on exactly why, one day things changed.

I suppose I first became aware of boys as a separate species when I was around eight years old. Nicola, startlingly pretty and, by then, pubescent, paved the way. She was ten and she started going out with a boy called Peter Bromley, who was very good looking.

She would go down to the dump to meet up with him for a good old snogging session and, naturally, I would be tagging along behind her. So, in order to distract this boring kid sister, she shoved his kid brother Simon at me. He was my age – eight years old – and I remember looking at this snotty-nosed little kid, thinking, 'Great, I get the ugly one!'

In actual fact, I wasn't that fussy to begin with. Ugly Simon was my first kiss. The momentous occasion took place down by the garages in Morant Place and I only did it for a dare.

One of our favourite pastimes was playing a game called Truth, Dare, Doubledare, Love, Kiss or Promise. When it came to my turn that day, I was facing Snotty Simon and, yes, I got stuck with a kiss. I remember thinking, 'Yuk. I can't see why they make all that fuss about it on the telly.'

Mind you, it can't have been that bad, because pretty soon I was up for it again. I met another boy, Gary Quinten, who was about ten, and started going out with him. This kissing lark was no worse than playing doctors and nurses and a whole lot better than eating school semolina or so I thought until I met his big brother Stacey who was twelve and better-looking. I dumped Gary and went out with Stacey instead. Now, kissing him *was* exciting. I had leap-frogged three years to join the twelve-year-olds in their learning-sex games. I felt quite on a level with them. In my book, I reckoned I was much more mature than the rest of my nine-year-old pals so I naturally gravitated towards the older boys. I inevitably fancied Nicola's boyfriends who were eleven or twelve. To me, super-sophisticate that I was not but wished I was, boys my age were just babyish and silly. I most certainly was not giggling and prattish like them.

In some ways, I always wanted to be older than my years. Perhaps it was the responsibility of looking after Mum and our home, perhaps it was a quest to find someone older to look after *me*, but I always wanted to play with the big girls – and especially with the big boys.

Around that time, I first realised that I was attractive. I already knew I was pretty; I could see that in the mirror and all Mum's family had produced beautiful little girls. My cousins, by now in their teens, were all stunners so there was never anything to be smug about. I was simply one of the pretty family females and, as the youngest, way behind the others in the appeal stakes. There was no chance of becoming big-headed or vain.

Outside the family, however I was rapidly becoming rated as a 'looker'. Now, suddenly, I saw what that meant to boys. I was in the second to last year at primary school and most of the boys in my class, and the class above, began to make noises that they fancied me. That's when I started to have a bad time with the other girls who did not take kindly to this little upstart who was beginning to draw all the male attention round our way, especially when they wanted a slice of it themselves.

Kids of that age have no concept of what beauty really means. They don't know that looks are transitory, looks are superficial – and that good looks can get you into all kinds of bother. I didn't know it myself, come to that. All they knew was that the boys liked me more than them – instant alienation for me.

However, there was one other key factor that served to distance me even more from the other girls. I wore make-up and had done since I was seven. It did not seem unnatural or precocious to me at all. Make-up and costume had always fascinated me, ever since I could remember. My favourite shop had always been the chemist – nuts to the sweet shop or the toy shop. Whenever I got any pocket money or money from an auntie or uncle, I went straight to the chemist and bought eyeliner, eyeshadow and lipstick.

My favourite present ever was a 'Girl's World' set, which I was given at the age of seven. It was a life-size doll's head, accompanied by a full set of make-up to practise with. It sounds horrendous; in fact, it *was* horrendous but I loved that decapitated plastic head with a vengeance.

I was also very fashion-conscious. At ten, I became a Punk. I wore my hair all spiky and used to dye it purple, blue and red with food-colouring. It was harmless but it certainly managed to upset a few people.

The neighbours all tut-tutted briskly when I walked past in all my finery, masquerading – or so I thought – as a glamorous superstar. Move over ordinary Mandy Smith, schoolgirl; in Dreamland I was transformed into Mandi, a glamorous and exotic creature of the catwalk, Miss World-in-the-making. Others, with a sad lack of such colourful imagination, failed to see this extraordinary transformation.

Sometimes my appearance generated a furore at school. I certainly must have brightened up dull mornings for many a teacher bored out of their brain. I went through a phase where I did my hair in tiny Rasta plaits with coloured beads. The teachers didn't half look at me strangely then. I really went to town for the end-of-term school disco when I slid into a pair of skintight, black satin trousers and a tiny pink satin vest. I suppose it was a rather revealing little number, even though my budding breasts were no bigger at that time than bee stings. Mum insisted I wore a cardigan over it to attain some level of decency. I was extremely upset, principally because the cardigan was blue and clashed with my outfit, but I always did what Mum said. So, on the day of the disco, I was sitting in assembly in this outfit when the headmaster suddenly broke off his daily sermon to say in a *most* disturbed voice: 'Miss Smith, will you stand up please. And *what* exactly are you wearing?'

He made me stand up and pirouette in front of the entire school. He thought it would be the height of humiliation but, frankly, he simply wasn't on the same planet as Mandi Smith, megastar. I thought I looked perfectly fine, thank you very much – apart from the cardigan . . .

CHAPTER TWO

The Butterfly has a Ball

I was always a precocious child, ahead of my years, probably because of the responsibility I had taken on so young, looking after Mum and the home. That was not a problem for me. I was never aware that it was a great weight on little shoulders. To me it never seemed like a burden. It was just something that had to be done and there was no one to do it except Nicola and me.

Nicola was a very different spirit. She was much more fun-loving and carefree. She didn't care if the house was a mess or there was no dinner in the oven. She lived in her own world of fun and games and relished the freedom that came from having no disciplinary figures around. She would take every opportunity to run off and play with her pals, zoom home, throw her wet, dirty clothes on the flooor, change and run out again.

To me, this was mayhem. I simply couldn't go out to play if the house was not clean and tidy and Mum settled in bed. There were things to be *done* before fun, but maybe I had my own way of compensating for the adult role I'd assumed so young.

When I had finished the household chores and given myself permission to go out and play, I went for it. I wanted to enjoy myself and woe betide anyone who tried to rein me in. I felt I had earned my right to do what I wanted. I did not resent looking after Mum or our home, not in the slightest. It gave me huge satisfaction to see our home gleaming from top to bottom and to have done something for my mother who was not able to do much for herself, yet who gave me so much in terms of love.

However, the flipside of this little angel was that, when I was out and away from those daughterly duties, I was a free spirit, in other words, a right little rebel – not in terms of being a hooligan, lobbing stones at greenhouses or sniffing glue, nothing like that, but I wasn't being told what, or what not, to do by anyone, oh no!

I felt like a mini-grown-up because of all the adult things I did around the home, so I wasn't going to put up with adults treating me like a silly litle girl. I always refused to let anyone patronise me, particularly people in authority. Maybe I had what might be labelled today 'an attitude problem' but I was not downright insolent, or even cheeky to people like teachers or policemen or the shopholders who used to keep their beady eyes on us; I just felt that, if I wasn't on a par with them, then I ought to be.

Because I spent so much time in the home and with Mum, I had developed a very acute awareness of adult issues. Mum leaned on me, she treated me as a friend and discussed things in a grown-up way with me. I didn't bring loads of pals home to play, like other kids did; I spent that time with Mum, talking as woman to woman. She was an avid TV watcher. It was her window on the world. When other kids talked to their parents about what they did at school, Mum and I discussed the items on the news.

So, when some grown-up came along and told me not to sit on the wall outside the garages for no valid reason other than to pull rank, I was damned sure I was going to sit there until I turned to stone. Exactly what harm was I doing? Was it their wall? What right did they have to impinge on my well-earned fun and freedom?

I have no doubt that I gained a reputation for being a right little madam but I didn't care. I never hurt or harmed anyone, I never damaged anybody's property. I had a strong sense of my own moral code – those long discussions about religion and right and wrong with Mum were deeply ingrained by now.

What irritated people most of all, however, was the way I looked. I had discovered early that I could be anyone I wanted to be through dressing up, which I adored. I had a very acute awareness of style from an early age.

Mum was always artistic. She deeply regretted not continuing her education and going on to art college. She had all the flair and talent to be a fashion designer but she had opted for marriage and a family, which, after all, was the standard option for women of her generation, the 'war babies'.

I had inherited her artistic eye, I suppose. We would spend long, happy hours together in Mum's bed, poring over magazines and looking at the changing world of fashion. Mum could only dream of wearing some of the incredible styles of the early seventies. There were lots of long, floaty dresses that we both thought looked so romantic. In my mind's eye, I used to see her all dolled up in some Zandra Rhodes creation, wafting down the stairs at the Ritz on the arm of an elegant and wealthy suitor.

I had great dreams for my mum whom life was passing by so unfairly but, gradually, I began to transfer the dreams to myself. I could become that princess. I could transport myself into another world altogether, just by putting on different clothes and becoming someone new, someone glamorous, exciting, privileged, someone for whom doors would open and men would bow. Oh yes, I liked the thought of that. I would no longer be little Mandy Smith. I could be Mandi, queen of all she surveyed. The trouble was, by the time I began to get into fashion in a big way, Punk had arrived.

Naturally, I gravitated towards this bizarre latest fashion and the philosophy that went with it – rebellion. I wanted to be an exotic creature with spiky hair and wild extravagant artwork all over her face. I wanted to wear slit mini-skirts and fishnets. I thought Punk was just brill! Best of all, no boring grown-ups could join in our fantasy; They were all totally repelled by the look.

Mum was not quite so appalled by it. A bit of a liberal herself, she saw it as a creative expression of youth and freedom and a stand against the recessionary climate of the times. To be honest, she probably just read that in *New Musical Express*, but she adopted it as her own view. All the same, she did not want *her* little girl going out looking like a refugee from a sex shop.

Of course, I did not want to offend or upset her. I always respected her wishes. I would just do it when she wouldn't catch me, which was not that difficult. Poor old Mum! Stuck in bed most of the time, she couldn't possibly keep an eagle eye on two self-willed kids. So, instead, she placed implicit trust in us. She had invested a lot of time and care in educating us in a strong, Christian-based code of ethics. I'm afraid to say, though, that her good faith was occasionally misplaced, not over the cardinal rules of home that were writ large in the 'Invisible Book of Right and Wrong', but sometimes in the little by-laws, the ones that were written in small print. Like: you will not breeze out of the house wearing a perfectly decent pair of dungarees and sneak off to change into an outrageous pair of skintight jeans and a satin top. Sorry, Mum, I did – on more than a few occasions.

And yes, I was that monstrous child who would pretend to go to bed at 10.30 pm, lie there until I was sure you were asleep, then pad up my bed with pillows in the shape of a slumbering body and sneak out at 11. I wasn't up to anything heinous. I would just go to my friend's flat downstairs, where he had the most fascinating invention I had ever come across – a CB radio.

If anything opened up my horizons at that tender age, it was the CB. Without the danger of actual confrontation, you could talk to hundreds of different people, about anything and everything. It was a very adult world, talking to truckers, insomniacs and various misfits who probably would have been locked up – and knew it – if they walked the streets.

It was great fun. My handle, precociously enough, was Sexy Lexy. Through the world of CB, I learned some very sophisticated people games. I very quickly mastered the art of projecting myself as someone much older. I was certainly articulate enough, courtesy of all the adult conversations I had been privy to with Mum, and easily passed myself off as an aware and rather pushy teenage dream doll.

The biggest problem was trying to suppress my laughter as some beefy lorry-driver made suggestive remarks to what he supposed was a naughty nymphet. I could always picture the disbelief on their faces when I eventually revealed they had been coming on to a ten-year-old. It was naughty, I suppose, but harmless enough. There was never any fear involved. I was safe behind my receiver. I would never actually meet any of those people of the night. I had learned how to tease.

It was around then that I really became aware of my latent sexuality. Up until then, my forays into the strange and fascinating world of boys had been a bit of snogging, first with Gary Quinten, then with his brother Stacey. Most of that had been executed as forfeits in Truth or Dare.

When I turned eleven years old and left junior school behind, however, I leapfrogged into a new sexual awareness. Suddenly I was mixing with girls up to eighteen – and the boys who went with them.

My sister Nic and my cousins, who were all two or three years older than me, had already entered this new world. I was pretty sure they were not going to leave me behind, even if I was a pain-in-the-butt little kid. If Mum was the only stable element in my life, Nic and my cousins were my guides. With their burgeoning hourglass figures, they were teetering on the threshold of young womanhood and they were going to take me, gangly like Bambi, ambitious and curious far beyond my eleven years, along with them.

To their eternal credit, they never got fed up with this much younger kid tagging along. It was accepted that I was family and they had to take a kind of responsibility for me – not that they needed to. I was probably the most forward of them all.

Nic and I had established a strong bond. Sure, there were the normal sisterly quarrels now and again over who had nicked the other's best T-shirt or the last ice lolly in the fridge but, basically, we were closer by far than most siblings. As Nicola advanced along the road of flirting, dating and snogging, I danced in her shadow, watching, listening, waiting and leaping in when I felt it was my turn.

When I started at my new school, the Holy Family Convent in Enfield Town, I took a quantum leap in boy-awareness. Suddenly Stacey Quinten looked very tame and I promptly dumped him for the deeply gorgeous (or so I thought) Stuart Bewley.

The Holy Family was an all-girls convent school and it is true what they say about convent girls. That strict hothousing of all girls together makes for some very hungry young flowers, starved of the company of boys. However, life always has a sense of balance and so there was, naturally enough, a boys' school just up the road. Their hormones were in a growth curve just like ours. It was the perfect situation.

The journey to and from school was the highlight of our day, when boys and girls mixed and flirted, giggled and teased and passed notes of unrequited and unremitting passion for one another.

I purposely made it known that Stuart Bewley was the one for me, and the poor, marked lad meekly complied. We met daily on the back seat of the school bus where we would make puppyish eyes at each other to the accompaniment of various catcalls from our unattached mates at the front. By mutual agreement, we sorted out that, yes, we could officially be considered 'an item'. We were dating, going steady, and we hadn't even kissed yet.

We didn't waste much time, though. Once it was made official, we got stuck in with a ferocity that defied belief and all the scientific laws of adhesion. We were permanently glued to each other's hands, eyes and hearts. Conveniently, my best friend Kim Jackson started going out with Stuart's best friend Alan. It was a perfect little foursome, ready and willing to participate in a bit of kissing and fumbling. Well, that was all right, wasn't it? We were practically engaged!

The lads immediately assumed their rightful, dominant, male roles and did all the organising. The first place they took us was a graveyard near Enfield. Very romantic! We used to sit there on the tombstones and snog for all we were worth.

Stuart was actually only eleven, the same age as me. Although he was too proud and macho to admit it, I think I was his first proper girlfriend, so, after all my practice with the Quinten brothers, I was way ahead of him when it came to snogging. It would take him up to half an hour of circumvolutory chatting before he would shyly pluck up the courage to pucker up. I can remember thinking, 'God, he's a bit slow. I wish he would get on with it.'

I was all for a bit of action – some real, relentless passion like you saw at the movies. Addicted to the notion of grand romance on a *Gone with the Wind* scale, I wanted him to grab me manfully by the arms, look deeply into my eyes, smoulder with pent-up emotion... and kiss me to oblivion. Fat chance. He just used to sit there most of the time, telling me about his gerbils.

Out of sheer frustration, I gradually took on a mantle of boldness and would initiate the proceedings. Even though I felt it was a bit of a cop out, at least that way we would get some action. He never protested and, gradually, with my expert tuition, he became a bit better at the art of snogging. In fact, in the hands of his hungry and expert tutor, he even developed a bit of a passion for it himself. The romance lasted several months, right through the autumn and into the freezing depths of winter, but we had our love to keep us warm!

One night, it was snowing quite heavily and the four of us were waiting for a bus back home from a heavy date at the Wimpy Bar. To me, it was a perfect night, straight out of *Dr Zhivago*. My Russian Prince and I were enveloped by swirling snow in the majestic, wild beauty of the Russian Steppes (yes, with a coat of snow and a bit of imagination, I could even transform Enfield High Road).

Stuart and I were wrapped up in each other and his bomber jacket, lost in a serious snogging session in the bus shelter, oblivious to the fact that Kim and Alan, who obviously had no finer feelings for the power of love, were totally bored and turning to blocks of ice while they waited for our passion to subside.

By now, I was calling all the shots. When the bus arrived, I had to make the decision whether we all clambered on into the warmth and fug of the number 29, or progressed a little further on the road to everlasting love. No contest – Kim and Alan could play the abominable snowmen a little longer. God knows why they put up with me but I was so self-assured in the world of grown-ups that I had naturally evolved as a leader among my peers. They put up and shut up and we snogged on. We stuck together as a foursome – there was safety in numbers – and no one might be tempted to get out of hand in the fumbling stakes.

Stewart and Alan would take us round to their homes and we would sit for hours listening to records, discussing the various merits of Human League (brilliant) against Haircut One Hundred (not so brilliant apart from cute Nick Heywood and that deeply gorgeous timpani player, Mark Fox). On Friday or Saturday nights, we would be taken to the cinema where we made a big show of squelchy kissing in the back row, much to the disgust of all the teenagers present, who, by then, had managed to perfect the art of silent and meaningful snogging.

Nic, meanwhile, now thirteen, had progressed beyond bus shelters and graveyards and, along with our cousin Julie, had started venturing into pubs. Like me, with the skilful application of a bit of lipstick, mascara and a few shots of hairspray, she and Julia could both look much older than their tender years. They did not drink but had discovered that the local pub was the source of all the action – and also the only place where you could meet half-decent-looking seventeen-year-old boys.

Directly across the road from our flat was a pub with a club in the premises above it, called Wheatleys. Locally, it was *the* place to go. Nursing a coke all night, Nic and Julie had the time of their lives flirting with the older clientele, some of whom were even sophisticated enough to sup the odd halfpint of snakebite.

There was no getting round the fact that Mum was bound to find out – from her bedroom window she could have caught sight of Nic slipping into Wheatleys any night. So Nic had little choice. She came right upfront and asked Mum if she could go. There was some heated discussion about the dangers of drinking and fraternising with older boys but, in the end, Mum capitulated. It was only fifty yards away, Nic was in the company of her older cousins and there were plenty of neighbours around to keep an eye on her, so she said OK, Nic could go – but no drinking and she was to come home bang on time as soon as the music wrapped up.

Naturally, I didn't see why I couldn't be allowed the same freedom. Nic could look after me. We were best buddies. Mum was not buying it. A daughter of thirteen going to a pub or club was bad enough; but a daughter of eleven was out of the question. Back into bed with your teddy bears, Mandy. Act your age for once. I resorted to subterfuge, trying the same tactics that had made me a CB afficionado. I would set off for bed, then, quiet as a whisper, slip into my wildest outfit, slap on enough make-up to make myself look ten years older and tippy-toe down the hall to freedom – only for Mum to yell out: 'And just *where* do you think you are going, madam?'

There was no way she was going to fall asleep with Nic still out. She would wait up until she heard her footsteps clattering up the stairs before she would relax. I remember that two-year wait as being frustrating in the extreme. Mum wasn't the only one lying awake wondering what Nic was up to.

I would prop my eyelids open and wait up in bed so that Nic could give me a blow by blow account of her evenings out. I wanted to hear every last detail, no wink or blink spared. What was the atmosphere like, who was there, what were they wearing, who got off with whom – and all about the men, especially about the men. By then, men were the most fascinating creatures in the world, creatures of mystery and captivating allure.

With no father in my life, no brothers and nothing real on

which to base my comprehension of the male species, I had, up to then, had to rely on my imagination when it came to grown-up relationships with the opposite sex.

Now my sister was in there, savouring all the delights of talking to fellas, being with them, kissing them. My scenes with Stuart Bewley at the bus stop began to pall. Vicariously, I thrilled to her stories of the good, the bad and the ugly blokes she would turn her heel on and walk away from. I was captivated.

It was not long after that that I started to develop physically. Although my periods had started early, at ten, I had remained slim and boyish, with no defined hips or boobs to speak of. Now, finally, my body was catching up with my imagination. At twelve, I suddenly developed a sizeable bust, which came as some surprise, although the family shape is fairly busty. I was rather entranced by these new assets of womanhood and I was suddenly, acutely, aware that boys – and men – were too.

The first time it really came home to me that there was some powerful advantage in being a *big* girl was when I was window-shopping with Nicola in Wood Green one Saturday afternoon. We were just sauntering along, gazing into the shops, when suddenly I was aware that we were being watched. I looked round and, sure enough, there were eyes on us – loads of eyes. From every window across the road, men were looking at us. Some of them would literally rush to the windows to get a better look.

It seemed to me a quite staggering reaction. I did not understand it but I knew it made me feel good. To know that you are admired is a basic human need. I had never experienced anything like this before. If this was a taste of male attention, I wanted some. It was quite different to being fancied by nine-ten- and eleven-year-old schoolboys. For the first time I felt really and truly confident about myself.

I realised that the two of us, Nic and me, looked pretty good together. I would usually be wearing plenty of make-up, certainly enough to make me look older. My hair was always done well and I would wear a mini-skirt with a nice jacket, hopefully not tarty. I had a dread of looking cheap. I was most certainly not that sort of a girl. I preferred trousers, really. I always looked good, and felt at home, in jeans.

Not long after that, as I was rising thirteen, Mum finally gave up her battle to stop me going out with my big sister and bigger cousins. At last, one wondrous day, beaten into submission by my constant ear-bashing, she gave me permission to go to the club over the road. It did not come, however, without a long lecture on safety and morality and a built-in warning that I should be aware of what boys were really after. Bless her, if only she had known she was talking to the veteran snogger on the block.

I had already successfully rebuffed the tentative, exploratory advances of the Quintens and Stuart Bewley, so I knew what boys would like to do to girls given half a chance. Naturally, I did not reveal this knowledge to my worried mother. I sat there dutifully listening to her telling me to be a good girl and how I must never let any boy pursue his advances beyond a goodnight kiss. Her exact words, if I recall, were: 'Don't let any of them touch you. Remember they never marry the ones they practise on.' She was dead right as well.

I took that sterling advice very much to heart. I liked kissing boys but I never went much further, never what us girls used gigglingly to call 'the below-the-belt stuff'. I felt that I was quite able to handle any advances I personally did not care for. I certainly had been up until then but now I was entering a whole new ballgame, to coin a phrase.

The fellas I now began mixing with were quite a bit older and more advanced. Sometimes they would expect a lot more than I was prepared to give. I had a few close calls but I inevitably managed to keep them under control. I was always a good talker and knew when to open my mouth at the right time. I knew of plenty of girls who did give in to the boys and I saw the reputation they got. I didn't want any of that, thanks very much.

I also shared all my experiences with Mum – well, maybe I withheld a little bit of the detail and cut down on some of the more descriptive moments. After I came home, I would go in to see her to prove I was all right and tell her that, yes, I'd had a great time. She, in turn, would give me advice on which boys sounded like the good guys and which ones I had better be wary of.

Mum was nearly forty and I was twelve, but there was no distance between us. We would sit there like teenage girls, giggling away into the small hours. It seemed perfectly natural to me that I should confide in her. Besides, it was Mum who rescued me from the nightmare that began happening at school.

I had completed the first and second years at Holy Family but, by the time I went into the third year, things were going very wrong for me. I was having a terrible time with the teachers and the other girls. The precedent that had been set in junior school had followed me. Because of the way I looked and dressed, and the effect I had on all the local boys, I was an outsider.

I refused to conform to the strictures of the school uniform. Sure, I would wear it but I would adapt it. Ever a nifty seamstress with a needle, I would alter my boring, knee-length, navy skirt, making it tighter and shorter. I sliced my tie to half its width – I mean, who wanted to wear a kipper tie in 1982?

Other girls were doing it too but I always seemed to be the one who was picked on. I had a sneaking suspicion – later to be proved correct – that, because they were jealous, other girls were grassing on me.

I became an alien. I'd walk into assembly every morning and the whole school would turn round and stare. I could feel their eyes burning into me, looking to see exactly what Mandy Smith had on today. Sometimes there would be traces of make-up on my face from the night before and that would always get me into trouble. Little things, like wearing blue socks instead of white, would cause me enormous problems. I'd be yanked by the collar by one of the nuns and marched off to see the Mother Superior for a terminal lecture on the sins of individuality.

I started shaving my legs when I was ten and that made me stand out a mile. All the other girls had horrible black hairs crawling up their legs. Well, I'm sorry, but if that was a precursor to being a blue-stocking, then they could keep it. There was no way I was going to look like that.

In the end, it came down to a few punch-ups when I had a couple of fights with other girls. One day I was standing in the dinner queue and a girl behind me made some caustic comment about the colour of my hair. My anger had been building up for days and I simply turned round and whacked her one. I did not have a single regret over it, either.

I felt totally isolated in the scholastic community, through no fault of my own. Although there were, in fact, a couple of teachers who were sympathetic, I was mostly made to feel like

27

a square peg in a round hole. Academically, though, they could not catch me out. For all of my appearance and increasingly late nights, I was not a bad scholar. I excelled in English but in those classes where the teachers criticised the way I dressed, I simply rebelled. I thought, if that is your attitude you can shove your maths tables and your geography maps up where they belong.

It was a typical, petulant teenage attitude and it did me no good whatsoever but it made me feel a whole lot better about being labelled a 'wild child'. Prophetically enough, it was a label that was to stick with me for an entire decade. In fact, I'm not altogether sure that people don't still think of me in that way, even today.

My convent schooldays were much more short-lived, however, as they were about to come to an abrupt and spectacular end. It all came to a head one day when one particular nun, who really hated me, met me in the school corridor. For some reason she didn't like the way I'd done my hair. It was in a plait, if I recall. There was nothing particularly subversive about that, was there?

None the less, this nun was on the rampage. She grabbed hold of my hair and ordered another, younger girl to run off and fetch some scissors. *Scissors?* I couldn't believe what was going on. I was absolutely petrified. The possibilities of what she would do with a pair of scissors frightened the life out of me. I was only grateful I was not a boy. I might have been a gelding before the day was out.

Thankfully, just before the scissors arrived, the nun spotted two other girls whose hair was far worse than mine. She let go of me for a second in order to reprimand them and I made a run for it – right out of the school, up the road and round the corner to freedom. There was no way I was ever going back there.

The school saw it differently, of course. The following day, the headmistress came to my home and tried to persuade me to return. Mum was led to believe that I was a brilliant scholar and that it was in my best interests to return to the place where they could nurture my special talents... and chop off my hair, as it happens, Mum!

At Mum's behest, I went as far as the head's car but then she made the mistake of turning to me and hissing that she would make me pay for this misdemeanour as soon as we got back. That did it. I turned on my heel and legged it.

When I got back later that night, I told Mum the whole story and she came down firmly on my side. She would take me away from school. Whatever the cost to her personally, she would see to it that I got a private education somewhere more liberal, somewhere where they understood that kids could be individuals, not herded like sheep.

Yet again, I owed Mum one. Unfortunately, I did not repay her concern with the requisite dutiful daughter behaviour. I was well into my total rebel stage by now.

A prime example of me disgracing myself happened at a family wedding shortly afterwards. It was one of those rarest of days when Mum was going to get out of bed and attend a family event at all costs, even if she had to take an oxygen mask and cylinder with her.

My cousin Kim and I arrived at the reception early and there were no adults around. We spotted a bottle of bacardi tucked away behind the bar, looked at each other as if of one mind, grabbed it and took it under the table. There, hidden from view, we quaffed the whole lot with whatever mixers we could find. For the first, glorious time in our adolescent lives, we were drunk out of our minds. As an attention-seeking device, it was a positive blinder. It did not take long before people detected this burping, giggling pair under the table and, to her total shame, Mum was forced to take charge of us and escort us home, even before the party had started. She was furious. All I could do was try to contain the laughter that threatened to burst out of me in a relentless flood.

As it happened, that was not the only thing that was to erupt out of me later in a tidal wave, when I was spectacularly ill!

I had screwed up my mother's big family event of the year, I had made myself a laughing stock – but I got a result. After that night, I never drank to get sloshed again. It was a lesson well learnt.

It was around that time that Nicola first took me to the Mayfair nightclub in Tottenham, along with our cousins Beverly and Julie. I'd been dying to go for ages. I didn't have a problem getting in and getting served wasn't a hassle because I usually settled for an orange juice or Coca-Cola, for obvious reasons.

The four of us would go there religiously once a week, either on a Friday or Saturday night. We looked good together but only Beverly was over eighteen. The rest of us were all under-age. The Mayfair was a great introduction to clubbing. It was huge and always packed but we quickly became part of the in-crowd. Everyone knew us. For us, it was not a pick-up joint, everyone there knew that we four cousins were simply out to have a dance and a good laugh.

Fellas would buy us drinks, of course, but in my book that was not a down-payment on anything to come later. The door-men were great and we got to know them pretty well. They would let us in for free sometimes because they knew we were decent girls and no bother, and having pretty girls around always attracted more male clientele so they always let us straight in. Even though there would be a huge crowd outside, we would walk straight to the door and stroll in.

I heard every chat-up line in the book at the Mayfair. It was a fair old education in coping with blokes with a few pints of lager in them and I was pretty good at a quick put-down. Sharp as I was, though, I never lied to them about my age. If ever a fella asked me how old I was, I would tell him straight out. That usually did the trick. As a quick escape route from the unwanted clutches of some opportunist, it was unsurpassable.

Besides, we felt that if we had any bother of any kind, we could always go to the bouncers to protect us. They liked us, they looked after us and it was they who gave us free tickets for various other clubs and events around town. Normally, we would chuck these freebies in the bin – too far to travel, too dodgy to risk – but one night they handed us tickets for something a bit different. There was to be a rock and pop awards ceremony at the Lyceum in the Strand. They wanted pretty girls who could look good for the cameras because the show was being filmed for TV. We took the tickets but didn't really think seriously about going.

I went home that night, threw the ticket on my dressing table and forgot all about it. Little did I know that that ticket would change my whole life. It was my ticket to Hell.

CHAPTER THREE

A Ticket to Hell

Tuesday, 21 February 1984 was a bleak, grey and bitterly cold day. I had not long transferred to my new school. It was midterm and Nic and I were at a loose end. We were mooching around at home, debating whether to go down the road to the Pizza Place, or stay in and rent a video, when Nic came up with a bright idea. 'What about these rock and pop awards?' she said. 'You know, the ones we got vouchers for the other week at the Mayfair?'

I'd forgotten all about them. We were given freebie tickets all the time and I had dropped these on the dressing table along with the others, never really thinking we would go. The Lyceum meant a trip all the way into the West End, but then Nic remembered that it was a daytime event, which meant we could get there by bus or tube. It was a more exciting prospect than sitting in all day so, spontaneously, we decided we would give it a shot. We could still be home by early evening if it turned out to be a dud event.

I was determined to be back home early because I was very keen not to blot my copybook with Mum by being out until the early hours of the morning, as had sometimes been my wont in the recent past. Poor Mum had been less than impressed by my performance of late. I didn't want to upset her any further so I was trying to toe the line a bit and respect her rules of the house.

First there had been the upheaval of me insisting I had to change schools or die. Mum had listened patiently to all my tales of woe and, luckily come down one hundred per cent in my favour, agreeing that my life at convent school had been a nightmare. She knew that if I was forced to stay there, I would consistently bunk off and it would be the end of my academic future so she had moved hell and high water to get me into a private school called Franklin House, done some juggling with the already overstretched family finances and reckoned that, if she scrimped and saved, it might just be possible.

Then, wonder of wonders, David had come to her rescue. David was Mum's knight in shining armour. A local builder, he had been Mum's boyfriend before the illness struck her down. Even then, he had steadfastly remained by her side and promised she could call on him if she ever needed help. He had never married after his love affair with Mum and still carried a torch for her. Instead of a lover, he had become the family's best friend and saviour. This time David really came up trumps. He promised Mum he would step in and pick up the shortfall in my school fees. So I owed Mum – and David – a lot there.

But how had I repaid her? By stopping out until all hours of the morning with the local gang. She had had quite a few sleepless nights lately, worrying about me.

Somehow, for all my tender years, I had turned into the neighbourhood little flirt. I had learned the effect a pretty face could have on boys and had turned it into a kind of currency, using it to set up lots of little games and deals. Flirting was fun. It made me feel desirable and the centre of attention – childish, naive, but true.

I had dumped Stuart Bewley. He had long since passed his sell-by date when he still could not get round to kissing without half an hour's prelude of mind-numbingly boring chat. I had moved on to the big boys – all of sixteen and seventeen years old.

My appetite knew no bounds. Hungry for love, I had not one, not two, but three or four boyfriends on the trot at the same time and I knew where I liked them best – under my thumb.

The first, Carl, was sweet sixteen and dotty about me. Sadly, this was his downfall. I knew I could play cruel games with anyone who was *that* keen on me. When I was out with him and my cousin Kim, I would wind him up horrendously. I used to say to Kim, 'Watch this' and then turn to Carl and snootily tell him, 'I don't want to go out with you anymore.'

Poor sap, he fell for it every time. On several occasions he would immediately burst into tears and I would crack up laughing. Yet he still kept coming back for more. Heartlessly, I soon tired of that game and announced that it *was* over, for real. Dear sweet doting Carl then took to following me around like a little lamb. If he could not be my true love, he would settle instead for friendship, just so long as he could be near me.

Then, to rub salt in his wounds, there was another local guy,

Stav, but he was a different kettle of fish entirely.

A bit distant and stand-offish, Stav was Mr Supercool. Not for him the wearing of his heart on his sleeve. True to his Latin origins, he was dismissive of girls he could have on a plate. I was *very* keen on him but not so keen that I could not cram in another two alongside. There was Ahmet and then another fella called Mitchell, whom I delighted in playing off one against the other.

However, I was still a 'no-sex zone'. I might be evolving into the world's biggest – or smallest at just turned thirteen – flirt but, when it came down to the nitty-gritty, I was not ready to take that plunge yet. Sexually, it must have been very frustrating for the boys. None of them dared to take things too far though, because I made my stance quite clear from snog one.

Stav was quite domineering and highly sexed and he would frighten me sometimes when I caught the passion and drive behind his kisses, but even he knew where to stop – basically, when I shoved him away with all the force of a WWF champ. He respected me for that.

As I was a regular clubber, coming into contact with lots of grown-up men, there were also times when older men tried it on. I already knew a way out of that one. It couldn't have been simpler. As they moved in for the kill – or kiss – I would smile sweetly and say, 'You shouldn't do that. I'm only thirteen.' You wouldn't see them for dust.

Poor old Mum didn't see much of me at that point in my life. She was more used to seeing a clean pair of heels as I made a speedy getaway to join my mates. I spent night after night in the local Broomfield Park in Palmers Green with Carl, his best friend John and their gang.

They were a wilder crowd than the schoolboys I'd gone out with before, older and quite a few of them jobless. Most of them were aspiring actors or artists but between parts and paintings they spent a lot of time hanging about and I had been hanging out with them.

We'd go down to the park and just lark about, musing on the meaning of life and the state of the country. Much of it was above my thirteen-year-old head but it was exciting to be with them and they were a laugh. If they could raise a few quid between them, someone would go to the off-licence for a few quarts of cider or, on a flush day, a bottle of bacardi. Then they would all get totally sloshed and set the world to rights. I did not drink but it all seemed terribly exciting and sophisticated to me, sitting on a park bench with a bunch of seventeen-year-olds, all out of their box on cider.

Mum would have been horrified so I used to bend the truth to protect her, naturally. I would tell her I was off to Carl's house, which, indeed, I was. Once there, I would pick him up, along with John and we would set off to meet the others down at the park. I just omitted the second bit.

Mum had met Carl, realised there was no romantic involvement between us and thought I was quite safe and snug round at his place with his parents, watching telly in the living room. I was bound to get caught out sooner or later – sooner, as it happened.

One night I was on my way to a late night party to meet Stav. The whole gang of us were fooling around, shoving each other and generally acting like a bunch of rowdy hooligans-in-the-making, when someone pushed me straight on to a fence of iron spikes. One of them made instant and unfortunate contact with my leg. It was not an experience I would wish to repeat. There I was, screaming in agony with a fountain of blood gushing from my ankle. An ambulance was duly called and I was rushed to hospital where medical staff deemed it vital that they contact my mother. The pain in my leg subsided compared with the pain of being found out by Mum who thought I was at home in bed where an effigy of me lay tucked up, snug and secure, between the sheets – I had resorted to my old CB escape route tactics that night.

The cat was out of the bag and, subsequently, this particular wildcat was grounded for a few weeks. Gradually, however, Mum eased up and let me start going out again.

So, on this particular occasion, on this day that was to change the course of my life, I did not want to rock the boat or let her down by disappearing on an all-nighter at the Lyceum. Nic and I were only going with the proviso that we would be home early. On top of all that, I almost cried off because I wasn't happy with my hair. I had recently experimented with a bottle of bleach and the results were a bit haphazard. I'd got bored with the varying shades of Crazy Colour and food dyes I had been playing with for the past year. In my various Punk and New Romantic moods, I'd had pink hair, blue hair, purple hair and every shade in between. Then I fancied blonde – and had loved the difference it made to the way I felt. As a blonde, I felt bubbly, funny and light-hearted. Being a brunette always made me feel a bit serious and older. So I'd streaked my hair blonde but my hairdressing skills were not a match for my adventurousness. It felt a bit dry and brittle, not unlike a haystack, if the truth be told. Like the despondent girl in the old shampoo ads, I couldn't do a thing with it.

Mum sighed in that long-suffering way she did when I'd gone over the top again and suggested putting some conditioning heated rollers in. Fair enough, I gave it a shot and it worked. Mind you, I didn't look at all like me when I looked in the mirror – all these bubbly, blonde curls – but, what the heck, another day, another dollar. I could change it the next week, couldn't I?

We got dressed in our clubbing clothes. I wore a flowery pale blue mini and grey top and Nic had on a white top and yellow skirt. Then we slapped on a bit of make-up and set off. Surprisingly, there was a large crowd outside the Lyceum when we got there; the event was obviously far more popular than we realised.

We were about to join this long queue when one of the doormen spotted us. It was one of our mates, the Mayfair bouncers, doing a spot of daytime moonlighting, if that makes sense. He ushered us in ahead of the queue.

I'd never been to the Lyceum before – it was way outside my league – and was surprised at how big it was. I was used to tiny little clubs like Wheatleys. This was vast by comparison. There were technicians and TV crews all over the place and music was booming out from the stage. We had arrived smack bang in the middle of rehearsals. Much to our dismay, we discovered that the afternoon would be taken up watching the various bands rehearsing for the actual event, which was in the evening. We wouldn't have a chance to dance or anything. They had laid on a spread of buffet food: curled-up sandwiches, vol-au-vents that looked as if they should have been put out of their misery years before and chicken legs that the chickens should have been happy to part with.

It seemed to be a bit of a non-event all round. We were

sitting around, gnawing tentatively on a chicken leg and feeling a bit bored, just watching the TV crews setting up their equipment and thinking we might as well hop off back home when this band, Freeez, came onstage. They'd just had a big Top Twenty hit and were currently a real-hot chart band. As soon as they struck up, Nicola and I fancied a bop. I said, 'I don't care if this is only a rehearsal, they're really good. Let's have a dance before we go home.' So we went down to the stage and started dancing in front of the band.

We just wanted to enjoy ourselves and weren't really paying attention to anything when Nicola suddenly prodded me and hissed, 'The lead singer can't take his eyes off you, Mandy. Look!'

I looked up and, sure enough, the singer was looking right down at me. As I looked up I met his gaze and he beamed me a great big smile. I was so embarrassed. I felt that everyone in the place must be looking at me but, of course, no one was paying the slightest bit of attention. Lots of the audience had also got up to dance by now and the TV guys were far too busy with their equipment.

Still, I felt as though a spotlight was right on me. The singer carried on, looking straight at me, and sang the whole song to me. I felt like I was the only girl in the world. It was terrifying but at the same time really exciting. I kept thinking, 'Some mistake here, surely? He's a pop star and I'm Mandy Smith, schoolgirl, aged thirteen.'

Nothing like this had ever happened to me before. I said to Nicola, 'Is my hair sticking up or something? Is my skirt tucked into my knickers? Why is he looking at me like that?'

Nicola, with all the sophistication of her fifteen years, laughed at me, 'Because he fancies you, silly.'

It was silly all right. For all my flirtation with schoolboys, and my kissy-kissy relationships with Stuart Bewley, Carl, Mitch and Stav, this was way out of my realm.

When they finished their set, the singer winked at me and, as he went offstage, he beckoned me over. I thought I was going to faint. I didn't know what to do. I said to Nic, 'He wants me to go over there. What am I going to do?'

She sighed. 'Go over and see what he wants, dopey.'

Not without her beside me, I wasn't. So, practically holding

36

my hand, Nic walked me over to him. He smiled that smile again and my knees turned to water. He said his name was John, John Rocca, and did we want a drink? I asked him for an orange juice and, suddenly, the chicken leg I had eaten earlier started churning round in my stomach. I felt sick with nerves, but, when he came back with two orange juices and started chatting, John Rocca turned out to be perfectly normal – a really nice, down-to-earth bloke. We were so busy talking to him that I didn't notice that the actual award ceremony had started.

He said he had to go, his band was due onstage and could he have our phone number? I scribbled it on a piece of paper and he said he would call us some time.

The whole dreary afternoon had turned out to be a main event after all. We had met a pop star and he was interested in us, or me, as Nicola kept reminding me. We went back on to the dance floor to wait for them to come on again and carried on dancing. I was on cloud nine. My feet were hardly touching the floor; I was laughing and giggling away to myself with the excitement of it. John Rocca was absolutely gorgeous. It was really scary but thrilling at the same time.

Then a combination of nerves, excitement and the greasy chicken suddenly began to have an effect on me. I felt queasy. It was getting late. We'd promised Mum we would be back by mid-evening and I felt it was time to go. Nic agreed but she said, 'OK, just one more dance.'

As we were having that last dance, some bloke approached us. He came up, caught my arm and said, 'Bill Wyman would like to offer you a drink. Would you like to come and join us?'

I looked at Nic. She looked at me. 'Who's Bill Wyman?' I hissed into her ear behind my cupped hand.

'He's one of the blokes presenting the awards, I think,' she said.

We looked over to where the man was gesturing and, sure enough, it was a special table, set apart from the audience, where the presenters were sitting. Nic, ever-adventurous, said, 'Come on, what have we got to lose? We're going home in a minute anyway.'

I was still dubious. I'd had enough excitement for one day and that fried chicken was threatening to turn into one of the biggest regrets of my life. Nic pulled the clincher. She said,

'John Rocca might come over.' Done. I was hooked!

We went across to where the guy, who said his name was Julian Temple, was leading us. There were people all round the table. There seemed to be women everywhere. It was obviously the important place to be. Then this guy sitting in the middle of the mêlée looked away from the girl who was chatting him up and said, 'Hi, I'm Bill. Would you like a drink?'

I didn't want to get caught up in this crowd situation. I felt light-headed. I needed some air. I shook my head and said, 'No, sorry, I feel really sick and we've got to go.' Those were the very first words I ever said to Bill Wyman and how deeply prophetic they were, as it turned out.

He was just an awards presenter, as far as I was concerned. The only award I wanted at that moment was one for getting home before I threw up. However, Bill would not take no for an answer, even when accompanied by a sickly smile that meant *sickly* with a capital S.

He said, 'Aw, come on, you've made it all the way across the dance floor. The least I can do is get you a drink. Have some champagne.'

There was something very charming and persuasive about him. Although he was old, he had a very boyish smile. I shrugged and said, 'OK, but not champagne, just an orange juice will do, thanks.'

I hadn't the faintest idea who Bill Wyman was but Julian Temple soon put me right about who everyone was in that elite little group around the table that everyone seemed to be falling over themselves to get to. He told us that he himself was a film producer – he had made *Absolute Beginners* and some other films I had never heard of and that Bill was one of the Rolling Stones.

I had heard of the Rolling Stones but, as far as I knew, they were a band from donkey's years ago. I knew Mick Jagger – I had seen his picture in magazines and the papers with Jerry Hall – and I had heard of the druggie one, Keith Richards, whose name was often in the papers, but Bill Wyman? Never heard of him, mate. To his credit, Bill did not even mention the band nor did he try to push his status at us.

It was fairly obvious that he was respected, judging by the way the waiters, the TV crew and all these women were fawning all over him but he couldn't be that famous, I thought, because he wasn't even presenting the awards himself. He had come just to accept one for a friend of his, a jazz musician (I later discovered it was Alexis Korner) who had died.

Bill Wyman did not impress me nor did he try to. He was just perfectly normal, chatting to us as if we were the girls next door. He asked our names and we told him. He asked if we had enjoyed the show and we told him. He asked how old we were and we told him and he nearly fell off his chair.

I said, 'My sister Nic is fifteen and I'm thirteen.'

His mouth fell open. He leant forward in his chair and practically toppled over. He said, 'What?' with a look of sheer incredulity.

Nic laughed out loud. She whispered to me, 'It's that hairdo that does it. Told you it makes you look ancient.'

Then Bill turned to his mates and smiled at them. Whatever the secret was, he was sharing it with them not with us.

I thought, so what is so peculiar about being thirteen? I've been thirteen for the last six months. It's not a problem to me. I felt quite defensive for a minute. I had never lied about my age and, although it had elicited a shocked reaction from a few blokes in the past, it had never seemed like a plus before. Previously, it had scared off blokes who were trying to come on to me.

Bill was different. Bill was enjoying this. He carried on as if nothing had happened, as if he was happier chatting to two schoolgirls than lapping up all the adulation from these other women and his cronies. He asked us where we went to school and what we wanted to do when we left. As one, we both said, 'Modelling'.

He smiled a long, slow smile. 'Right,' he said, 'I might just be able to help you there. A friend of mine runs a model agency. It's quite well-known. It's called Models One, in the King's Road, and I happen to know they are always on the lookout for new young models. It's impossible to get through the door because everyone wants to be on their books but I could make an appointment for you. Maybe I could take you both to lunch afterwards. I live not far from there.'

It was a line, all right, but there was something nice about him. He was kindly in a sort of avuncular way, not predatory

39

like other older men. He had to be forty if he was a day but he didn't seem like a dirty old man. He seemed to be genuinely interested in helping us. If he had his pick of all the women around him, he was surely not going to be chasing us. Why bother? He was very, very charming and that certainly wasn't a quality I'd become much acquainted with among the boys I'd met up until then.

However, I was feeling desperately queasy right at that moment so I nudged Nic that, this time, I really meant it, I was going. We turned to Bill and said we were off and he said, 'OK, let me have your phone number. I'll speak to Models One for you.'

Nic wrote it down on a napkin for him and we left.

I really thought no more about Bill Wyman that night. Above the waves of nausea left over from the salmonella chicken, I had one thought – maybe, just maybe, gorgeous John Rocca would ring me.

Sure enough, early next day the phone rang. Mum picked it up. As she spoke to this mystery caller, she glanced at me quizzically. My heart leapt. She said, 'It's for you – a man.'

'Hi, Mandy,' said a male voice. 'It's Bill. Bill Wyman.'

My heart sank. I tried to cover up the disappointment in my voice. It was nothing to do with him personally, just that, given the choice, I would rather be hearing from John Rocca at that precise moment in time.

'Hi,' I said, with as much enthusiasm as I could muster. 'How are you?' although, quite frankly, I couldn't have cared less.

'Fine,' he said, 'I've managed to fix you up with an appointment at Models One. They owe me a favour so they said they could squeeze you in today, about twelve noon. I could meet you after that. I'll take you both to lunch. Do you know Thierry's restaurant in the King's Road?'

'Sure,' I bluffed, not having the faintest idea where the King's Road was, never mind a restaurant with a name I couldn't pronounce.

'Great,' he said, 'I'll meet you in there at 1.30, OK? Good luck with the modelling appointment. If they've got any sense, they'll snap you both up.'

That was sweet, I thought.

Well, what the heck! If John Rocca wasn't going to ring, I

might as well see if I could get myself started on a modelling career but I knew at that moment which I would rather have.

It was a bit of a frantic dash after that for Nicola and me to get ourselves spruced up and down to the King's Road for the noon appointment. We didn't have time to be nervous. On with the make-up, into the gear, shove a bit of hairspray on and off we went. We didn't really hold out much hope of winning a slot on the cover of *Vogue* the following month – we were a little more realistic than that – but it was an opportunity not to be missed.

I guess it took all of five minutes for the boss at Models One to give us the once-over and, oh-so politely, tell us that we were very pretty girls but, really, models tended to be on the taller side than my puny five foot four inches and a little older than thirteen. Perhaps in a few years' – and six more inches' – time? As it happened, I did grow another three and a half inches over the next two years so she wasn't wrong there. She instantly recognised a child that had a fair old way to go before she reached womanhood, never mind a catwalk.

I got the impression that she was just humouring us and could have shown us the door the minute we stepped inside, as I was certain she did with plenty of other schoolgirls with good bone structure and grand delusions. So why bother with us? Bill had persuaded her to – but why?

For a second, it crossed my mind that we weren't the first young girls he had sent on this mission, with hopes of being the next Marie Helvin on their minds. We trawled down the road, not too despondent over our hopes being dashed, and found Thierry's, the restaurant where we had agreed to meet our mentor. We walked in and there he was at a corner table – 'his' table, I was later to discover. He greeted us with a big smile.

The restuarant was chic, dark and expensive but I wasn't nervous at all about it. Why should I be? Bill was very charming during the meal. Nic and he had pasta and I just had a salad because I was still feeling a bit dodgy after the Lyceum chicken lurgy. Embarrassingly, I had to go to the loo a couple of times because my stomach was still a bit unsure of itself but Bill thought this was quite funny. He said, 'You're a sensitive little soul, aren't you? At least your intestines are!'

I found it really easy to talk to him. That was appealing.

Most of the guys I knew were in their teens and had little or no conversation. It felt really comfortable sitting there chatting with Bill. There were no awkward pauses or clumsy chat-up lines. He could be boyish too though; he had a really youthful charm, especially when he smiled. And he was funny.

When I asked him his age, he joked, 'Twenty-five', then he actually blushed and told the truth. 'Forty-seven, really,' he admitted sheepishly. 'Just about to pick up my middle-aged pension.'

We laughed. He certainly didn't strike me as being ancient because I wasn't looking at him in terms of a boyfriend, not at all. He was just a nice, charming man. He was interesting, too. He had lots to say. He talked about his life, his son, his work – but he wasn't boasting. He was very good-humoured and quite at ease with us. I didn't feel he was being at all flirtatious and, sitting opposite him, a little germ of an idea had begun to form in my head.

We had told him all about Mum and what a terrific woman she was, coping so well with her illness and bringing up her dreadful daughters all on her own. How we both longed for some magical cure for her and some magical prince to sweep her off to happiness. Then suddenly I thought, 'I wonder if Mum would fancy him?'

I wasn't in the habit of looking out for men for my mum but suddenly the whole thing seemed to fit into place. They were from the same era. She would remember the Rolling Stones. He was just a bit older than her and terribly charming. If they hit it off, well . . . I might be facing my future stepfather here. I was smiling away to myself at this when he went to the Gents.

No sooner had he excused himself from the table than Nic grabbed my sleeve and pulled me to her. 'You'll never guess what he said when you went to the Ladies,' she hissed, with a look of manic glee on her face. 'You'll never guess in a million years!'

I shrugged. 'He said I was drop-dead gorgeous and what was I doing with a drongo sister like you? But as you know, there's always an ugly friend somewhere in tow. In my case, it just happens to be my sis . . .'

'Do drop dead,' she said laughing. 'He said, wait for this . . . "I really like your sister."'

'This is completely understandable,' I replied. 'No one in their right mind could fail to feel the same way.'

'No, you twit, he *meant* it. He *fancies* you.'

'Don't be daft,' I retorted, 'He's old enough to be our grandad.'

Both of us collapsed into fits of giggles just as Bill returned. Nic was so beside herself that she had to go to the loo as well at that moment.

Bill wasn't fazed at all by this silly schoolgirl giggle attack. He looked me straight in the eye and said, 'I really like you, Mandy. I just can't believe how old you are.'

For the first time in a long while, I could feel myself turning bright scarlet. I was desperately embarrassed. I had never been in a situation like this before. I didn't know what to say or do. I just looked down at the table and felt this red-hot blush setting my cheeks on fire.

He was so complimentary to me. He said he liked my hair, what lovely eyes I had, what a beautiful, open smile. I had never, ever been talked to like that before. I was relieved when Nic came back to the table.

However, Bill had had a curious effect on me. He said things that made my ears stand up and listen. He had somehow taken charge of me. For once, I became very quiet and felt as shy and gauche as a five-year-old. It was a very bizarre situation, one that I had not anticipated at all.

When the meal was over, Bill suggested we pop into his office, next door, for a coffee. Even before the suggestion of 'What's he up to now?' had crossed our minds, he covered himself. He said, 'You must meet my secretary Karen. She's my right-hand girl. I'd be completely lost without her. You'll like her. She's great fun.'

So no threat there, then, but, to be honest, neither of us felt in the slightest bit threatened by Bill. Normally, we would have baulked at 'just popping in to some man's flat for a coffee' but there was nothing menacing about Bill at all. We both felt he was a genuinely nice man, a safe man. Even if he had deeply unnerved me with his compliments, I knew he was not the sort of guy to try to jump on me. So off we trotted next door.

We walked up a narrow flight of stairs – meticulously clean, I noticed approvingly – in the door and there was the office. A pretty dark-haired woman – around thirty years old, I guessed –

was sitting at a desk, surrounded by neatly organised files, papers and phones. On the pale cream walls were loads of pictures – mostly of Bill and his friends. There were several of him with a little boy and others of him with a dark-haired young man – obviously the little boy now grown up.

He noticed me looking at them. 'That's my son Stephen,' he said with a cursory nod.

He introduced us to Karen, who just had time to say, 'Hi' before one of the phones started ringing. As she answered it, Bill beckoned us to follow him up a further flight of stairs.

'I'm not in,' he mouthed to Karen, who nodded in understood agreement.

'I'll bring you up some coffee in a sec,' she replied, with her hand over the mouthpiece of the phone.

'OK,' he said and led us up to his sitting room.

Later, I wondered just how many hundreds of women he had charmed into walking that path up to his bachelor flat. One day the spectre of a never-ending stream of women and a thousand footfalls padding up and down those stairs would haunt me relentlessly but at that moment I felt completely at ease. Bill had been the perfect gentleman. Already, I felt I would trust him with my life. I could never have foreseen how much of my life he was ultimately to take.

CHAPTER FOUR

Tramp!

I *was* intrigued by Bill Wyman. Here was this lovely, charming man who seemed to have his life in complete order. He wanted for nothing yet he was paying an inordinate amount of attention to me. It was deeply flattering.

I had never known attention from a grown man. My own absentee father showed his affection in the only way he knew how – a perfunctory visit and a token fiver on birthdays and at Christmas, but Bill showed his interest in me with his eyes, with words and with his presence. Even if I had understood these strange feelings that were drawing me to him, and the emotional ropes he was playing in to get me hooked on him, at thirteen I had no experience to fall back on. It was new and uncharted territory for me. It was rivetingly exciting.

Although I had not the slightest inkling about his past, Bill had plenty of experience to draw on. He would not waste any time. He invaded my life without giving me time to draw breath. Barely twenty-four hours after Nic and I had lunch with him, he called me at home.

This time, when I answered the phone, I had no feelings of disappointment nor the reluctance I'd felt the previous day when waiting for John Rocca to call. I was delighted, and surprised, to hear from Bill again so soon. It was a very casual phone call. He said he would love to see Nic and me again and, primed by all our chat about Mum, would love to meet her.

Perfect! He and Mum would surely hit it off. If nothing else, they would become good friends. They would be absolutely terrific together. There was just one teeny problem. Mum, as cute as a cat with her sixth sense for trouble, would surely suspect that she was being set up. This was going to be a game of outstanding skill if I could remain undetected as matchmaker and pull it off.

Oh so terribly casually, although my heart was thumping with excitement, I said, 'Sure, why don't you come round here for dinner tomorrow?' It never entered my head that this man might be more used to dining at the Ritz than downtown Wood Green. It never crossed my mind that a man who lived in the chic King's Road might sooner cross the Amazon than cross the 'great divide' to a north London council estate. Not for one second did I imagine that this was a man who was at home rubbing shoulders with millionaires and megastars, or, indeed, that he was one himself.

Bill agreed that that seemed like a nice idea and if he was in the least put out about lowering his standards in order to slum it not far from the soon to be universally notorious Broadwater Farm Estate, he never showed it. The date was set. Our place at eight. Dinner jacket *not* necessary.

Ever-so-casually, I breezed in and told Mum that Bill Wyman would be coming to dinner. Nic and I had already told her about meeting him at the Lyceum. She knew, too, of our abortive mission to launch ourselves as supermodels, courtesy of Bill's introduction and, down to the last detail, she was intimate with the layout of his office and living room in the King's Road.

Unlike my boyfriends, I had not been sparing in describing Bill. There was no reason for Mum to be suspicious here. He was simply a man who had befriended us. Naturally, Mum was a little more impressed than we were. Yes, she had certainly heard of, danced to, and hummed along with the songs of the Rolling Stones but personally, she told me, she had always preferred the Beatles.

She was not at all perturbed by the thought of a Rolling Stone coming to dinner. She insisted on meeting all our friends and all our boyfriends. Lots of them were actors. Bill was not special simply because he had been on telly or made records. In her mind, the Rolling Stones were part of her past. She knew they were still around but so were the Tremeloes and Sweet, whoever *they* were.

So, she rang the butcher for a rare treat, some steak. Her main concern about the whole thing was that he was not vegetarian, even though we assured her he was not. (How the heck did we know? He had had pasta on the only previous occasion we had seen him eat but we bluffed it anyway, just to put Mum's mind at rest.) For her, a 'proper' meal for a man was steak and three veg. She would not let herself down by serving anything less to a guest.

46

The following day, she carefully prepared the meal for the four of us and muttered quietly about how he had better be on time, as steak did not warrant overcooking.

Bang on eight, the doorbell rang and there stood Bill, a bunch of flowers in one hand, a box of Milk Tray in the other and a shy smile on his face. He was off to a head start. Mum thought it was an extremely nice gesture. It was only countermanded by his smoking. Somehow, Bill managed to juggle a lit ciggie along with the chocs and flowers. He dragged nervously on it as he entered the flat.

The very first thing I said to him that night was possibly only marginally more attractive than my first words at the Lyceum when I forewarned him that I was about to throw up. I said, 'Sorry, you can't smoke that in here. It affects Mum's chest. It will make her sick.'

To his eternal credit, Bill immediately stubbed it out. He might well have been thinking he had walked in on a right bunch of hospital cases but he never faltered. I noticed then that Bill was really quite nervy in certain situations. I did not yet know, nor would I for many years, what dictated the terms of that nervousness, then, all I noticed was that he was desperately uncomfortable without a ciggie in his hand. He chainsmoked menthol cigarettes like they were going out of fashion – which, indeed, they had done years before, but Bill, as I was later to discover, was totally unaffected by fashion of any kind. It did not just leave him cold, it simply passed him by unawares.

After the initial introductions were made, the evening took a very peculiar tone. It was, quite frankly, a bit strange, all of us sitting round the dinner table in our humble Formica kitchen. The only other male grown-ups we had previously dined with there had been family, such as our many uncles or Mum's friends like David. Here was someone who fitted neither category and who, despite that, was not the slightest bit perturbed.

He did not attempt to impress us with any tales of his days on the road with the Stones. He turned the spotlight back on to us and made clever little jokes about situations in our own lives that we found ourselves telling him about. He complimented Mum on the meal and said he had rarely eaten a finer steak, which went down a treat with Mum. I could see the potential relationship shaping up very nicely, thank you, although naturally, I did not give away the slightest clue.

Over coffee, because he was lost without a cigarette to hold, he began to play with the cardboard and wrapping paper from the box of chocolates. Watching him, and by now spellbound, I realised that he was actually sculpting a pretty little doll. When he had completed this mini-masterpiece, he presented it to me with a great flourish. He smiled: 'You're not too old to play with dolls, are you, Mandy?' I thought that was really sweet.

Then the evening, which had thus far been a great success, began to fall apart. Mum, unused and unable to cope with all the cooking, the heat in the kitchen and sitting around the dinner table for so long, began to feel faint. She had tried to do too much all at once. Doggedly she sat there, smiling politely, far too concerned about not letting the side down to give in to a fainting fit. Recognising her flushed look as the first symptom, I whispered to Nic that we should let Mum lie down for a bit. We could do the washing up together. Nic agreed. She would tackle the dishes if I saw Mum to bed.

Mum was profusely apologetic to Bill but he could see how pale and tired she suddenly looked so they politely said goodnight to one another and I helped Mum upstairs.

By this point, Bill had got through the entire evening without a ciggie. When I came back downstairs a few minutes later, I could see he was dying for one so I said, 'Why don't you go out and have one on the balcony?' and he agreed.

Suddenly, and inexplicably, I felt apprehensive. Mum was upstairs in bed. Whatever juvenile schemes I had envisaged for her and Bill had suddenly disintegrated. In a blinding flash, I practically heard myself wonder aloud, 'What's going to happen next?' I soon found out.

As we walked through the hall from the kitchen to the lounge, he suddenly stopped, turned to face me and, grabbing me by the arms, pulled me to him. Then he kissed me full and hard on the lips. I was totally stunned. Absolutely unprepared for this turn of events, I was stiff and unresponsive, not yielding to his kiss at all. He was holding my arms very firmly down by my sides.

I didn't kiss him back. I was thinking, 'What is happening here? How has this happened?'

Then he said, quite simply, 'That was something I had to do.'

I was really, truly shocked. Up until then I had wondered if he really did fancy me but that seemed too silly. I had dismissed the thought in favour of the, to my mind, far more realistic notion that he would be attracted to my mother.

At the moment of that hard, stolen kiss, however, I knew, with blinding clarity, that, yes, it was me; Bill Wyman definitely wanted me. At the same time, I was totally aware, 'This is dangerous. He is famous, he knows my age – and my age is too young.'

Everything I had known and learnt about boys went out of the window at that precise point. Where the hell did I stand with a grown man like Bill, for whom I had already developed affectionate daughter-father feelings? I knew that I liked him and felt really comfortable with him but now everything had turned on its head and I was worried. I just didn't know what would become of, this whole situation.

All these conflicting thoughts were jumbled in my head as we walked into the lounge. I knew I hadn't led him on. I had not flirted with him nor encouraged him. I was wearing ordinary comfy, at-home clothes of jeans and a T-shirt. Mum had made all the effort. Why was he kissing me, not her?

In an awkward silence, we sat down together on the settee and lost the embarrassment of the moment in watching television. I have no idea what was on the screen, it was merely a distraction to focus my attention on, away from what had happened. I could hear Nic banging around in the kitchen, washing up the pots and pans. It was a perfectly normal domestic setting, except that I was sitting on the settee with a man I barely knew, a man old enough to be my grandfather, and he had just kissed me.

Now he was sitting next to me, silent, watching TV as if nothing had ever happened. It was bizarre.

There was some distance between us. Bill made no attempt to snuggle up next to me, cuddle me or even touch me. I was perched on the edge of my seat, leaning forward as if engrossed in the mindless babble on the box. After I don't know how long, although it seemed like an eternity, I tried, ever so casually, to sink back into the settee, still leaning away from him. He never flinched. He sat motionless, his eyes glued to the screen.

I risked a glance at him to see what his expression was and, as I slid my eyes sideways, I caught his, looking straight at me.

His eyes were smiling and his face, as I turned to him, broke into a big grin. Still he said nothing. Then, as one, we both erupted in giggles. My laughter was an automatic reflex, a nervous response to break the tension. Bill's? Well, he sounded for all the world as if he was thoroughly enjoying the situation. He was certainly not ill at ease. Who knows? Maybe he had found himself in this situation a hundred times before. Then Nic came back in to join us and the moment was lost.

Shortly after, Bill said he should be going and rose to leave. Politely, I got up with him and went to show him to the door. He said how much he had enjoyed himself. It was not often he was afforded the luxury of settling into a cosy family evening. He gave me the impression that, perhaps, he was a bit sad and lonely. After all, he lived on his own; his son Stephen was grown up. He obviously missed the comfort of family life.

I felt very tenderly towards him at that moment and, as I opened the door for him, he picked up on my feelings. Gently he leaned over and kissed me on the cheek. 'Perhaps you'd like to visit my family home?' he said. 'It's in the countryside, at Gedding in Suffolk.'

I registered a moment's surprise. I had assumed that the King's Road flat was Bill's home. How silly of me. He went on, 'I'll call you and let's see if we can fix something up.'

Then he was gone. I rushed straight in to Nicola and nearly fell over myself in my attempt to tell her what had happened. 'You'll never guess,' I giggled. 'He kissed me!'

'Ssshh!' she said. 'Or you'll wake Mum. She'd have fifty fits!'

United in our secret, we giggled gleefully all the way to bed, but I couldn't sleep. I kept thinking about this weird turn of events. I couldn't get what had happened out of my mind. No kiss had ever affected me in this way before, that was for sure. It was so confusing. I liked him, but what did I *really* feel for him? I barely knew the man, so why was I feeling this way?

I made a promise to myself that, next day, I would do some research. By now, I was curious to know a bit more about Bill Wyman.

When I awoke next morning, it was with a single-minded sense of purpose. I was going to do a trawl of the local library, record shop and newsagent, to see what I could find out about Bill. In my heart, I felt he was not just an opportunist. I felt he genuinely liked and cared about me but all I had to go on was my gut instinct and, at thirteen, I really wasn't too sure that I trusted my barely developed female intuition. Just who exactly was he? Had he really been a big star? What exactly had he done in the past?

Before I left, I gave an update on how the evening had gone to Mum, carefully glossing over the part about the stolen kiss. I felt quite sure that she would definitely not have approved. She was not romantically interested in Bill and would probably have banned him from the house. I did not want that to happen. Already, I felt that Bill had made an impact on my life. I did not want to lose that before I at least knew *why* this should be.

In the library I found a book on the Stones. I flicked through it. Sure enough, there was Bill Wyman, bass guitarist. The silent one, it said. Well, that fitted sure enough, judging by the episode on the settee.

There were countless photos, faded old black and white ones that seemed to me to have been taken at the turn of the century. Five long-haired blokes in funny trousers. Bill looked like the only normal one out of the lot of them. Bill in dark suits, dark jeans, dark shades, his eyes hidden in most of the photos. Funnily enough, he looked much older *then* than the Bill I knew now. He had certainly got better looking as the years had rolled by. I did not take the book out. I wanted to find out about Bill myself, not absorb some writer's opinion.

Next I went to Our Price record shop. A cursory look at the R section revealed a real shock. There were *dozens* of Rolling Stones albums. No wonder he has no family life, I thought. He must be working all the time, judging by the Stones' output.

My research had served its purpose. It presented a rather different picture to the flesh and blood ordinary man I had met but at least I knew he had been totally honest. He had not been spinning me a line or trying to impress me. He simply was who he said he was.

He rang the next morning, asked how I was and, very directly, asked me out to dinner that night. My instant reaction was, 'Oh, he's very keen.'

He seemed to assume that this was something I did regularly. Well, I had dinner fairly regularly – on a daily basis, actually. I even went out to dinner occasionally, like on family anniversaries, but I had never, ever been *out to dinner* on my own with a man before.

I said I'd be delighted to come and would bring Nicola but Bill immediately said, 'No, you, on your own. At Tramp. We'll be meeting friends, Keith Richards and his wife Patti and some other people with the Stones.'

I was a bit perturbed at the prospect so I said I would have to ask Mum and could he call back later to see if it was OK? He said he would.

Tentatively, I went to ask Mum. To my sheer amazement, she said yes, almost without demur. She had met Bill, she liked him, she felt I would be safe with him. She felt that a man in his position, with his age and experience, would never get into any trouble with such a young girl. Besides, if I was being chaperoned by Bill I could only come to less harm than I did with Carl at the local park. In the grand scheme of things, she would rather I was having a civilised meal with some adults than mooching around on a park bench with teenagers.

My next concern was what and where on earth was Tramp? And how would I get there and back? I did not have to worry. Bill sent a taxi for me that evening. The driver had been instructed to drop me at his flat first so that we could make our way to Tramp together. I sank back in the cab and thought how lovely, how blissful to be looked after like this. To have someone make decisions for you and take care of the preparations. It was a luxury I had never known before.

When I arrived at Bill's flat, I was a bit nervous but excited at the same time. I had wondered what people were expected to wear to places like Tramp. My own wardrobe was very limited and, quite frankly, very teen-queen. It was fine for Wheatleys but would it be out of place at a West End restaurant? After much deliberation, I had settled on a very plain white top and a pastel yellow skirt.

Bill met me at the top of the stairs and said how nice I looked, which immediately put me at ease. Then we sat down and had a chat before we went out. I said I was apprehensive about going to a place I had never been before without the support network of my sister and cousins. He told me not to worry, he would look after me. There was just one small item he should really mention... 'Look, Mandy,' he said, 'if the question of your age comes up, you'd better say you are a bit older than you really are. Say you're seventeen. It could be just a bit of a problem, what with the place being licensed and such like.'

He could tell by my face that I was not too happy with this. I had never been good at lying. 'You can say you're a student,' he went on. 'Then it won't really be too much of a lie. Just say you're studying for your A-levels.'

I had never lied about my age before. If it had been up to me, I would have come straight out and told anyone who asked the truth, that I was thirteen, but I could see that, from Bill's point of view, it might cause problems. I was, indeed, much too young to get into a place like Tramp and it might be embarrassing for Bill.

I really wasn't comfortable with the idea but what could I do? Bill had asked me to do this for him and he was being nice enough to take me out. Catch 22. I just prayed that maybe the matter of age would not come up at all but, of course, it did, straightaway.

At Tramp, which struck me as much the same as the clubs I had been to before – small and dark with a tiny, overcrowded dance floor – Bill introduced me to Keith, Patti and the others. They seemed very nice and were all interested to meet me. Then someone – and I can't remember who – asked how old I was. I was a bit flabbergasted. Not until much later did I learn that this was always the question on everyone's lips whenever they met a new girl of Bill's. His partiality for teenage models was well known in Tramp and among his friends so it was automatically the first question they asked.

I hesitated for a second, caught Bill looking at me, and muttered the line exactly as he'd told me to. I felt such a fraud. I was sure my voice sounded false and staccato, as if I had learned this line parrot-fashion. To my amazement, no one seemed to doubt me. Unbeknown to me, seventeen was a favourite age for Bill's girls.

After that stumbling block, I felt a bit awkward but Keith's wife Patti took me under her wing and chatted to me while the others talked about people and places I had never heard of.

Then my worst nightmare came true. I had been terrified that I would use the wrong cutlery during the meal or make some huge social gaffe because of the lack of experience of my thirteen years but those things paled into insignificance when I was faced with a far worse disaster. The zip on my skirt split. Worse, it did it in slow motion, giving me an eternity to realise exactly what was happening.

I was sitting there, nibbling my salad, trying to appear cool and sophisticated and interested in their very adult conversation, when, suddenly, I began to feel it give way. Tooth by tooth, I could feel it separate, all the way slowly down until the whole thing was unzipped and broken beyond repair. I glanced down. Under the table, I was sitting in my underwear. I went alternately hot and cold. What the hell did I do now?

Then – and this was proof of how comfortable I felt with Bill – I turned to him and whispered, 'Bill, help me, my skirt has just split totally apart.'

Bill looked at me in astonishment, not sure at first whether I was playing a trick or not. Then, as he realised I was both serious and panic-stricken, he burst out laughing. He pulled Patti to him and, discreetly, to save my further blushes, explained the situation. She handed me a largish – although barely large enough – table napkin to wrap around me and we sidled off to the Ladies where the woman who looked after the place stitched my skirt back together. I would not be able to visit the loo again that evening, nor bend over in a hurry but at least the night, and my dignity, were saved.

As we returned to the table, we could barely contain our mirth, so Patti let the cat out of the bag and everyone had a good laugh about it. In a way that broke the ice and I became an accepted part of the assembled company.

It was a turning point for me in the way that I felt about Bill, too. I felt then that I could always turn to him for help. He knew what to do in all sorts of situations. He was not embarrassed by my lack of experience in any way. Rather, it seemed to appeal to him. We just got on so well together. It was all clicking into place, but there was one warning sign that I should have noticed on that very first date.

I love to dance and always had done but Bill refused ever to go on the dance floor. I only ever knew him to dance once in all our time together. That night was no exception. After dinner, when we moved to a table beside the dance floor, I felt sufficiently comfortable to get up for a bop on my own, as I often did. There were many other single dancers on the floor, simply enjoying the music but Bill was not concerned with them. I could feel his eyes on me every second. He just sat there, watching me, taking in every movement, totally passive, saying nothing.

Later I was to learn that if ever another man approached to dance with me, Bill would give him the evil eye, warning him off and letting me know that there would be hell to pay later. On one bitter occasion, he would flare into a storming rage and stomp out of Tramp, leaving me stranded, simply because I dared to dance with another man.

On this first night, however, his look was more light-hearted. It said, 'Aye aye, having a bit of a flirt with the other men on the dance floor, are we?'

In fact, I wasn't. I always turned my back on men who approached me for a dance, to let them know that I was not available. I simply loved to dance but Bill's interpretation was something quite different. With hindsight, I could have spotted the tell-tale signs of his towering jealousy there and then but what did I know about jealousy? It was a lesson I was to learn very painfully in the years to come.

That night, however, nothing could spoil my fun. I had already decided I was deeply attracted to Bill. He made me feel secure and that was something I had never felt in my life before.

Later, we went back to his flat for Bill to order my taxi home. It had been a lovely evening but it was now very late, about 2 am, and I was concerned about getting back to north London. I did not have school next day, which was a Sunday, but I knew Mum would be awake, waiting for my safe return.

He didn't try to rush me. He called for a cab and suggested we have a coffee until it arrived. He switched on the TV and we sat on the settee. Then, very gently, he took me in his arms and kissed me. This time, I kissed him back, properly, for the first time. It was a revelation. I was really surprised at what a good kisser he was. I thought, 'He doesn't kiss like I imagined an older man would.'

I had half-expected it to be different, I don't know why, sort of out-of-date and old-fashioned, like in those grainy old black and white movies where the hero dryly and briskly plants a chaste peck on the heroine's rosebud – and closed – mouth. Very prim.

Bill's kiss was nothing like that. It was a lovely, slow, lingering caress. Then we talked. He kept repeating, 'It's such a shame you're not older. We could be open about your age and about our relationship.'

Two things struck home very forcibly. One, that Bill thought we would have a relationship, so this was not some one-off, one-night stand. Second, that it was my fault I was so young. A little seed of guilt about my age was planted, very skilfully, on that very first night. He was not too old for me. I was too young for him. My fault. My problem. So if we were to continue in a relationship, it was down to me to lie about it. 'Well,' a tiny voice inside me was saying, 'That's not so bad, really, is it? I had just broken my own rule by lying to Bill's friends about my age. It would seem quite plausible that I should do it again, then.

I could never have imagined the immense and irreparable repercussions that that single lie would have. At that moment our relationship was built on deceit and, like all things built on lies, one day it would crumble to dust.

That was where we went totally wrong. My Catholic upbring-ing and my own strong code of morality told me that what I was about to do was wrong but by then I was used to fighting with my conscience about going out with boys when Mum believed I was fast asleep in bed. On those occasions, I never actually lied to her, however. I just made sure she did not find out the truth.

Lying about my age was something very different. It was a lie about me, Mandy Smith, north London schoolgirl. Just as I was beginning to forge a picture of my own identity, on the threshold of adolescence, I was forced to build a picture based on lies. I was, at Bill's insistence, to create a different creature – Mandy Smith, seventeen-year-old sophisticate, college student, woman of the world in the making. I was not only altering my identity, I was altering my personality. Up until then I had always been very open and honest, even to the point of bluntness, as children so often are, unrestricted by the constraints of politeness and the politics of adulthood. Up until then, people had often been shocked when they first met me because I would always say the things that other people thought but never dared to say. I had prided myself on being like that, down-to-earth and always upfront, with the confidence of extreme youth.

That lie was the first step in a whole new me. It changed my entire character. I couldn't be who I wanted to be. I had to say goodbye to Mandy Smith, schoolgirl, aged thirteen. If I wanted to see Bill, which I undoubtedly did, I had to assume the new role of Mandy, seventeen, girlfriend of Bill Wyman. That lie changed my whole life.

I guess we talked for the best part of half an hour, keeping the cabbie waiting outside, but Bill did not seem to care. I knew by then that, so long as I fitted in with his picture of me, we would be seeing a lot more of each other. Bill was the perfect gentleman during that time. He didn't press me for anything more than that initial kiss and cuddle. He seemed respectful, wanting no more than to talk about the two of us – *us* – I liked the sound of that. Stav and my other schoolboy flirtations had been fun and light-hearted but it was always *them* and *me*. The concept of us, a couple, a pair, was infinitely more exciting, and reassuring.

As I finally extricated myself from the comfort and warmth of Bill's arms and got set to leave, he said, yet again, wistfully, 'I wish you were older, Mandy, so you could stay longer.' Put that way, I felt so too. Damn my age. Then Bill kissed me goodnight and promised he would call next day. I floated home that night totally unaware of the time or the traffic or even the real world outside as the taxi cruised along.

Although I was shattered from lack of sleep and the aftermath of all the nervous tension and the excitement, when I finally collapsed into bed, I could not even close my eyes. My thoughts were in turmoil. It felt so very right to be with Bill but it was so very wrong, too. What was I sure of any more? Only that I liked him and found him attractive and a joy to be with but, beyond that, what did I know? Eventually, exhausted, I settled for the most simplistic solution, so typical of a little girl. I thought, 'We'll stay good friends. I really don't want to get serious. Let's face it, I'm only thirteen.'

That was it settled... until the following day, when Bill rang and invited me to his country home, Gedding Hall, for the weekend. I might have settled for the easy option but there was to be no let-up on his part. Bill was not just older and more experienced than I, he was also hungrier. He had hooked me, now he was going to reel me in.

CHAPTER FIVE

Country Life

Mum was not too thrilled with me on the morning after my date with Bill at Tramp. Lying sleepless in her bed, she had watched the minutes ticking into hours and the hours slip by until it was gone 3 am. Then she finally heard my tiptoes creeping silently, so I had hoped, but obviously not silently enough, up the stairs. Bill Wyman or no Bill Wyman, no thirteen-year-old daughter of hers was stopping out until that time of the morning. She let me sleep on until midday, when, through the blackness of deep, deep sleep, I heard a distant phone ring.

I was up and out of bed like a shot, reaching it before Mum had managed to clamber down the stairs from her own room. I knew it was Bill. I hoped it was Bill. I wanted to speak to him before Mum gave him a piece of her mind for keeping her daughter out half the night. Still bleary-eyed and half-asleep, I thanked him for a lovely, lovely evening and I meant it. I could hear the smile in his voice as he said he had really enjoyed it too.

He said, very quietly, 'You're a very special little lady, Mandy.'

I wasn't sure if I half-imagined he had said that. No one had ever called me a lady before. Little girl, little nuisance, little devil, maybe, but little lady was a first. His voice was very soft and sincere. Maybe I was still asleep and dreaming this?

Bill went on: 'I wanted to sit up all night talking to you, Mandy.'

Whispering, for fear that Mum might be able to overhear this intimate conversation, I said, 'I think I'm in deep trouble, Bill. It was terribly late when I got home. Mum will not be happy. She'll think I've broken her trust.'

He said, 'But we didn't do anything wrong, did we? We weren't up to anything naughty. We were just talking. Listen, if your mum gives you a problem over this, let me talk to her.' Bill to the rescue again. He was very quickly shaping up as my knight in shining armour. I gave no thought to the fact that it was Bill who had persuaded me to stay an extra hour when I had been worried about being late home and who had refused to let me jump into the taxi at a half-respectable time.

'How would you like', he went on, 'to come to Gedding next weekend? Then we could talk right through until dawn if we feel like it.'

Instinctively, I hesitated. I knew that would be dangerous. Bill and me, away from it all, just the two of us. That would be putting opportunity and temptation too much in our way. Although Bill had been very sweet and caring the night before, there was no mistaking the urgency behind his kiss. He was turned on by kissing me. I had had experience of what that meant with Stav.

Boys reach a certain point when they are necking and then they want more. I had always been able to stop Stav in his tracks and I knew I could do the same with Bill, given the right circumstances. In other words, the opportunity to say, 'Time to go, then. Must be getting home.' At Bill's home in the country, miles from London, miles from a taxi rank or a bus stop, there would be no such chance. Not that I felt worried about Bill taking advantage of me in that situation. I didn't. Unlike Stav, he was a grown man, quiet, caring and more in control of himself, but I did not want to risk it.

I said, 'I can't do that, Bill. I can't go away with you on my own. It wouldn't be right.'

There was silence for a second, then he said, 'So why don't you bring Nicola? I'll show you both around the place. You'll love it, it's very peaceful and very pretty, deep in the countryside. How about it?'

It sounded lovely to me but first I had to clear it with Mum and, before I did that, I had to apologise for my lateness the night before. Again, Bill said, 'If your mum is at all worried, just let me speak to her. She knows you'll be in safe hands with me.'

Bill rang off and I delicately picked my way through to Mum's room where she was sitting, glasses perched on the end of her nose, pretending to read the Sunday papers. 'Welcome home, the Prodigal Daughter,' she said with just a hint of a jagged edge of sarcasm.

'Er, hi, Mum,' I offered, then, looking at her eagle eyes watching me squirm, I backed down, 'Can I get you a cuppa?'

'Certainly, dear, most kind of you,' she said. 'But first, you can tell me what the heck you were doing until 3 am?'

OK, here goes. Both feet in . . . 'Dancing, Mum and chatting.' (The truth.) 'Honestly, I swear. Tramp doesn't close until 3.' (The truth.)

She looked at my earnest expression and said very slowly, 'I have always trusted you, Mandy. I know you're a good girl. Please don't abuse my trust and faith in you.'

'I won't, Mum,' I promised and I meant it. I would rather have cut off my own head than let my mum down. I knew what she meant. She had been badly scarred by my father's illicit affairs. She felt that if a woman gave herself sexually to a man, he would use and abuse and finally dump her as shoddy goods. She had indoctrinated Nic and me with this philosophy. Men never marry the ones they sleep with. Hang on to your virginity until a really, truly decent man comes along. One who loves and respects you. They are few and far between, so don't muck about with the no-hopers who will destroy your self-respect.

I was not contemplating a sexual relationship with anyone, never mind Bill Wyman, but I was keen to explore the new avenue of emotions that had opened up when I discovered boys and that quiet little avenue had suddenly become a busy main thoroughfare now that I'd met Bill.

Mum could read me like a book. She saw from my expression that I was telling her the truth. 'Come on, then,' she relented, 'tell me all about Tramp. What's it like?' So I curled up next to her on the bed and told her about Bill and Keith and Patti and the incident with my skirt and we were both convulsed by fits of giggles. I loved my mum so much. I could tell her anything. She was always on my side.

Then I broached the subject of the trip to Gedding. How Bill had offered to take Nic and me for a weekend in the country. 'Sounds lovely,' she said. 'So long as there are two of you.' Perhaps naively, she had failed to spot any sexual motives in Bill. His charm, his chocolates and flowers, his comfortable presence in our own home made her feel he was entirely trustworthy. Like me, she felt he was a bit of a lost soul who had sacrificed a happy home for the sake of his career.

She said, 'Bill really is very kind, isn't he? He reminds me of David. I expect he longs for a family of his own. It's sad, really, isn't it? You can have fame and success but, at the end of the day, you can't have it all. If it came down to choosing between family and fortune, I know which I would rather have any day.' And she gave me one of her great big cuddles.

The weekend was on and the breakaway had begun.

The week came and went with amazing speed and suddenly it was Saturday morning. Nic and I frenziedly threw a clean pair of jeans apiece into an overnight bag, along with a couple of toothbrushes.

Bill had told us not to bother bringing any luggage. The house had everything we might need and we could rely on his house-keepers, Monique and Louis, to provide any extras for guests. They were used to catering for Bill's friends and business colleagues who often popped down for the weekend. Suddenly, I had a vision that Gedding Hall might be a bit on the splendid side if it was a regular weekend retreat for all Bill's chums. What the heck, you only live once. At least Nic and I would be out of place together in our jeans and T-shirts.

At midday, when Bill was due to arrive at Morant Place to pick us up, Nic, who was looking out of the window, suddenly let out a yelp. 'He's here,' she said, 'Ten out of ten for punctu-ality. I am impressed!'

More used to being kept waiting by boys with no sense of time and even less sense of decency, it was a treat to meet some-one like Bill, on whom you could rely. He beeped his horn impatiently and we kissed Mum goodbye then rushed downstairs to where his silver-grey Mercedes 500 SL was waiting.

I swear we could hear every pair of lace curtains twitch along the length of Morant Place as we stepped into the car and sank back into the sumptuous leather upholstery. It was one in the eye for those patronising neighbours who had sneered at us Smiths for years and made us the object of all their totally unfounded local gossip. Well, this time, for once, they *did* have something to bitch about! This would keep a few coffee mornings in tittle-tattle for the rest of the week.

We cruised down to Gedding, laughing and joking all the way. All three of us were in great spirits. It was the beginning of March, cold and crisp, but clear and sunny with the promise of an early spring already on the way.

I had always thought of myself as a town girl, brought up in the city and enjoying all the hustle and grime of London life. The countryside held no particular allure for me at thirteen. I was on the threshold of those teen years where discos, clubs, the cinema and theatre are the only places to be. Stuck in the middle of nowhere with only cows for company is a typical teenager's idea of death by slow and agonising boredom.

On this first occasion, however, Gedding was a treat to be savoured, but I knew it was Bill's presence, not the country nor the mansion, that gave me pleasure.

At first sight, I thought Gedding was a forbidding old house. Rather dark and gloomy, it stood out in its isolation, detached from the surrounding rolling fields by a long, winding, gravel driveway. Bill parked the car outside and led us through the porticoed entrance and into a marble hallway. He made no reference to its history or grandeur but waved us through to the sitting room to meet his French staff, who were waiting there, obviously very pleased to see him.

Monique offered us tea in the drawing room but Bill was keen to take us on a guided tour. The house was quite clearly his pride and joy but, to be honest, I found it a chilling place. You could never call it a home. It was too small to be a stately home, although that seemed to be what Bill had been aspiring to when he had had it renovated and decorated. It was dark and stuffy with antiques and oil paintings strategically placed to draw maximum attention, but the whole presentation did not add up to a happy package. It felt like it was a show-piece, loved but unlived in. The only room that had a friendly feel to it was the guest bedroom, a peaceful harmony of muted cream and pastel hues. Welcoming and mellow, it stood in stark contrast to the rest of the house. Nic and I dropped our bags next to the twin beds and moved on on the guided tour with Bill.

As Bill showed us round, he gave us a potted history of various antiques and the structure of the building, right down to the last gnarled beam. He admitted he was a bit of a history buff but his pride and joy was his own bedroom – and, I was later to discover, a fair bit of history had been made by Bill himself in there.

As he ushered us in, the first thing that met my eyes was a great monstrosity of a double bed. This massive – and massively ugly – four-poster dominated the entire room. It was huge and ornately carved in heavy dark wood. It made the room look dark.

It was really quite spooky. I hated it on sight.

He proudly revealed its chequered history. Mick Jagger had owned it before him and the film star James Coburn before that. Elizabeth Taylor had slept in it and many other movie and music business stars whose names were unfamiliar to me. I looked at Bill. His joy in this bed was plain to see. What sort of memories did he have of his own time between those dark burgundy sheets? How many women had he shared this bed with? I felt ashamed of this sudden and unexpected emotion. Why should I be suspicious of Bill all of a sudden? Yet his feelings about his bed were written all over him – in the way he looked at it and then at me – in the pride in his voice when he described it. For no apparent reason, that bed haunted me.

Later, I would beg him many times to get rid of it. When I finally discovered all about Bill's Lothario past, when he finally confessed that he had bedded over a thousand women before me, this bed became rooted in my mind as the symbol – and the scene – of all those sordid sexual encounters. It was a monster, a constant reminder of his womanising ways.

The whole room was dark and oppressive with burgundy and cream wallpaper and drapes to match the bed. It made me shiver.

'Seen a ghost?' laughed Bill, unaware of the real reason for my sudden discomfort. 'As it happens, there is a ghost here. Several guests have seen her. I've often thought I've heard her myself – especially in the dead of night at full moon, when there's a ghostly hush all around.'

He was laughing at me, my nervousness and my little girlish fears. He would not let up. He told us all about the sad tale of the resident ghost; the spirit of a young girl whose family had originally owned Gedding Hall but had been forced, through mounting debts, to hand it over to an unscrupulous landowner. Forced into marriage with this elderly charlatan in order to save her parent's lives – they faced imprisonment and certain death as the penalty for their debts – the young girl, her heart and spirit broken, refused to eat and finally starved herself to death. I knew nothing of anorexia then but I knew I did not like this tragic tale, nor the thought of a lost and lonely ghost wafting through the dark and gloomy Gedding hallways.

I was much relieved when Bill then led us downstairs to dinner. Monique, the cook, had laid on a sumptuous feast for us.

With typical French flair, she had created a cordon bleu master-piece of great style and subtlety. Although Bill had not thought to forewarn her that Nic and I ate little red meat, she had thoughtfully prepared an exquisite free-range chicken dish, basted in oil and swathed in herbs.

There were several kinds of vegetable, crisp and buttery, and freshly baked French bread. Bill offered us some red wine from a bottle he had brought up from his wine cellar with a great flourish – he said it was a rare vintage and very, very sought after. I sipped a mouthful. It tasted like vinegar and I told him so.

He laughed. He said, 'You know what I love about you two? You always speak your mind and you tell the truth. Plenty of people have sat here and knocked back the most undrinkable plonk and said how superb it was in an attempt to impress. But if you think something is horrible, you'll let me know, right?'

Nic and I did the meal proud and polished off every scrap. Bill, I could not fail to notice, only picked at his.

'Ah,' said Monique, not in the least bit offended, but clearly quite used to this blatant waste of her efforts, 'Bill likes only his food if it has ketchup with it. But I prefer he should not kill my cooking with tomato sauce. I am teaching him the French way of food – but it is taking more time than I thought!'

As the plates were cleared away, we moved to the adjacent TV lounge where Bill had a library of hundreds of videos, arranged in alphabetical order in neat rows.

I sat on the settee next to him but, again, I could not concentrate on what was on the screen. There was a feeling, almost tangible between us, that something was about to happen. There was an electricity, the air was positively charged.

Nicola was oblivious to the fact that she was playing gooseberry. Over in a corner armchair, she was laughing uproariously at the video. Eventually, she yawned dramatically and said she was off to bed.

Bill turned to me and said, 'Where are you going to sleep, Mandy?'

'With Nicola,' I replied, 'in the guest room.'

Then he smiled and said, 'Why don't you come to my bed?'

I looked at Bill and suddenly there was no doubt in my mind. I knew I would sleep with him that night. It was all so straightforward. He just asked me outright. No pressure, no fumbling, no stops and starts. He was being completely honest and sincere. He wanted to sleep with me. I was flattered, I was reassured. I felt needed, wanted and loved. His honesty, his directness and his need just touched my heart. It was as simple as that. So he led me up to his bedroom on this first step on the biggest adventure of my new life as Mandy Smith, child-woman.

I was extremely nervous, scared even. Although I liked, trusted and fancied Bill, there was no getting away from the fact that he – and this – were virgin territory to me. It was the first time I had ever been to bed with a man and there was one thing of which I was very very sure. We were not going to have sex. I was one hundred per cent positive about that.

Beyond that certainty, I was a jumble of feelings. Above the nerves and fear, I was deeply embarrassed at the thought of someone seeing me naked. Not even my mother had the dubious privilege of that! I was at that tender age where nudity is terri-fying. My body was still developing and, although I was hugely assured of my figure in nice clothes, when I was stripped bare, I was, well, just that . . . stripped bare. My confidence went out of the window along with my clothes.

I felt like a little girl again as he led me into the room but at the same time I felt like a woman. This was a very grown-up thing to be doing and I felt curiously in control.

I believed I knew Bill enough to know that he would not touch me if I did not want him to, which I didn't. This was just like the next step on our adventure together in a Mills and Boon romance. For added comfort, I fell back on my Rule Number One with boys: 'No sex until sixteen'. There, I was quite safe, then. Then we got to the bed and my shyness overcame me. I couldn't do it. Playing for time, I asked Bill for a T-shirt. He turned away to a chest of drawers, pulled one out and handed it to me, smiling.

Escape! I slipped off to the bathroom and took my clothes off ever so slowly, thinking, 'What am I doing? What am I *doing*?' I would keep my knickers on, just for good measure – a cotton chastity belt to preserve my virtue. Then I slipped on the T-shirt and looked at myself in the mirror. 'Mandy. You are thirteen. Bill is a man.' I said to myself, several times so that the importance of it would sink in. Although I didn't know what good it would do, it was comforting just saying the words.

Bill knocked on the door. 'You all right, Mandy?' he said, his voice muffled through the heavy oak panels.

I came out of my trance. 'Yes, just coming. Got to brush my teeth.' Damn and blast. My toothbrush was in the guest bathroom.

I used Bill's, brushing fervently and wondering if a hundred brush strokes would eliminate the taste, and worse, the smell of garlic. Oh God, Bill had not really touched the flipping chicken. How could I kiss him when I smelt like a kitchen garden?

Another knock. 'Ma–andy,' he said. 'I'm not going to eat you . . .'

'Not if you didn't already eat the chicken,' I thought wryly to myself and then, gingerly, I opened the door, ready to meet my destiny. Bill, still fully dressed, walked straight past me and into the bathroom. 'Desperate for a wee,' he said. 'Too much wine at dinner.' So much for Mills and Boon.

I took the opportunity to slip quickly between the sheets. At least then I would be completely covered up and Bill would have to undress in front of *me*. I wondered if I would know where to look. I had never seen a man take off his clothes before. Should I look at the ceiling? Pretend to bury myself in a book. I looked around the bedside tables – paper tissues, a hairbrush, a digital clock, pot pourri – no joy there, then.

Bill came out of the ensuite bathroom and paused, staring at me lying between the sheets. 'You are the most beautiful creature I have ever seen,' he said. He walked to the bed and sat down beside me, stroking my hair lightly with hs fingertips.

Holding up a strand between his fingers, he smiled. 'You've never been to bed with a man before, have you, Mandy?'

'No,' I said.

'Well, I won't hurt you. I promise,' he said and turned round to remove his sweatshirt, then his white T-shirt underneath. He bent then, removing his trainers and socks, before turning back to face me with a shy smile. 'Bit skinny, aren't I? But not bad for an old dog who's had his day . . .' He made me laugh by being so gentle and self-effacing. I felt he was trying to put me at my ease. Then, slowly, he unzipped his jeans and slid them down over his skinny boyish hips . . . Oh my dear God, he was wearing Y-fronts!

Suppressing the roar of laughter that was welling up inside

me, I shoved a metaphorical hankie in my mouth and blinked hard to stop myself from choking. Did men *really* still wear Y-fronts? I had seen them on washing-lines, big and baggy and boiled grey, the natural wardrobe of tired old grandads – I knew from school gym lessons that boys had moved on to that modern invention, boxer shorts or even plain and simple underpants. Blimey, Y-fronts went out with the Ark!

Oblivious to my suppressed mirth and still with a look of loving tenderness in his eyes, Bill gently sat down on the edge of the bed, gazing steadily at me. Then, trying to be as sexy as possible, he hooked his thumbs into the waistband and deftly slipped off those giant pants. I did not dare take my eyes off his face. God help me, if I laughed now...

He slid one arm under my shoulders and the other over my chest, then he pulled me to him for a tender kiss, but he didn't try anything else at all. We lay there for an age, him holding me tight, cuddling and kissing, but I didn't have to fight him off. He was happy just to be there, to have me in his bed and in his arms. Me? I loved it. I felt so secure lying there next to him. There was nothing threatening nor sexual about it. Just tender, gentle, comforting care and complete peace. It felt like I had come home.

My lifetime of need and longing for a father figure, to pick me up, hug me and love me, was made flesh that night in Bill's arms. I would never forget that total, blissful sense of security. It was a landmark, a cornerstone, on which, for many years, I would build my illusion – my delusion – of Bill.

Not that he looked or felt like a father. He did not seem to me to be an old man at all. He was so slight, small-boned and slim. He was my first love, my first man, and, ever after, I would be drawn to slender, slim-waisted men. Bruisers pulsating with gym-toned body mass and rippling muscles remain to this day an instant turn-off. Bill was my mentor and my sculptor. That night he carved himself into an effigy of the father I had always longed for. In return, he won my total love, adoration and devotion.

I had fallen for him without reservation and when you fall so hard you don't even notice a wrinkle here or a grey hair there. You fall for the whole package. That was the way it was with Bill that night. The only thing I wasn't mad about were his hands. I love hands, I have a big thing about them. Some women love men's bums, or shoulders but I adore long, slim, artist's hands. Bill had tiny hands, with short fingers. I remember feeling sad about that. However, when he put his arms around me and we eventually fell asleep, it felt just right.

Unfortunately for Bill, the seeds of fear he had sown earlier came home to roost in the middle of the night. All my life I've always been scared of the dark. It was no different that night. All Bill's talk of ghosts had infiltrated my subconsciousness and then erupted in some monumentally bad dreams. I was being chased by some unknown terror, racing against time, and it was gaining on me, breathing hot and heavy behind me. I could feel its breath on my neck, its evil hands reaching out to ensnare me then, suddenly, I was falling, falling into a never-ending bottomless, black hole. Perhaps it was just my guilt surfacing but I woke in a very real terror. Nudging Bill, I made him, not once, but twice, get up and open the separate sets of curtains that closed out the light of the night outside and cloaked us together in darkness.

Even so, I could not fall back into sleep. I lay there, listening to the sound of my own shallow, fearful breathing, and the deeper, sonorous tones of Bill's breath. I needed to go to the bathroom but to cross the few feet to the ensuite door was to cross the great divide between sanctuary and danger. I could not do it on my own. Again, I prodded him into a bleary wakefulness. Pitifully, plaintively, like a little child, I whimpered, 'Bill, I need to go to the bathroom.'

Somnabulent, he took my hand in his and walked me those few treacherous feet across the room. 'Please don't go back to bed,' I pleaded. 'Please wait here for me.' So my man lover waited dutifully, comatosely, outside the heavy oak door while I did what a little girl had to do. Then, stumbling, still half-asleep, he led me back to his bed.

That night, and often thereafter, I would lie next to Bill and think of the ghost of poor, tragic Elizabeth. Sometimes I could feel her presence. There would be a sudden chill from nowhere or perhaps an inexplicable waft of an untraceable smell – fresh freesias, or flickering candles and pipe smoke. I was terrified and yet, at the same time, I felt for lonely, lost Elizabeth, whose life was so wasted and whose death so unnecessary, torn between a family she loved and a man who destroyed her. In my young terror and naivety I could never have foreseen how prophetic this vision of Elizabeth was to be for me. How my own young life would follow in her ghostly footsteps and lead me to the brink of destruction too.

For then, I was just glad to have the comfort of Bill's body next to mine, keeping the ogres of the night at bay. I always fell asleep in his arms and when I woke we would be tangled up in each other, lovers in the deepest, truest sense of the word, untainted and unsullied by sex.

That first morning I woke to feel the glorious, warming sunlight of the countryside beaming through the mullioned windows on to my face and to hear the sound of ducks quacking noisily on the duckpond directly outside in the gardens. Next to me, Bill lay crumpled and creased and utterly lovable, like a little teddy bear.

Alerted to the change in each other's breathing, we would often wake as one and so it was on this first occasion. His sleepy eyes met mine and he squeezed my hand. We were like a couple of schoolkids, tucked up in bed, tickling each other, teasing and giggling away. Bed became our haven from the world. Free from rules and regulations, oblivious to our differences in years, experience and background, we became as one. We were so happy in bed that we would often stay there until two or three in the afternoon. And so we did after this very first night.

Before me, Bill had always been a prompt riser, up at 8 am, but now we couldn't bear to get up; we were so happy there together. When we finally did get up, to face what remained of the day, the staff would look at us very oddly, as if we had been practising the *Kama Sutra* from back to front all night. That added to our joy. It was our little secret that we were still celibate.

However, I still had a major juvenile hang-up. I was much too embarrassed to let anyone other than Bill see me in bed so he told the staff we were never to be disturbed in the bedroom. Let them think what they might, we knew the truth and that truth, in its innocence, bound us closer.

My biggest problem that next day was facing Nic. She, of all people, would not settle for surmising what had happened. She would want to know it all, right down to every last detail. We had always shared everything together but that night I had crossed a bridge and now a river flowed between us. I had crossed over to Bill's side and there was no going back. I had done something she would find unacceptable, beyond the bounds of anything either of us had done before. How could I explain that to her?

Naturally, because we always shared all our secrets, as soon as we surfaced and Bill had disappeared into the kitchen to fetch us coffee, she asked me directly: 'What happened?'

For the first time ever, I snubbed my own beloved sister, my erstwhile confidante and my best friend. It was an automatic reaction. I said, dismissively, 'That's a bit personal!'

It was not the sort of reaction she had ever had from me before. She saw the widening gulf and she knew she could not cross it. She retreated and I shut myself off from Nic at that very moment. From then on, I began to turn against her. After that, whenever she asked about Bill and me, I felt she was prying and resented her intrusion.

Poor, blameless Nic was not prying. In the only way she knew how, she was being protective, the elder sibling in defence of her baby sister. But little sis was gone. In her place was Mandy, big girl, several steps ahead of the game or so she thought.

In fact, it was my own fear and guilt over my quantum leap that night that I had turned into another emotion altogether. Unable to cope with what I had done, I looked for someone else to blame, to shut out. That person was first of all my sister, later, it would be my mother. I had broken the strong family moral code and I simply did not have the wherewithal to cope with my feelings about my behaviour. Far easier, then, to shut them out and go along with what Bill said and did and told me to do.

When I started sleeping naked with him, then I really felt utterly, totally vulnerable. There were just the two of us and our secret. When you are flesh to flesh with someone, you become very close. How could I then turn to my mum or Nic and talk to them about that, when it was forbidden? So I turned towards Bill, which was exactly what he wanted. He had already planted the seed in my mind that I would be all right with him; that he would look after me.

His next step was to undermine my mum. To sever the bond completely, to free me from being little Mandy, someone's thirteen-year-old daughter – and turn me into his very own nymphet. The process, insidious and subliminal, started that very weekend.

When I returned to his room after my confrontation with Nic, Bill was swift to reassure me that I had done the right thing. 'She might be your sister, but some things are best left unsaid,' he nodded sagely. He was so much older and wiser; already I was under his sway.

'How can I face my mother', I wailed, 'when I can't even cope with my sister's attitude?'

Bill's answer was simple, straightforward and designed to close the door between me and my mother forever. 'Parents aren't right about everything,' he said. 'They make mistakes and misunderstand, just like the rest of us.'

For the very first time, I began to question Mum. I thought, 'Bill's right. She is wrong sometimes.' I knew, without question, that she would never understand the momentous step I had taken just hours before, sleeping with a naked and aroused man. A man who wanted me – but all of me, not just my body. Bill wanted my heart, body and soul and Bill always got what he wanted.

As we drove back to London later that evening, the journey was in stark contrast to the one we had taken to Gedding just the day before.

I sat in the front with Bill, united in our secret bond. Nic sat silent, watchful, wary in the back. In just twenty-four hours, I had lost my childish innocence. I had slept with a naked man, his body interlocked with mine. At that point I had shut out all I had known before. Now I listened only to Bill. He had sucked me into his lifestyle and his life.

CHAPTER SIX

Child by Day, Woman by Night

Returning to school on the day after my weekend at Gedding Hall with Bill, I knew I was a changed person. I adored Franklin House because it offered me such respite after the bitchy hot-housing at my previous convent school, and also because it was mixed. By then I knew that I got on better with boys than girls and I had developed some good friendships among the boys in the years senior to me.

I had settled down very quickly there and, despite my pre-deliction for make-up and blonde streaks, was getting no hassle from the teachers. There was no rigid uniform rule, the emphasis being on academic excellence rather than pristine appearance.

I had quickly adapted to the regime and began to excel in classwork, largely because I felt all pressure on me had been removed. I was relaxed, I felt I could be myself. However, no sooner had I settled in than I had met Bill. It was all very well to be myself? But just who was I now?

I had left school on Friday, books clutched under my arms, muttering the usual moans about homework . . . and I returned on Monday, having just slept with a man. I sat behind my desk and all my thoughts were of Bill, the feel of his skin, the smell of him, the taste of him. Geography, maths, French – they were all history as far as I was concerned. With the intensity and fervour that only first love can produce, I was lost in a mist of the here and now, longing to be a million miles from the dry dust of the classroom and back in Bill's arms. I could not wait for the day to drag by so that I could rush home and wait for his call. There was no doubt that he would call. By some miracle, he seemed to feel the same desperate need to be with me. He had told me he wanted to be with me all night long, each and every night. I was a schoolgirl by day, but a woman, and the object of a man's desires, by night.

I could tell no one. Isolated in my half-world of awakening sexuality, I distanced myself from my schoolmates. What did they know of men and love and lust? Theirs was only fantasy, storybook stuff of dreams about pop stars like Tony Hadley or Marty Pellow. My love was real. My man was real. And he said he loved me too.

The trouble was, love like this was so huge, so overwhelming, that it had to be shared – either moony-eyed and confessional with a best friend or questioning and seeking reassurance from my mother but my first love was forbidden love, so how could it be shared? That weekend I had been forced to move into in a shadowy, twilight world of lies and half-truths.

I had glossed over the events at Gedding when we returned home to Mum. I left it to Nic to fill in the finer details – a test, in some ways, to see whether she would spill the beans and split on me. She did not. Perhaps it was too big an issue even for Nic to broach with Mum but she did not betray me.

Mum, happy enough with our description of the house, the staff and the food, did not pause to ponder that I might not have slept the night in the guest bedroom with Nicola. She trusted me. How could I face her when I had let her down? I didn't. I turned instead to Bill.

True to his words of love that night, he called me, almost daily, over the next few weeks. We talked of school and his music and the day-to-day trivia that others would no doubt find too insignificant even to mention. To me, in love, they took on the significance of world events. I wanted to know about every minute of Bill's every day and he, mine.

Mum marvelled at this closeness between us but, hearing us talk on the phone, she assumed from my childish banter about lessons, lateness and how the dog next door had given birth to seven pups, that this was a relationship founded on genuine fatherly friendship on Bill's part. Indeed, he would repeatedly tell me – and Mum – how he had always longed for a daughter. One of the great regrets of his life was that his marriage had not worked out but at least he had his son. Thus, he lulled Mum into thinking that his attitude to me was purely paternal.

If I wanted to see the sights of London, he would show me. Bill's name was a passport to places I had only ever dreamed of but the only place he ever took me on those early dates was Tramp. That, and Bill's flat, gradually became as familiar to me as my own home. I started seeing him on Friday and Saturday nights, first for dinner at Tramp, then back to Bill's place for coffee and kisses. Then the weekends stretched into the week, and I began visiting, at his behest, on Tuesdays and Wednesdays, too. Initially, I would try to get a taxi home by 1 am but, gradually, the time slipped back, later and later.

Mum started voicing concern but I shrugged it off. She knew I was in safe hands, didn't she? Then Bill would call and pour oil on stormy waters and she would relent again, for the time being.

Overall, however, she had begun to feel that enough was enough; that there was something unhealthy about the way Bill was taking over my life. She told me to call a halt to the relationship – whether it was purely platonic or not, it was leaving no space in my life for my family, friends or school. By then it was too late. I weighed up the influence of my mother against Bill and Bill won.

There were several barn-storming rows over the isssue, each one culminating in me storming out of the house and over to Bill's where he would calm me down, stroke my hair, reassure me that he would look after me and call Mum to let her know I was safe with him.

Mum, bedridden, worn out by the constant battles with me, and worn down by Bill's reasoning charm, was powerless. She could not, would not, condone the relationship but she would not give it her seal of approval, either.

We formed an uneasy truce, whereby, every time I went out, I promised to call her from Bill's to let her know I had arrived safely and again, later, to let her know what time I would be on my way home.

Bill had cut a swathe through my relationship with my doting mother. Equally as destructive, he had effectively terminated my studies. I could no longer cope with retreating into schoolgirl mode by day when I was developing so fast emotionally and sexually by night.

Although we did not have full intercourse, I was by now sleeping almost naked with Bill. It was a natural progression from our first night together, when I had kept on my T-shirt. Slowly, tentatively, he was teaching me how to be sensual and enjoy the pleasures of flesh on flesh. He would beg and plead with me to take off my T-shirt, until finally I did. Then he would coax and cajole me to remove my panties, but I always refused. Penetration would mean he had taken all of me. I needed to keep that to myself until I was stronger, older, more sure of this love between us. In my head, I still lived by the dictum: no sex until sixteen.

I knew every inch and every contour of his body. I knew what it meant when he was aroused and I knew what to do about it. Bill had shown me. I was happy to oblige him. Sleeping naked with him made me feel like a vulnerable child. Bringing him to orgasm gave me power over him, just for a few fleeting minutes. I loved to give him that sweet ecstasy.

We would lie together, on the rug in front of his fire, stroking, kissing, just being together until the early hours of the morning. I would always go home before dawn – but only just.

Night after night, I would fall into bed at 4 am, then stumble out again at 7.30 for school. Day after day, I would fall asleep at my desk. If I could make it through the morning without closing my eyes, I would be all right. Then, at lunchtime, I could find myself a quiet classroom, put my head down on a desk and pass out for an hour. It wasn't long before I was nodding off during lessons as well. The teacher used to crack his blackboard eraser on the desk to wake me up. If only he had known why I was falling asleep or what I was dreaming about. I couldn't concentrate. So far as I was concerned, school was out for the summer.

Eventually, I had to crack. I had to talk to someone about my dilemma so I took my dearest friend, Jason, into my confidence and spilled the beans about Bill.

Jason, who had been a child actor, was a bit of a star himself. He played the role of the teenage son in the Oxo family ads and, if anyone understood the problems of being in the public eye, he did.

Bill had always been at pains to point out that he could not afford to be seen in public with me. Tramp was OK, he was best friends with the owner, Johnny Gold, and regarded it as 'his' club. He felt safe there. His fame and public recognition were things I found very hard to deal with. To me, he was my boyfriend and my love, a normal human being, not a star. Jason understood. To people in the street, he, too, was a famous face but to me he was ordinary, down-to-earth Jason.

I gave him the works. A blow-by-blow account of how I had met Bill, how I had lied and cheated to my own family to cover our love and every intimate detail of where we went and what we did. Jason was fascinated, intrigued and the soul of discretion. I was massively relieved. At least I had got it all off my chest and, somehow, in the curious way that sharing secrets with an outside source does, it brought me even closer to Bill. I began to move some of my things into his flat. I was spending more and more time there so it was expedient to have a few changes of clothes, make-up and a toothbrush there.

Mum never noticed I was squirreling things away from home. By now, I felt I had two homes, which was exactly what Bill wanted. His attempt to transform me from schoolgirl into his own nymph was almost complete. He would often persuade me not to go to school in the mornings but to stay in bed with him instead. I left school, and my family, behind. My head had been turned by the glamour of Tramp and the excitement of dancing, then loving the night away, had completely taken me over.

What young girl wouldn't rather spend the day in Chelsea having a lazy lie-in, followed by a bit of browsing in the boutiques along the Kings Road? I felt grown-up now. I had rushed headlong out of childhood, without even stopping for adolescence. I was later to learn the devastating consequences of that precipitous leap. One day I would pay a high price for missing out an entire stage of my personal development and find myself teetering on the edge of madness and death. One day I would be reduced again to the helpless child I was forced to leave far behind when Bill took me over, but what did I know of that then?

I looked to Bill for my guidance. In some ways, he was the father I had never had. He slipped easily into the dominant parental role and I complied with his orders. When he told me to come over for the evening, I would. When he told me I should stay the night or stay home with him the following morning, I did. Bill was calling the shots and I was happy to collude. I had longed for that paternal influence for years.

Yet, at the same time, somewhere along the line, somehow, I had also evolved into Bill's woman and, very rapidly, I grew to fit that role. Sometimes, when he'd persuaded me to stay overnight, next morning he would hole up in his study and get on with his work at the computer, completely absorbed.

Right from the beginning, Bill revealed a great affinity for his computer. He would spend hours on it every day, writing his memoirs or composing songs. He took his music and his writing very seriously. It was man's work. So it fell to me to do the woman's work. I would go out and fetch some shopping for the kitchen, then cook him dinner, usually something simple like pasta and salad, or roast chicken with all the trimmings. He loved that. He adored me in the kitchen almost as much as in the bedroom. He relished me in the role of wife and little housewife. Of course, it was a role I was already used to. I had had a young lifetime to prepare for all this, looking after my mum. Other thirteen-year-olds might have protested at having this premature domesticity thrust upon them. Not me. It was my destiny.

Neither did I worry any longer over missing school. In his whispered avowals of love in the night, Bill would promise me the world. I was his little girl, his woman, his wife. He would look after me, love me and never leave me. What did I need academic qualifications for? My future was secure with him.

There were many bridges to cross in this journey from my mother's little girl to Bill's woman but we met most of them together. School was not a problem. No truant officer chased me up, no letters from the local education authority suggested I should attend more regularly. They simply let me slip through the net.

Mum, initially frantic with worry, had settled into an unhappy acceptance of this situation. After several capillary-bursting rows, she had realised that if she forbade me to see Bill, she would lose me altogether – until such time as I came home brokenhearted.

She could not bear the thought of that. Bill soothed her fears with his charm and reasoning. He promised her faithfully that he would look after me. He suggested, very early on, that he would pay for alternative private education. That he, too, was concerned that I had dropped out of school. He assured her, time and again, that ours was not a physical relationship and that he looked on me as a daughter. That last line was the clincher. Mum, ever concerned that her headstrong younger child might one day turn wayward, had long felt I needed a strong, steady male influence in my life to guide me. Well, here he was. The gospel according to Bill.

However, if I thought I had surmounted all the obstacles in the way of having the perfect relationship with Bill, I was wrong. There was one final stumbling block – Bill himself. I thought I knew him with his funny old-fashioned bachelor ways, his neatness, his need for space on his own, his fussy, funny habits like always having HP sauce on the table at dinner. He had been a long time single, I thought, but there was one fairly major element of his prolonged bachelor lifestyle that I had absolutely no prior knowledge of: his appetite for other women.

I came to Bill with an unblemished record in love. It simply had not happened to me. Ridiculously, I assumed his situation was similar. Despite his thirty-three years on me, like a child I assumed that, after his marriage had failed, he had been so hurt that he had never found another woman he could love and trust – until me. If anything revealed my extreme youth, that gullibility did. Bill, I was to discover, had had more women, literally, than I had had hot breakfasts.

He had told me of his longstanding affair with Astrid Lundstrom. He told me they had really been no more than just good friends for the latter years of their relationship and how she had had a serious drink and drugs habit that forced him to stay with her, largely out of pity. It was certainly not the love he felt for me.

Very soon, however, I began to feel that perhaps Bill was not being one hundred per cent honest with me in this area. For a start, the phone calls were a bit of a giveaway. Whenever we returned to the flat from a meal out, there would be a stack of calls on his answerphone – most of them from young-sounding women. They all said much the same thing; for example, 'Hi, Bill, where have you *been*? Call me as soon as you can.'

Fine, so he had lots of female friends, but even I was not silly enough to buy that one. Still, I let him fob me off with the perfectly reasonable excuse (given how often he told me he loved me) that he had had plenty of girlfriends before me but now he was happy to confine his attentions to me – until I looked in his secret dairy.

Curiously, on all the days and nights he was not spending with me, there were female names pencilled in. I totted them up. There were dozens, and one name, Kelly, came up time and time again. The only woman I knew that Bill saw on a regular basis was his masseuse and her name was not Kelly.

I seethed at this incontrovertible evidence of his duplicity. He had sworn I was the only girl for him. He had talked to me of eternal love and marrying me at sixteen. He had sworn to me that fidelity was high on his list of life's priorities. I had believed him, because it was that way for me. I fumed. I waited. I picked my moment the following night to confront him.

Always upfront, I could not let this pass. As we lay in bed that night, I said I was thirsty and got out of bed to get a drink of water. I returned with a glass of water – and his diary. Bill paled visibly.

'Mandy, have you been going through my private things?' he said accusingly, in a desperate attempt to turn the blame on to me.

I was having none of it. 'Yes,' I said. 'You led me to believe there was nothing private between us. We share everything, remember?'

Point taken. He looked sheepish. I came straight out with it. 'Bill, have you been seeing other women behind my back?'

He was equally straight. 'Mandy,' he said, without a moment's hesitation, 'If you won't have sex with me, I have to get it somewhere.'

Bang. He had thrown it right back in my face. It was my fault, again. Just like my age. He know he had hit the bullseye. I was mortally wounded, backing off, questioning myself, not him any more. His thirty-three years' advance on me had won through again.

'You can never be my proper girlfriend, Mandy, until you have sex with me.'

To any self-respecting woman with any knowledge of male emotional blackmail, the red light would have gone on. To me, at thirteen, in love with a man who had taken the place of the father I never had and the lover I had only begun to dream of, it was tantamount to being hit in the belly by a sackful of wet cement. I was utterly, totally crushed.

Whoever coined the cliché, 'Sticks and stones may break my bones, but words will never hurt me', was totally misinformed. I bled over those words. The man who had said I was his everything was now saying I was nothing until I had sex with him. He was saying: 'Sleep with me now, Mandy, or lose me forever.' It was only a matter of time, then . . .

That night, however, I was calling the shots. Distraught, furious and petulant, I told Bill it was over between us, I would never tolerate an ultimatum like that and I went back home to weep on Mum's shoulder. She wept too; tears of pain because I had been so hurt and tears of joy to have me back. Then I plunged into the nightmare of pain and depression that only the failure of first love can evince. I couldn't eat, I couldn't sleep, I thought I would never smile again.

I had loved and lost and I tried desperately to come to terms with my decision but I knew I was right. I had given everything to Bill but the one thing I had to retain was my self-respect. I could not let myself be treated like some little bimbo. He might treat those other women that way, but not me. To me, he was not some rock star, he was just plain Bill. He had said, right from the start, that that was what was so refreshingly different about me. I always treated him as Bill, not Bill Wyman, Rolling Stone. Well, if he could indeed have his pick of women, he could find plenty of others to treat that way, but not me.

And yet, no matter what I thought, my heart said differently. I loved him.

I refused his calls. I had to get him out of my system. He would only hurt me. I stayed strong through the pain of those endless tearful days and nights, and then, just as my resolve was gaining strength, Bill did an about face and caught me with my guard completely down.

It was the week of my birthday on 17 July 1984. I was opening the usual family cards when there was a knock at the door. A messenger was on the doorstep, bearing a huge bouquet of flowers and a tiny package, a small red-velvet box. 'For you, Mandy,' the card read, 'Happy 14th birthday.' Inside was the most exquisite antique ruby and diamond ring. The date on the inscription engraved on the gold band read 17.7.1884. It was a hundred years old to the day.

Who could fail to be moved by such a gesture? I swallowed the lump in my throat, put the ring on my wedding finger and rang Bill. 'It's lovely, Bill,' I said, through tears.

'Come home, Mandy,' was all he said.

I went. He sent a taxi for me and met me at his door, a huge smile on his face. 'I missed you,' he said simply. It was enough.

I knew then that although the road we were to travel together might be rocky at times, there would always be some force that pulled us back together.

He told me that, yes, there had been another woman, Kelly Wynn. She was a model, aged twenty-two, and he simply had not had the courage to tell her it was all over when he met me. He said – and we both laughed – that he could not bring himself to tell a twenty-two-year-old that he had fallen for a younger woman – aged thirteen! But my departure had made him see sense. He knew he loved me. He had taken the plunge and dumped Kelly Wynn. There was no one else but me.

Then we went out for a lovely celebratory reunion meal – at Tramp, where else? But when the curtain fell on our evening out, however, I stood firm. I could not forget the pain of our split, nor the reasons for it. We might be back together but it was one step at a time or else, who could say, he might hurt me again. I kissed him goodnight and went home to Mum. I would stick to home and hearth for now until my heart could sort itself out.

I pulled away from Bill a little and tried to get some balance back into my life. I went back to school in the autumn term, just a few weeks later, and started trying to make up for time lost the previous term, when my thoughts and waking hours had all been with Bill.

I proudly displayed my ring at school. There was no need now for total secrecy. I was not embroiled in a big love affair with Bill. I was not living with him any longer. No one need ever know what had happened between us. This was a genuine gift from a genuine friend.

'He's a musician,' I revealed to all my classmates who were agog at my glittering band of stones. 'In the Rolling Stones. He's a family friend, kind of like my godfather...' Kind of appropriate, as it turned out.

In the meantime, having re-opened the lines of communication if not the sensual and emotional relationship, Bill had evolved a plan to win me back. He invited me to France.

He had already taken Nicola and me there once before, for a week at Easter at his villa at Vence in the South of France. It had been a strained week. Nicola, my supposed confidante and chaperone, had been left to play on the sidelines, ousted by the intimacy between Bill and me. She had only agreed to go in the first place after I vowed that, although I was sleeping with Bill, we were most definitely not having sex.

The rift between us was partially healed and we had spent the week sunbathing, swimming and lounging around – but never facing any of the very real issues that were in hand.

Bill had spent most of the time in his basement office, working on his computer. He hated the sun. He had work to do. I got the feeling he had actually wanted Nicola to come along so that I would have some company during the day.

At night, however, he had wanted me all to himself. On that trip, I had been made fully aware of this dichotomy in Bill's character. In London, I understood why he wanted to work during the day and restrict his playtime until the evening – but while we were on holiday?

Bill was a diehard creature of habit. He worked during the day, wherever he was. It was as simple as that. He got withdrawal symptoms if he went more than a day without his computer. I did not have particularly fond memories of that week in Vence.

This invitation was different, though. Bill would be working officially. He was going to Paris with the rest of the Stones to record their latest album.

We had driven through Paris on that Vence trip. Bill, who had a phobia about flying, had insisted on driving all the way to the South of France and back – a long and arduous car journey that had left us all numb, aching and travel sick. The only highlight had been passing through Paris – that beautiful city of love and romance. Bill, grumpy and tired from the drive, had muttered in a disgruntled fashion when I suggested that, one day, we should do what all lovers dream of and visit Paris in the spring.

His impending recording visit had obviously struck a dimly remembered chord. He knew I would probably find the thought of Paris with him hard to refuse. He was right, but I let him think I needed a bit of persuading.

He would be with the rest of the Stones, he cajoled, so I would have lots of good, fun company. That was a lie. I knew that Bill rarely mixed socially with the rest of the Stones. In our months together, I'd become aware that he had his own coterie of friends, most of them culled from outside the Stones' camp.

They were London's glitterati, not Jagger and Richards and co. I let him sweat a bit more.

He went on. I could visit all the sights: the Left Bank, the Eiffel Tower, the Arc de Triomphe, the pavement cafés, the nightclubs. And I would be there in an official capacity, not just tucked away and hidden from sight. I would be his friend, his girl. Done!

I had made some careful calculations of the dates. As it happened, that week was school midterm. I agreed to go and Mum did not stand in my way. She saw the way I had managed to cool the relationship with Bill. She need have no fear. It had been a schoolgirl crush and I had got back my sense of perspective about life. It was, I persuaded her, a fantastic opportunity, not just to see Paris, but to watch the group in action. She let me go on the proviso that I was to be escorted on the journey, there and back, by a Stones chaperone. Letting a girl barely turned fourteen cross the Channel and make her way to Paris on her own was out of the question. So it was that a Stones minder was duly appointed to accompany me by hovercraft to France, then on by train to Paris where I would join Bill at the Hotel le Warwick on Thursday evening.

I would not allow myself to get overexcited. I had to remain calm at all costs and keep my emotions in check but the thought of seeing Bill again was uppermost in my mind, sending a shiver down my spine. Never mind Paris!

It was a long journey and a rough sea crossing. The combination of the swell of the sea, the hovercraft's motion and my nerves combined to make me feel extremely sick. The French train was crowded and smelly. It was with huge relief that I finally arrived at the Hotel le Warwick where Bill always stayed while in Paris.

He knew the staff very well and felt comfortable there. I felt too nauseous to protest when I was ushered in without checking in first. Then I realised that, by handing over my passport at reception, I would have identified myself, and more importantly my age, to the staff. Protective or not, they would have been alerted to a scandal going on under their roof. So I was *not* here in an official capacity, then. I was expected to be a secret stowaway in Bill's suite. At the same time, I understood the risks of the staff knowing about me.

That was not all. Bill was no longer staying in a suite; he had just moved into a double room just that day. It suddenly became blindingly obvious what was on Bill's mind. He wanted us to sleep together again. Unless I fancied the floor or the bath, I had little option. Exhausted and still feeling queasy, at that moment all I wanted was a bed.

I knocked tentatively on the door of room 14 and a muffled voice answered, 'Come in.'

Bill, bleary-eyed, lay in bed still half-asleep. He had been up all night, recording, and had only fallen into bed at midday.

'Mandy,' he smiled sleepily and stretched out his arms for that first, long-awaited embrace. Holding me, kissing me tenderly, all the old feelings rushed back. It had been so long since I had lain next to him like that, felt his soft kisses on my face, my neck, my shoulders. I slipped off my coat and my dress and slid in beside him in my bra and pants. With each kiss, it was like we had never been apart and yet, because we had, there was a fire and a hunger in us both that we had never known before.

All my apprehension about being alone so far from home and the pain of our parting and reunion faded in the heat of his kiss. He was different somehow. He was stronger, more demanding, more dominant. He was taking control. Tired, happy, over-whelmed by the moment, I was powerless to resist.

Bill unhooked my bra and slid it gently over my arms, kissing me every inch of the way. Then he hooked his thumbs into the lace of my panties and gently slid them down and off. I was naked, for the first time ever, lying next to him, kissing, touching, exploring, somehow the barriers of the past had been broken down and swept away.

We reached the point of no return, the point at which we had always stopped before. He pressed himself against me urgently, moaned my name and stroked my hair back from my face. I saw then, in that instant, what was written in his eyes. He could not, he would not stop. For a split second he paused, looked deep into my eyes and we both knew. Then he moved again, hard, sharp and fast. He was inside me. We were making love.

It was over very quickly. There were no streamers or fire-works, no waves crashing on shores. I was so surprised. Like most people, I had expected the first time to be something special, earth-shattering. It was special, but only because I felt over-whelmed by a sense of peace and security. I was just so happy to be with Bill. Now we had done it, we had taken that final step. The last piece of the jigsaw had slotted into place. We were as one, we were committed to one another.

Bill rolled on to his back and lay there smiling. He looked like the cat that got the cream. Then he turned to me, tutted, and said, 'You naughty girl.'

CHAPTER SEVEN

Sympathy for the Devil

My first thought afterwards was, 'Oh no, that's it. I've done it now.'

There was an overwhelming sense of loss. Not just for my virginity but for my principles, my moral code and, most of all, for my childhood. I had given away so much in just a few seconds, and Bill's words of admonition had rammed home the message – I was to blame for this happening, I was the guilty party, it was my fault.

The guilt was terrible. I knew to my very core that what we had just done was wrong. I should not have let Bill make love to me. I couldn't help but feel dirty. Mum's words rang in my ears: 'Soiled goods'. That feeling, so firmly implanted in my mind, would leave a lasting scar. It would stay with me whenever I made love with Bill while I was still under-age. From that moment on, sex could never be the natural culmination of a loving, passionate relationship. The seed of guilt that Bill had planted in me at that moment would grow into a snarling beast of self-loathing.

For many years, until I found the courage to face that beast and destroy it, for me sex would always be bad, rude and dirty, even when I was in love with the man. I had seduced Bill. Not he, me. I was a naughty, naughty girl.

I felt, at that moment, apologetic for leading him astray. Subconsciously, I needed my dad to put his arms around me and tell me it was all right. I had been wicked but if I made it up to him and did exactly what he told me, then he was not going to punish me. He did not need to. Racked with guilt, I was punishing myself.

I was completely confused. My age and lack of experience left me ill-equipped to deal with such a momentous step and the way Bill was handling it. At the same time, there was a germ of indignation burning away inside me. How had Bill managed to turn round the fact that he pushed himself inside me ... into my fault? I had *not* consciously seduced Bill. It was never my intention to let him have sex with me that night. My only crime, if I had committed one as Bill was insistent I had, was in not fighting him off, but how could I have fought him off at that moment? I had no idea he was going to press on, to push further, to break down the physical and emotional barrier of my virginity.

What strength did I have to resist at that moment in time? I loved him, I had missed him so much, I was so happy to be with him again. Above all, I was exhausted and still feeling nauseous after the long journey. I had no reserves to draw on, no powers of resistance to pull him up short at the point where he had always managed to stop before. I was, literally and metaphorically, wide open for Bill's advances. So how could it be my fault?

I lay there next to him, my mind in turmoil. While I should have been suffused with the warm glow of love, I was perplexed, anxious and desperately in need of reassurance from this man who had just taken my virginity.

But Bill was not offering tea and sympathy, just tea. 'Fancy a cuppa?' he grinned. Not, 'Thank you for giving yourself to me.' Not 'I love you.' Not even a token sentiment of appreciation like, 'That was wonderful.'

Not Bill. He lit a cigarette, inhaled deeply and said, 'I could murder some tea and biscuits.' And that is exactly what he did. He celebrated his conquest with a ciggie and a cuppa and several digestive biscuits.

He immediately rang room service and, as usual, his every whim was catered for within minutes. Tea, sir? No problem. Biscuits? Certainly. Young virgin? Why, we had one here a minute ago . . . but I was not cynical then. I was simply young and confused. A voice inside me said it should not be like this, so dismissive, but what did I know? It was all new territory to me.

I drowned my misery in a pot of tea and set about demolishing a whole tray of chocolate biscuits. I suddenly realised I was ravenous. There were crumbs everywhere, all over the bed and in the sheets. Bill watched me munch my way through this mountain with the voracious appetite of a just-turned teenager and promptly burst out laughing. 'Biscuit!' he said, spluttering out a mouthful of crumbs. 'I'm going to call you Biscuit.'

Ever after, whenever we were out in company, if Bill felt

the urge, he would turn to me and say: 'I'm hungry. Time for a bit of biscuit, eh?' It was our secret code. I knew exactly what was on his mind – and it wasn't chocolate digestives.

At that moment, however, all I wanted was to get up and have a shower to wash away my sins, to absolve myself of blame but Bill wouldn't let me. 'Don't get up, Mandy. Stay here. It's taken me six months to get this far. You're not going anywhere now.'

He ordered dinner through room service and we stayed in bed for the rest of the evening, just cuddling, watching television and talking. I needed to talk. I needed to know that Bill would not walk away from me again. I had given myself to him. In turn, I need him to give himself to me.

Never previously open about his feelings, I expected this to be a turning point in our relationship. Now all the barriers were surely broken down. Now, having given him this precious gift of my virginity surely he would no longer need to look for other women to satiate his sexual needs. I had come across with the goods, now I could be his proper girlfriend. He had promised me that, but, right now, there were no avowals of love or tenderness. Bill would not be drawn any further. It was not a time for words.

I was not aware of it but there had been an intangible shift of power in that single sex act. Reticent about his emotions at the best of times, Bill no longer needed to tell me I was the best thing that had ever happened to him. He no longer needed to blackmail me, or coax or cajole me with words of love and promises of how he would look after me. He had got what he wanted. The ball was in his court. I had nothing to fall back on. I had to keep on playing this game if I wanted to keep him. What need was there for a bottle of champagne? Bill had taken what he felt was his by right.

He never once mentioned my virginity. I did not realise it then but, in his head, he had decided that I was not a virgin, but a child temptress, a seductress who had used my charms on him – and therefore probably on other men before him. It was nonsense but it got him off the hook. It turned the situation into my fault.

I would soon discover that this incident was not singular in any way. Bill was a man who had long since discovered every conceivable means to avoid wrestling with his conscience. He turned everything into someone else's fault. He had buried his conscience very deeply many years before when his marriage had failed and he had embarked on a quest to screw as many women as possible, as a kind of twisted vengeance for what he saw as his wife having screwed him emotionally. So there was certainly no need to resurrect that conscience now, simply because he had taken the virginity of a fourteen-year-old child. As he saw it, I had led him on.

He was a very happy man. He kept smiling to himself. His silence disturbed me. My own mind was, by now, running riot as another fear surfaced through the troubled waters. What if I was pregnant? Sex without contraception meant babies. My Catholic upbringing had rammed that one home, too. There was no use in crying over spilt seed but another terror had taken root in my head and would continue to grow through all the years I was to share with Bill. 'You won't get pregnant,' he promised me. 'I was careful. I withdrew in time. Trust me. I'll look after you, Mandy.' Condoms were out of the question. Bill was allergic to them.

'The rubber brings me out in a rash, Mandy. It's murder.'

I believed him, so the onus – and automatically the guilt, the fear and the worry – rested firmly on my shoulders.

By some incredible good luck, I never fell pregnant in all my time with Bill but the fear of it hung over me like a tumultuous black cloud. My knowledge of sex education was practically zero, mere rudiments culled from a Catholic education and girlie gossiping, married to a bit of furtive groping on park benches. I was entirely in Bill's hands here, as in every other area of my life. Eager to know more, now that I had supplanted the theory with the practical, I sought information from books. A few weeks after we first made love I read a book which revealed that the withdrawal method was by no means a guaranteed way of avoiding pregnancy. That sent me into a real panic.

Bill laughed it off. 'I've had a lot of sex with a lot of women – in the past, Mandy,' he was quick to reassure me. 'And I've only got one child. So how safe do you think the method is? I've got it down to a fine art. Don't you worry your pretty little head about it.' He did confess that other women had tried to claim that he was the father of their children but he dismissed them as gold-diggers, one of the problems that went with fame and fortune.

That night, Bill fell into the deep and easy sleep of a man gratified, at peace with himself. I lay next to him, snuggled up like spoons, his back against my breast, my arms around his slim, smooth chest, with my cheek pressed into his back, listening for his heartbeat as if it was driving my own.

We made love again the next morning. When he woke, Bill was always aroused, his ardour pressing against me. Before I was even properly awake, he would be making love to me. It became a standing joke with him. 'I can't help myself, Mandy. It's him, Wicked Willy. He's got a mind of his own.'

The pattern was set. In a way, I was deeply relieved. This was not a one-off occasion then. He was tying himself to me with the threads of sexual encounter. It was not until much later that I would discover how slender those threads were and how easily they snapped.

Three days later, with my credentials as Bill's little lover firmly established, we drove back home. I had met the rest of the Stones for the first time, seen them in action in the recording studio and become firmly established as 'Bill's girl'. It was a long journey in every sense of the words.

It was a leisurely drive back home, with Bill at the wheel of his beloved Mercedes, light-hearted and jocular, the mood of a man in love, and me content to snuggle up next to him in the passenger seat, my head full of dreams for our future. I had gone to France a little girl, I would go home a woman.

As we approached England, however, the fairytale began to disperse and the clouds of black anguish were gathering over me again. My sojourn with Bill in Paris had been an unexpected fantasy. Cocooned in our hotel bedroom, we were shut off from the outside world and safe to indulge our fantasies together. Now the real world beckoned again.

What now? Back to Mum, school, my fourteen-year-old friends with their heads full of the boys in the class above.

Bill, unaware of my change in mood, wanted to stock up on his duty frees. I left his side and went up on deck, the now-familiar waves of nausea rushing over me. Holding on to the ship's rail and watching the white cliffs of Dover hove into view, I had never felt so lost and alone as I did at that moment. If I was not with Bill – and how could I be, because I was too young to join him in his life as his lover or his wife – then who could I turn to now? 'This time, you're totally on your own, Mandy.'

I stood there, staring over the choppy waves of the English Channel. It seemed like a metaphor for my life. Miles and miles of murky water stretched in front of the ship but it ploughed its way relentlessly on. I'd come this far in my own life; there was no turning back. There would be a lot of rough water to ride before I was home and dry but I would get there and I would have to do it on my own.

A young couple came up and stood alongside me, he in a herringbone greatcoat, she in a lightweight suit. She was cold. He opened his coat and wrapped her inside, smothered her with his love and she gazed up at him adoringly. I longed to be her, and for Bill to do that for me one day.

Self-pity made way for strength. Thinking the situation through, it was no longer intolerable. I shifted my focus to Bill. How was the situation for him? Dangerous. It was down to me to protect him. I felt suddenly defensive. I knew I couldn't breathe a word. It was a very serious situation and we had Bill's position to think about. I would defend him to the end. Thus encouraged, I went back below deck to find him stocking up on menthol cigarettes. My spirits lifted as I watched him pick up two packs and make his way to the checkout. He looked up and smiled as he saw me watching him, then turned and, grinning, picked up a bottle of Miss Dior. 'For you,' he mouthed as he pulled out his credit card to pay.

I had come down firmly on Bill's side. I would cope with my own problems in order to prevent him from angst. The decision was made. There was never to be any thought or discussion about the effect our sexual relationship might have had on me. Bill did not offer it, I did not expect it. He was the one with so much at risk – his status and his fame. They were tangible, manifest in his lifestyle and his possessions. The effect on a fourteen-year-old mind was invisible.

Nothing of my dilemma was mentioned as we drove off the ferry and back up to London, stopping off first at King's Road for a cup of tea. Bill loved tea and punctuated practically every event of the day with a cuppa. Later, it would strike me as yet another sign of the old woman in him. A world crisis might be looming, but Bill had to stop for his tea first. Then he ordered a taxi to take me home. 'I'll speak to you tomorrow,' were his parting words. I never questioned that he might be unconcerned about me facing my family. I chose to believe he had implicit faith in me, he knew I would not betray him, that I was strong.

I felt anything but strong as I walked back into our flat to find Mum waiting with a welcoming smile. I summoned every ounce of the fast-developing actress in me and tried to beam back. I failed, miserably. You can fool some of the people some of the time – but not my mum.

I felt everyone must know I'd become a woman. Surely it showed? Mum picked up on it. She noticed something was up. I was quieter, withdrawn, not my usual larky self, despite my highly descriptive tales of the rest of the Stones and the recording studio and the music and the meals and...

Mum interrupted my breathless monologue. 'Are you all right, Mandy?' She was to ask me that question repeatedly over the next few days.

Repeatedly, I bluffed, 'Yes, fine, Mum. We had a lovely time. But the sea crossing was a bit rough. I still feel a bit seasick.'

It was the perfect excuse. Who better to understand the debilitating effects of nausea than poor sick Mum. Thankfully, she took that one on board, insisted I go up to bed with a hot drink and never pressed me any further. When I think about the duplicity now, it makes my blood run cold. I had been ringing her every day from Paris, and sometimes I would be lying on the phone to her with Bill next to me in bed, only a little while after making love. There was already a gulf between us and sex had made it wider. I was now ever more drawn to Bill and the tissue of lies was becoming a wall between me and Mum. There was no way I could tell her. I knew it would destroy her.

So I took it on myself. I knew I had to sort out the guilt in my own head. I had taken those steps on my own, now I had to deal with the aftermath on my own, but I wasn't prepared for what Bill did next.

We resumed our relationship as it was before. We would speak to each other daily on the phone and I would go to his flat at the weekend, for our outings to Tramp or San Lorenzo for dinner. I felt our love was strengthed by sex, that we were closer than ever before. I was deluding myself.

A week or so later, Mum got a phone call at home one night. It was one of those rare evenings when I had gone out with Nic and my cousins to a family party. We had made arrangements to stay overnight at my cousins' house.

Mum, at home alone, was perplexed to hear the phone ring in the early hours of the morning. Ever fearful that something might have happened to one of us, she rushed to pick it up. It was Bill. He said he was ringing to let her know something he felt she really should know. He had slept with me – and without pausing to draw breath, he added the rider that it was my fault; I had led him on.

Mum told me later, much later, when we were finally able to address the issue without her blood pressure going through the roof, that she felt her heart stop at that moment. She could recount every word of that phone call verbatim. It was etched indelibly in her mind.

He said, 'Hi Patsy, It's Bill. I've got something to tell you. Something you really should know. When Mandy came to Paris, we slept together – but it was her fault. She was the one who initiated it.' Like it was some kind of sex ceremony.

Mum was so flabbergasted that her immediate assumption was that Bill was joking. Of course it couldn't be true. He had to be drunk. She asked him if he'd been drinking. He admitted he had. Gathering her wits about her, Mum decided she wouldn't listen to this drunken tirade and told him she would speak to him later when he had sobered up. Then she put the phone down on him.

She had plenty of time that night to sit and ponder on the veracity of his words. Sitting alone in the cold light of dawn, she wondered, worried and waited for me to come home.

Unsuspecting and still elated after a fun night out with Nic and my cousins, I breezed blithely back into the flat early next morning. Mum was sitting at the kitchen table with a look on her face I had never witnessed before.

'Is everything all right, Mum? You look terrible, as if you've seen a ghost.'

She came right out with it. Hit me straight in the solar plexus with her words. 'Have you had sex with Bill?'

My stomach lurched over. I could feel the heat of embarrassment rush to my face, turning my cheeks scarlet. I could say

Here I am with my uncle Harold who gave me away when I married Pat. It was Harold who introduced us in a wine bar in North London.

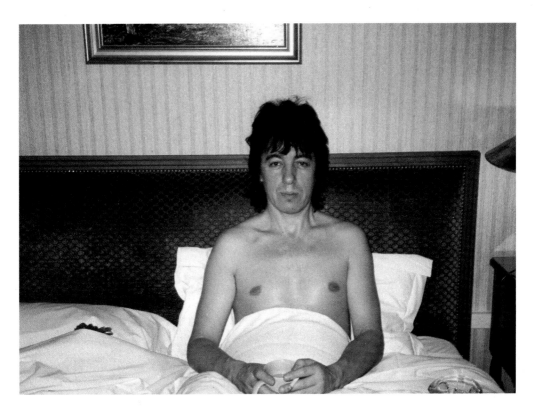

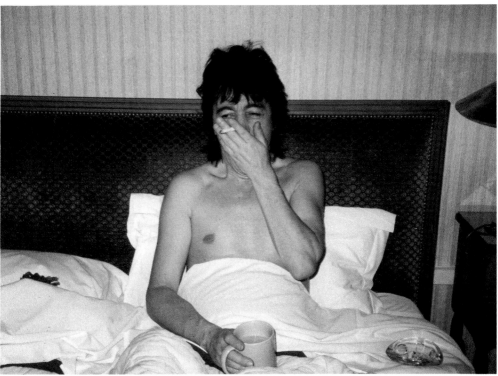

The real Bill Wyman. Every morning His Lordship would insist on a cup of tea and a cigarette to start the day. I took these pictures at Le Warwick Hotel in Paris in October 1984 when I was 14. I think they are proof that love is blind.

Top: This is one of my favourite pictures taken after the wedding at Bury St Edmunds, Suffolk.

Above: Here we are celebrating my 15th birthday. Bill took me to a restaurant near his flat in Chelsea with some family and friends. Half way through the meal a Gorilla – gram arrived and stripped off in front of me – that was Bill's little surprise.

This is my Bond girl pose! The picture was one of Bill's favourites and was taken during a Boy clothes promotion in 1986.

Still ill but on the mend. Here I am shopping near my home in Muswell Hill a few months after coming out of the Cromwell Hospital. My weight was down but at last my confidence was up enough to venture out.

Top left: My favourite nurse. I made Reggie dress up in the outfit when he came back from a match one night. Doesn't he look sexy? Pat's mates nicknamed him Reggie because when he's playing he becomes a Psycho – just like Reggie Kray.

Top right: Reggie gets revenge by making me dress up as a man. I decided to test out my disguise with a trip to the local 7 – Eleven.

Above: Here's Reggie dressed up for a party at my gran's. None of my family recognised him when he walked in with his red wig and dress. We introduced him as Helga and the fellas immediately fancied him.

What a lovely couple! Don't you think my Reg looks smashing in a dress.
We even shaved his legs!

This is one of my favourite pictures from my wedding to Reggie.

Brutus jeans campaign – my first big modelling assignment. I look a bit bleary eyed because minutes earlier I was crying after the make up girl did an appalling job on my face.

Top left: My ticket to hell....The rock and pop awards at the Mayfair on February 21 in 1984.

Top right: This is my first picture with Bill. Nicola took this on our first visit to Gedding Hall in 1983.

Above: Bill and I together in the South of France for the first time. He took me to visit his friends Carol and Craig. They were obviously well used to Bill turning up with his latest girl.

In a beauty competition on the Costa. I was representing Cuba, the club where I worked as a ticket girl, and for once I won!

Top: Getting ready to board the Orient Express in London in 1985. The compartment was tiny and the bunkbeds made passion impossible – unless you were Bill Wyman.

Above and opposite right: Bill in holiday mood. Resting and reading the papers. *zzzzzzz.*

Opposite top: Waiting for yet another meal on the Orient Express.

Top: At the launch of Bill's Kensington restaurant Sticky Fingers with Barbara Bach and Ronnie and Jo Wood.

Above: Jo and Ronnie's wedding in 1985. Bill made me take this picture because he was scared of me being spotted. I was only 14 at the time.

My first singing appearance at the Hippodrome. I loved that outfit.

Nic and I at one of our favourite clubs, the Limelight, in 1986.

nothing. The fire in my face spoke volumes. A silence hung in the air between us like some fog.

'So it's true, then.'

Her voice was so small, so wounded that I wanted to run to her, put my head in her lap and say, 'I'm so sorry Mum. I never meant to let you down.' Instead I stood there like some disobedient schoolgirl, awaiting the just punishment for my sins.

She went on, 'Bill rang me and told me you had.'

If I was already on my knees with the crushing weight of confrontation, then that was the body blow that keeled me over completely. I was aghast, dumbfounded, suspended in complete disbelief. It simply could not be true. I had never in my wildest dreams expected Bill to do a thing like that. One look at my mother and I knew he had, sure enough. 'What did he say?'

'Never you mind that. You just tell me if it is true or not.'

'Yes, Mum. I'm sorry, but what he said is the truth.'

Our eyes met but neither of us moved. Then it all came spilling from me like a torrent. A tidal wave of emotion that had been held back for far too long by a dam of lies. I needed to tell her, I wanted to tell her. I was so exhausted dealing with it all on my own.

Out it gushed, all the pressure and the emotional blackmail. How Bill had expected it of me, said he loved me, adored me, wanted to marry me and have our children but I could never be his wife, or his love, or his proper girl until I cemented our relationship with sex. If I did not give it to him, he would need to seek it elsewhere, as he had done before when we split up.

Mum sat, saying nothing, just listening to this anguished monologue. Then she reached out and put her arms around me. I was crying then, bitter tears for all the losses I had taken on board for Bill. Loss of my self-esteem, my virginity, my relationship with my mother. 'Oh Chicken,' she shushed me. 'But don't you see? He's conned you. Mandy, if a man really, really loves you, he will respect you and wait. No way would he go with other women.'

By then of course, the whole thing was academic. It was too late. No matter how I rationalised it, my heart held sway. I was in love with Bill, faults, flaws, selfishness and all. He had stepped into a gaping chasm in my life and filled it completely. I would rather die than give him back and retreat into that aching void again. Besides, I was so immensely relieved to have finally off-loaded all the secret guilt that, somewhere in my heart, I found it easier to forgive Bill for that bizarre and treacherous breach of trust. At least it had closed some of the distance between Mum and me. At least I had got it all off my chest. We sat there, Mum with her arms around me, for a very long time.

'Well, the damage is done now, Mandy. We have to build our lives from here. No painful lesson is a waste. Just know that somewhere there is a boy who will love you for you, not for what you can give him.'

It was over, consigned to the cupboard of our personal experiences. Mum would never bring the subject up again. It had happened but I had learned from it. She believed the rift between us had been healed. That was the good that came out of the bad, but what did Bill gain from it? I was never to find out because he never even acknowledged that phone call.

When next we met, days later, it was as if nothing had ever happened. I could not confront him over it. The whole episode had left me traumatised. All I knew was that I did not want to lose him because he had become a part of my life.

Much later, I would learn that this was a customary pattern for Bill. If he did something of which he had cause to be ashamed or which embarrassed him – and he often did, especially when drunk – by the following day he would have erased it from his mind. He was quite capable of blocking things out completely. It was so much simpler, really, than compounding a mistake with confrontation. Bill would simply never face up to an issue if there was the slightest chance it would put him on the spot or cause an argument.

So, he came to pick me up, sat outside the flat and beeped his horn, unable to brave the possible wrath of an irate mother – and down I dutifully went. The merry-go-round was still on.

Mum wrongly assumed our sexual encounter was a one-off event. It didn't cross her mind that, by now, we were in and out of bed all the time. She saw how much he meant to me and, rather than risk putting me through any more pain, she settled for a straightforward line of thought: 'Mandy is happy, I'm happy. At least he will look after her.'

The irony was, I was looking after myself and after Bill, too. I believed that, one day, when I was old enough, then Bill would take care of me. He had promised often enough.

For Bill, sex now took on an increasingly important role in our relationship. Ever a creature of habit, he liked sex last thing at night, as guarantee for a good night's sleep, and again in the morning to set him up for the day. His loving was confined to the bedroom. There was no spontaneity, no sudden rush of love when we were out together or simply pottering around the flat. Sex was like medicine for Bill; every night and morning, on the hour.

It was enough for me. I had read no authoritative tomes to instruct me that there were other means of expressing love than a perfunctory act in bed twice a day. I had no previous lovers to set standards by. I had no one with whom to compare notes.

On the positive side, I had grown with our sexual experience. It freed me from inhibition. I became more aware of my own body, more confident in my own nakedness and assured of the powers of the flesh. Finally, I was able to stand naked before Bill and watch him become aroused.

Despite my lack of experience, I quickly realised that I did a lot more for Bill in bed than he did for me. He would moan at the sight and taste of me and lie quivering with the pleasure of me making love to him. He talked as he made love, repeating over and over that this was special, amazing, something he'd never known the like of before. No one had ever brought him such sexual fulfilment. I didn't have any tricks up my sleeve but Bill was always satisfied.

For me, the pleasure was simply in the warmth and tenderness of the act. I did not expect to surrender to earth-shattering orgasms. I did not know that women could experience those thrilling heights so I was happy to bring him pleasure. My thrill was in kissing and caressing him, along every inch of his slim, smooth body. He never asked for more. There was never any suggestion of bondage or anything kinky. Our lovemaking was always very straight.

The man I knew and loved never once suggested anything out of the ordinary. Not once did he ask me to pose naked for him or dress up in my school uniform. There was something I had sexually that meant that he didn't need the thrills. Perhaps it was just the fact that I was so young, unspoilt and innocent. That seemed to be enough for him.

Although Bill was always telling me how he wished I was older, he certainly liked the fact that I was so young. When we were alone together, he often encouraged me to act my real age. On the one hand, he expected me to pass myself off as seventeen when we were in public, on the other, in private, he liked me to be that little girl of fourteen.

He was most turned on when I looked babyish and vulnerable, when I woke first thing in the morning or when, late at night, I would curl up on the settee and twiddle with my hair like a sleepy little girl. He would take me on his knee and hold me like a child in his arms then start to explore my body with his kisses. When I stepped out of the bath, all freshly scrubbed, with my hair wet and face bare of make-up, he always wanted to pick me up and kiss and cuddle me before carrying me through to the bedroom where he would show his mastery by pressing me forcefully on to the bed for a session of sex.

He loved to tell me, time and again, that I was his precious little girl, such a sweet child. I did not then understand the sexual connotations of his desire to love a little girl. I interpreted it as his need and want for a daughter. Just as he was a father figure to me, I believed I was a daughter to him.

However, if I was unaware of the complicated psychology of Bill's sexuality, then he was not. The thrill of the forbidden and the edge of danger in the relationship added an extra piquancy and spice to it. He was well aware of the dangers he was exposing himself to. He loved it. It was like the devil dangling a carrot for him. It was the biggest turn-on of all.

Within a few months of the first night in Paris I became more dominant sexually. Bill liked that and would encourage me to start the proceedings and take over while he lay there, motionless, trying to control the urge that was building up inside him. Yet, at the same time, he liked to be mothered. He would ask me to stroke his hair and his face and cuddle him like a little baby in my arms. He was vocal during lovemaking, too. It excited him that he had transformed me from an innocent child into a little sex nymphet who knew just what to do and exactly when to do it. He said I thrilled him, I chilled him, he had never, ever known sex like it. It completely blew his mind.

In a moment of confidence, he told me that he had developed a taste for sex at a precocious age. As a child of seven or eight, he would spend a lot of time with three of his young aunts – then in their teens. Sometimes they would all go to bed together and his aunts would swop secrets and giggle, while encouraging their little nephew to go under the sheets and explore their 'secret places'.

Thus he had been initiated into the mysteries and sexual allure of young teenage girls. It had been a turning point in his life but for Bill it was simply a lucky experience, a passport to the delights of the flesh many years in advance of the norm.

I believe those incidents scarred Bill and left him unable to communicate with women on an intimate level, left him feeling that sex should be on tap, freely available, as his right. It left him, too, with an insatiable appetite for new girls, new experiences, without the need to invest emotionally.

I was well aware that he still kept his little black book, full to bulging with the names and numbers of a bevvy of young beauties whom he had known before me. Even though we were sleeping together, I found it hard to banish the ghost of suspicion about Bill's whereabouts on the nights I did not stay with him. I was not quick to accuse him of anything, but a developing female intuition told me that Bill was not being honest with me.

I knew from past experience how much he was fawned over and fêted by women hungry for his star cachet. He had always been at great pains to point out that that was what made me so special to him. The fact that I cared not one whit for his rock star status. The fact that I loved him for being 'boring old Bill'.

However, they were still there, hovering in the shadows of our love affair, like ghosts from his past. I knew he simply had to ring and they would be there within five minutes. Not just in London, either. He had women everywhere – in Sussex, in the South of France, in Paris – he could probably pick up the phone anywhere in the world and find a girl delighted to fly to his side without a second's hesitation.

He loved French women and Canadian women in particular. He said the accents really turned him on. 'But that, Mandy, was in the bad old days. Before I met you.' Like a fool, I believed him.

CHAPTER EIGHT

Sex and Drugs and Rock'n'Roll

Bill had an uncomfortable relationship with the rest of the Stones. Outside their work context, he rarely mixed socially with any of the others. He was friendly enough with Charlie, who was the world's easiest-going guy, even when out of his mind drunk, which he was a lot, and also with Woody, who was relentlessly cheery and cheeky. Even when the recording sessions had stretched into the night and tempers were getting frayed, Woody would lighten everyone up with a cheeky quip.

When the instruments were packed up, though, Bill would take off and do his own thing. We spent a lot of time in Paris over the months they were recording *Steel Wheels*. I would fly out to join them for the weekend, often with Karen.

Sometimes the other wives and girlfriends would be there. They were friendly enough on the surface but made no attempt to get to know me. I was not bothered by this. Curiously, they seemed old to me. Without the intimacy that Bill and I enjoyed, there was a generation gap between them and me that was greater than that between Bill and me.

We were, indeed, a generation apart. Jerry, Jo and Patti were in their thirties, Shirley in her forties. I was fourteen. They were old enough to be my mother and sometimes I felt they looked at me with the disparaging eye of a displeased parent.

Once, when I mentioned this to Bill, he was dismissive. 'They're jealous,' he said simply. 'They're over the hill. You're fresh, young and beautiful – and they don't like that.'

Sometimes we would go out with Jo and Woody for dinner but we never visited the others, even though Mick and Jerry were only up the road from Jo and Woody.

On the rare occasion when they did all go out together, Bill was often the butt of Mick's jokes. When all the Stones were together, Jagger always had to make his presence felt as the kingpin. He had to assert his authority and he did it by being disparaging about other people, mostly Bill.

Mick would try to wind Bill up about anything and everything – from his clothes to his sombre appearance to his age. He did not need an excuse to have a sly pop at Bill. It was simply his favourite sport if he was in a bitchy mood, which he often was.

Bill would inevitably remained unperturbed by Mick's waspish asides. He would either shrug them off or laugh them off, but he would never retaliate, which used to infuriate Mick.

Bill had got used to it over the twenty years they had been together but, when I appeared on the scene, it gave Mick fresh fodder for his childish games. I was not specifically the target, even Mick would not stoop so low as to insult or goad a child, but he could have a go at Bill about our relationship and especially about my age. Mick loved the fact that I was just thirteen. I think it depressed him when I turned fourteen because it took the edge off his jibes. He made a point of telling everyone just how very young – and underage – I was.

The inference, of course, was that Bill was no longer a stud but a dirty old man, taken to molesting schoolgirls.

Over the years I was to spend with Bill and the rest of the Stones, I gradually realised that Mick had a special grievance about Bill.

In the sixties and seventies, the Stones were a global success but they measured themselves not so much in terms of financial and chart gains, but in their prowess with girls. They pitted themselves against one another to see who could score the most with the best-looking girls, and how often.

Mick, as undisputed frontman, laid natural claim to his pick of the groupies who would virtually queue up to be laid by the world's number one rock band. To his eternal chagrin, however, Bill won, hands down. For every one that Jagger had, Bill would get two. I assumed it was Jagger's innate arrogance that put many girls off. Bill, unassuming and sweet, was a far more attractive proposition.

I did not yet know that Bill had a point to prove; that his own deep-seated insecurities drove him on a relentless quest to bed more women than Mick, than the rest of the band put together, than any man ever born – not that his insatiable sexual appetite meant that he could keep going long after Mick had retired with a Budweiser and a book about himself.

Whatever the reasons, Bill's performance with women had always rankled Mick. He wanted revenge and here it was on a plate.

Bill, secure in the knowledge that sharp, shrewd Jerry had Jagger well and truly trussed up in a relationship, did not care about Mick's jibes but, as far as I was concerned, on one particular occasion in London, he really overstepped the mark.

We had all sojourned from the recording studio to a big showbiz party hosted by Valerie Perrine, the Oscar-nominated actress. It was a fairly low-key affair, with lots of rock stars and celebrities trying their damndest to look superior and outdo one another with their coolness. Mick was bored. He must have been to a million dos like this before. He was hanging back on the sidelines, rebuffing all comers and talking in hushed tones with his great pal, David Bowie. I caught his eye. He was looking at Bill and me and whispering something to Bowie. Bowie registered a look of sheer disbelief and spluttered into his glass of wine. Jagger smirked. Then they approached us.

'Awright, Ma–andy?' he said with that curious broken-syllabled drawl he had cultivated over the years. 'Bill lookin' after you, is 'e? Eh, Bill, you lookin' after Ma–andy, are ya?' A big grin was spread across his face – and, with Mick, that is big. 'Innit about time you took 'er 'ome, Bill? Past her bedtime, innit?' And both he and Bowie exited stage left, in guffaws.

It became the pattern of the night. Mick and Bowie kept looking over and then Mick would look at his watch and pull a face in mock-admonishment. He came over again and hissed loudly enough for everyone to ovehear, 'Time for beddy-byes, Ma–andy.' Then he made his way through the throng, telling everyone: 'Ere, how old d'you think Mandy is then? Tell you what, she's thirteen!'

I had had enough by then. Bill stood back and did nothing. 'It's just Mick and his puerile games. Let him get on with it. Everyone else thinks he's just being a total prat, too.'

But I was incensed. First, that Jagger should take the piss like this but, second, and more important, that Bill was not strong enough to tell Mick to knock it off. I felt it was tantamount to a betrayal so I stepped into the breach. 'We're going,' I told Bill. 'Let's get the coats.'

Bill did not demur. I felt he secretly enjoyed being the centre of all the party gossip. In his book, it was another notch on the bedhead of his reputation. In Mick's eyes, he might be a dirty old man, but weren't the rest of the assembled male company thinking, 'Blimey, old Bill's still got what it takes if he can pull a thirteen-year-old looker like that.'

On our way out, I stopped at the door. This was no cowardly retreat, no sir. I coughed loudly and, as all eyes turned to us, I said, 'By the way, Mick got it wrong. I am not thirteen at all.' (Pause for effect.) 'I'm fourteen actually.' With that, I took Bill's arm and sashayed out, leaving them all open-mouthed.

It was a minor skirmish but after that I didn't have much to do with Mick. I felt he was consciously staking me out, watching for me to put a foot wrong, looking for ammunition to bait Bill.

From then on, my age was out in the open with the entire Stones entourage. It was just a laugh to them but it was not a joke for me. I was, typical of a child on the edge of adolescence, deeply serious about affairs of the heart. This, my first love, was the be-all and end-all, Mills and Boon, *Gone With The Wind*, *Doctor Zhivago* all wrapped into one. It was real, it was devastating, how could anyone joke about such a big thing in their lives? The divide between Bill and me and the rest of the Stones grew wider.

From my stance as a young outsider, I could view them all with a detached eye. I was not swayed by their previous track record of fame, fortune and acclaim. To me they were just people and I felt there was a curious aloofness to them all as if they felt their position in the band had elevated them far above the mass of the rest of us ordinary mortals.

Even so, there was little cohesion among them as members of a group. They all maintained their individual status. Only Mick and Keith had retained anything that looked like a normal relationship. To my mind, they were like brothers. They slipped in and out of fraternal love and enmity with consummate ease. If they were not fighting and feuding, they were in each other's pockets. They had much in common, the same wicked, sometimes vicious, sense of humour, the same wry asides that separated them from everyone else, the same basilisk look that could turn you to stone if you said something out of turn.

When I had first met them, in London and then in Paris, I had initially adopted silence as my defence, not because I was overawed in the presence of such superstars – far from it – simply for fear of saying something childish and naive that would prompt a barely disguised sneer from Mick.

Keith always seemed to be on another planet. If he was not on drugs, then he had the mad, blank look of someone who ought to have been. He was out of reach, on some cosmic ray somewhere, disinterested and disenchanted by the humdrum of daily trivia and idle conversation.

The others were more accessible. Charlie was everybody's friend. I always felt he would never harm a fly. He was always sitting in the background, the same benign smile on his face, always a glass in his hand. I never heard him be rude to, or bitchy about, another person, not once, and I never ever saw him with any other woman than his wife.

The Stones' women were another ball game altogether. Playing second fiddle to a star was not their style, not for any of them. They defiantly retained a *soi-disant* supremacy over their sister race. Not for them the chumminess of girlfriends. These were men's women, but there was an air of desperation about their determination to stay resolutely by the side of their man – or 'mah ma–y–an' as Jerry would refer to Mick when he was not around.

Woe betide any other floozie who ever dared to make eyes at their men, and their own constant presence by the Stones' side made sure that no hapless female ever did. All the women, but especially Jerry, had a second skin of metaphorical spikes to repel all would-be boarders after their men. Look at Jagger and you could practically feel them cut a swathe through the air.

To his credit, Jagger never came on to me, but, when Jerry was not around, there was always some other long-legged beauty waiting in the wings with a ready, seductive smile.

Jerry was intriguing. Internationally famous, before we actually met she was my heroine. Pictures of Jerry Hall in the glossiest of magazines stacked by my mother's bedside had helped to inspire my own fantasies when I would dress up and pretend to be a top model or a beauty queen.

To me, Jerry Hall was Miss World, megastar – far more exciting and glamorous than the Rolling Stones. I was amazed when I first met her in Paris. She was not as tall as I had expected. At five foot ten inches, she was not the stunning six footer I had envisaged. I thought she was not nearly as gorgeous in real life as she was in her glossy picture spreads. Her blonde mane was not so much of a crowning glory as a bird's nest. To someone like me, obsessed with silky hair, her's was astonishingly out of condition.

I can remember thinking, distinctly – and bitchily – 'This is the world's top model? Hey, maybe I could do that.'

With her lazy, Texan drawl, she at first came across as warm and I wondered if she would take me under her wing. She did not. Behind that carefully draped cloak of warmth I felt there was the steely determination of a woman interested in two things in life, her money and her man – not necessarily in that order.

Then there was Patti, like Keith, in her own little world. Like Jerry, she lived for her man but did not seem to have so much of a point to prove. Patti was content to be always at Keith's side, letting him soak up the attention, the accolades, the booze, whatever. Woman as accessory. How totally different to Jerry, who portrayed herself in a very firm and forthright fashion as 'woman in her own right'; who always knew that the only way she would hold on to Mick was by proving her worth in the glamour and independence stakes. Even at that tender age, it was obvious to me that Jerry worked so stoically for her independence for one reason – to keep Mick's interest from flagging.

Charlie's wife, Shirley, was elegant and stylish and largely detached from anything to do with the band. She rarely joined us. Older than the others, she had seen what Charlie had to do, sighed and let him get on with it, carving a comfortable home life for herself and their daughter Seraphina back home at their farmhouse in Cornwall. It was a stable base for Charlie to slip home to when band business was done. Of them all, Shirley was the one who struck me as the most secure, the most serene.

Jo Wood was the one Stones wife who reached out to me. Like Woody, she was open and funny, with the most infectious giggle. Nothing about the Stones' fame impressed her too much either. Woody had joined the band several years down the road, some time after their guitarist Brian Jones had died, drowned in mysterious circumstances in a swimming pool after a booze and drugs binge.

Woody and Jo were therefore never blighted by the founder Stones' struggle to get the band on the road and to fight out their place in the hierarchy. They had slipped in, later in the day, into a fun thing and they saw it as just that.

Totally irreverent, Jo would sometimes take me to one side and whisper bits of gossip about a fight between Mick and Jerry – of which there were a few – or how Keith had ended up in a complete stupor after a recording session and it had taken three minions to cart him, featherweight but fighting all the way, back to the hotel and the oblivion of bed.

However, one thing prevented Jo and me from becoming bosom buddies. I longed for a best friend to confide in, to share the woes of first love and to give me astute advice on how to handle it but I simply could not condone Jo's drug-taking. I had been inveigled – albeit wittingly – into a world of glitz and sex but I could still – and always would – say no to drugs.

In the studios, there was inevitably a spliff, or several, being passed around and, although cocaine was not lying in tubs on tables, there would often be lines drawn up on the piano, or in the dressing room adjoining. Once, I saw Jo snort a line. It turned my stomach. She was heavily pregnant at the time. All the time there were drugs around, however, none was ever offered to me. Just as Jerry bristled when there were other women around, perhaps I gave off intangible signals of disapproval when there were drugs around. Bill, too, stood apart from the others in his anti-drugs stance. For him, as for Charlie, booze was better.

I often wondered if it was Bill's straightness, too, that got up Mick's nose. Increasingly, as our relationship became more solid, there were more and more disparaging remarks about us from Mick. I began to notice, for the first time, that it was affecting Bill. After a run-in with Mick during a session, he would head back to the hotel under a black cloud of gloom or simmering anger. I could never decipher which and Bill, typically unable to express his feelings, was reticent about divulging this. Instead he would head straight for the phone and order a cold bottle of Chablis to dispel his mood. There was certainly no love lost between Mick and him.

I felt distinctly uncomfortable. Whatever their long-standing differences, I had no part in it. It was unfair of both of them to embroil me in some twenty-year-old feud but, increasingly, I felt I was the catalyst that caused all sorts of buried resentments to come bursting through the veneer of their working alliance.

Instead of turning directly to me to air his grievances about Mick, Bill would manifest his discontent with occasional, off-the-cuff, petulant remarks after Mick had been throwing his weight around. 'Who does he f*****g think he is anyway? God?' was typical after a long hard day at the studio.

Sometimes they were warranted, sometimes not. Gradually, it dawned on me that cool, unflappable Bill, was bitterly jealous of Mick and, to some extent, of Keith, too, probably, most of all, of their friendship. They were the leaders; people always listened to what they said. Together they were doubly invincible. Bill resented that. He wanted to be in charge.

To add piquancy to their hostility, I realised that, just as Jagger resented Bill's success with women (increasingly as Jerry reined him in relentlessly), so Bill harboured a long-term grudge against Mick because Mick had once screwed Bill's own woman – Astrid. In Bill's eyes, even though he played the field constantly during his years with Astrid, it was one rule for him and another for her. She had to remain faithful while he slept around. But to f*** his friend! Unforgivable.

Naturally, he preferred to believe that Astrid had not put herself Mick's way, but that Mick had wheedled and cajoled her into it for one reason – to get at Bill. He was very, very bitter about that little *coup de grace*.

I would watch Mick with his wandering eye and his easy way with any gorgeous girl who happened to be around and wonder about his fidelity to Jerry. No wonder she tried to be with him as much as possible.

And Bill? I never saw Bill flirt with another woman or even look at one when I was around. After our earlier debacle over Kelly Wynn, he had chosen to walk the path of apparent fidelity. At least, that was the picture he presented to me and, as far as I could make out, to the rest of the Stones' entourage. I was now accepted as Bill's girl but there was little evidence to prove it.

I was still kept tucked away in his flat. He clung to his old line about not being able to be seen with me in public. Our only forays were to dimly lit restaurants, private parties or Tramp.

However, the net was closing in. A paparazzi snapper caught us dining together with Woody and Jo one night at Tramp and a picture duly appeared in the *Sun* and the *Daily Mirror* gossip columns next day. I was identified as Jo Wood's younger sister. We laughed about it but I was not happy. There were plenty of people in north London who knew me, tabloid readers who would spot Mandy Smith, schoolgirl being wined and dined by Bill Wyman. Many might suspect there was, indeed, something between us. Many might not stop short of calling the papers to put them right on their error.

Bill was unfazed. He loved having his picture in the papers, especially with a beautiful blonde by his side. It enhanced his image. He collected his own publicity with a passion, scouring all the papers every day. In his absence abroad, he would instruct Karen and others to do it for him and he would pore lovingly over them on his return. It was his reassurance and his prime hobby. Every single press cutting and photograph was neatly filed away, by Bill himself, in a vast library of publicity, charting the Stones' success from day one. Notes on the cutting, the publication whence it was culled and the date were punctiliously stored in the database in his computer. One day Bill would write his memoirs, based on this meticulous diary and it would be just like Bill – boring – concerned only with his image, not with reality at all. Devoid of feelings and emotion, it would read like the mountainous wodge of press cuttings it was.

However, in that first year of our relationship, there was little more than a local north London buzz about Bill and me. I, for one, was certainly not flaunting my affiliation with a Rolling Stone. It was he who insisted on turning up on my doorstep in his Mercedes to pick me up. He who seemed to get a belt from flaunting his wealth and status in the depths of a council estate. He loved that risk, that hint of danger. It made a non-sense of his reasoning that I should remain undercover and never be seen with him, when he adored to be seen with me on my own territory.

It was inevitable that this show of ostentation would cause local comment and, sooner or later, that these whispers would reach the ears of the national press.

It happened sooner rather than later. Although the scandal of our three-year affair would not break world-wide in the news-papers until after my sixteenth birthday, the press were on to us a long time before that. I did not realise it and lived in trepidation of anyone ever finding out the truth about us but Bill, with his battery of top-flight Stones lawyers, was well versed in the techniques of avoiding scandal. He knew that even if they did get a sniff of our liaison, the papers could do nothing about it. All they had to do was print rumour and hearsay and Bill would have swept in with a massive claim for libel. Before they could print it, they had to prove it.

Naturally, he said nothing of this to me. My closest contact with the law had been walking past a bobby on the beat. My only knowledge of the press had been my mates distributing the local free-sheet for a fiver a neighbourhood – up until the day a reporter approached me in the butcher's shop.

It was about six months into our love affair. I was standing in the queue, minding my own business, when suddenly a voice behind me said, 'Excuse me, Mandy Smith? I wonder if I could have a word about your friendship with Bill Wyman?'

I froze. As it happened, I was wearing the ring that Bill had bought me for my birthday a few weeks earlier. Automatically, I put my left hand in my pocket and surreptitiously slipped it off. I thought to myself, 'If she sees that, she'll ask me who bought it – and I can't lie to her.' I knew I would be caught bang to rights if she started asking direct questions. I still found it impossible to look anyone in the eye and tell them a blatant lie. 'Excuse me' I mumbled, 'Can't talk. Got to go.' And I turned on my heel and walked out.

She followed me, asking questions, but I kept my eyes on the middle-distance and, gaining pace, strode the hundred yards home and slammed the door behind me. I did not then realise what a persistent bunch the press were, how they would sit and wait on your doorstep for hours, days, possibly longer, until they got the quote and the picture they wanted. It was best, in the long term, to give them what they required.

On this occasion, though, after my first confrontation with the press, I had no knowledge of what the heck to do next. Instinctively, I called Bill.

'I'll send a cab, Mandy. Say nothing, do nothing. Just wait until the taxi arrives, get in and come over here.'

When I arrived at the flat, later, Bill was curiously tight-lipped about the whole episode, not at all supportive as I had expected him to be. I had a sneaking suspicion that he felt I had invited this near-disaster by flaunting my ring on my engagement finger but I never did. He never voiced his suspicions in this area but it was like an unspoken accusation.

Before long, he would start pressuring me to leave my local school and the neighbourhood, in order to be nearer him. He would say how I would get a better education in a posh Chelsea private school. How we could be closer together, living as man and wife, while I went to school only a few streets from his flat.

In reality, I always wondered whether the truth was that he wanted to snatch me away from the real world, first, to be his little slave and second, to prevent me from having any contact with normal life, ordinary people – and press reporters.

Whatever the reason, Bill was certainly not trying to buy me with promises of private education or anything else. In all the time I lived with Bill, money played a very low-key role in our lifestyle. Bill was incredibly frugal, to the point of parsimony. He would never buy anything unless he could get a deal on it. He was always on the lookout for the next money-making venture. He would moan incessantly about how people were always trying to rip him off but he never cast any of those aspersions at me. He could not. I never asked him for a penny.

I went to one of Mick Jagger's parties in Paris once, dressed in a long yellow T-shirt that my gran had bought me for 5p in a jumble sale. I wore it as a mini dress with a matching yellow jacket. There I was, rubbing shoulders with the other Stones' women in their designer outfits that cost (as well as revealed, two arms and two legs) and I was in a 5p jumble cast-off.

However, I wore it with aplomb. By now I had become well versed in spotting designer labels and reckoned that most of them were a shocking rip-off, bought and worn only for their snob value, as opposed to their tailoring.

I tried to make a point of not asking Bill for cash because I knew he had a complex about women who only wanted him for his money, but there had to come a point when I had exhausted the dozen items in my wardrobe. I had worn them time and again to Tramp and parties, dressed up with different accessories and mixed'n'matched in every conceivable combination. The bottom line was that everyone had seen me in my jumble sale and high street store outfits time and again. In the end I had to bring it to Bill's attention. Sartorial elegance was never Bill's personal

111

thing – he insisted on wearing fifteen-year-old outfits himself but I knew he wanted me to look smart. (I also knew that his favourite outfit, as far as I was concerned, was my birthday suit, but I sure as heck wasn't walking into Tramp in that.)

So, I plucked up the courage, after many months, to suggest that if he wanted to take me to these parties and nightclubs, he would have to help me get some new clothes. I was deeply embarrassed, I felt as if I was begging but I had no choice. I'd simply run out of things to wear.

As it turned out, I needn't have worried. Bill's response was typical – he confessed he simply hadn't thought about it. He got the address and phone number of a lady tailor he had had recommended to him – so he said – and dispatched me to see her. She made me a spine-tinglingly beautiful blue leather suit.

It would have made far more economic sense for me to have spent the money on half-a-dozen cheaper outfits but I was deeply grateful for this wonderful gesture. I wore the suit until it groaned at the seams and vowed to buy Bill something exquisite for Christmas – our first together.

To this end, I decided to get myself a job. Aged fourteen, but none the less a keen worker, I passed myself off as sixteen and landed a holiday job at the local shoe-shop, TipToe Shoes, in Wood Green High Street. If I remember rightly, my basic wage for a Saturday shift was around £10. You could earn half as much again on commission on the old dud lines that nobody really wanted to buy but which a charming sales assistant might eventually be able to push.

By Christmas, I had saved enough to buy Bill a lovely cashmere sweater from the Scotch Shop in the West End. Fashion was not Bill's strong point. For someone who was vain enough to dye his hair and eyebrows to match, he was surprisingly unconcerned about the clothes he wore. He favoured Rolling Stones style *circa* 1970 – scruffy, flared jeans that flapped round his ankles (always too short for him) and nasty acrylic jumpers with zig-zaggy patterns, inevitably several sizes too small. He had had them so long that they had shrunk to half their original size through years of washing.

I had previously tried to initiate him into the comfort and ease of sweatshirts or at least jumpers that fitted. He would summarily dismiss them. 'I'm not wearing this, it's too baggy.'

Whatever he wore had to be skin-tight and shrink-wrapped to fit. Tiny though he was, his clothes were tinier still.

I was really pleased with my gift for him – I thought that the only reason he dressed in ancient gear was because he was mean. I was wrong. He simply had no taste. He opened my present and smiled sweetly before putting it to one side to give me a hug. No more was mentioned about the sweater but I noticed Stephen wearing it the following week.

It never struck Bill as curious that I should want to work in a shoe-shop. It never crossed his mind that it was all in aid of having a little bit of financial independence. He would drop me off each morning and pick me up from the shop at the end of the day in his silver Mercedes. Scrunching my bri-nylon overall into my bag, I would switch instantly from Mandy Smith, Tip-Toe's assistant to Bill Wyman's live-in lover. From Wood Green to Chelsea in the blink of an eye.

I used to laugh to myself about this sudden transformation. It was like being Cinderella, tripping out from her chores and drudgery into the arms of her waiting carriage and Prince Charming. I never saw the actual job as drudgery, however. I enjoyed working there. It was an effective antidote to school and my other life with Bill.

It never crossed my mind that it was a bizarre life for a child, traipsing between school, work and lover. Bill, in contrast, was always going on about how tough *his* life was as a child. It was his all-time favourite topic. He was so sorrowful about how he had suffered, it was almost comic in the relaying.

In his mind, he saw himself as some poor Dickensian waif like Oliver Twist, begging for some more gruel and being soundly punished for his audacity. He was at pains to get across just how poor his parents had been. I always felt he was deeply embittered about his humble beginnings. This obsession manifested itself time and again. His tightness with money was a hangover from his childhood poverty and yet Gedding Hall was always stiflingly hot. Bill insisted that the central heating was always turned on at full blast because he was haunted by memories of his childhood when the family couldn't afford to heat their home.

He felt so sorry for himself. He had absolutely no happy reminiscenses about his childhood whatsoever. He would regale me with these tales of woe and misery and I'm afraid to say my interest very quickly waned. I would switch off, put my head on his knee and nod dutifully in the right places. Bill never even noticed that it all washed over me, even less than he was aware he had told me the same old stories a hundred times. He just like to talk about it. No harm in that. It was certainly effective in sending me to sleep...

Apart from spending money on clothes, Bill loved to spend it on himself. His cars were the best, the furnishing in his flat and at Gedding were the best – yet he would often complain if a restaurant meal was too expensive. He would not, however, complain to the proprietor, only to me. It was a signal that we would be eating in for the next night or two, dining off cheese on toast to compensate for him being ripped off.

The one area in which Bill did not scrimp was in paying his staff. He knew how to make sure they were loyal to him. He surrounded himself with people who could not afford to betray him. He paid them too well for them ever to turn their backs on him.

His secretary Karen had been with him for years when I first came along. Very quickly, she and I formed a friendly allegiance. We would sit in her office for hours over pots of coffee, swopping stories about Bill. I was an avid listener. In one confession session, she admitted that, for a long time, she had had designs on Bill. She had fallen for him when she started working for him but, by the time I met Bill, she was at pains to point out, their relationship was strictly professional.

Karen was a great PA to Bill and a great friend to me. She knew to a T exactly how to keep Bill's life organised. She knew all about his different friends and would deftly sideswerve their calls and fit them all in around his work schedule.

As I had discovered very early on, these friends were ninety-nine per cent female, young and beautiful. I spent so much time in the office with Karen while Bill was working that I could hardly fail to notice the preponderance of women who still rang him. All the old insecurities started stirring again. Karen, ever keen to keep the peace, would assuage my doubts and confirm that Bill loved only me.

We had been together for a year, much of the time spent together, in London, Paris or at Gedding. We had spent the first anniversary of our meeting together, wrapped in each other's arms, making mad passionate love all night in the Hotel le Warwick.

Yet I still did not feel totally convinced of Bill's love for me. He was increasingly more and more wrapped up in his pet project, his own band, Willie and the Poor Boys. This was Bill's chance to be big boss, with no Jagger waiting in the wings poised to leap out and steal all the thunder. Without the self-assurance of a grown woman, I was easy to shunt into second place behind Bill's big career move. His job, his music, came first.

What I did not realise was that, along with the job, came a far greater threat to our relationship – other women. By now confident of my love, Bill was too weak to resist his own compulsion. When he was with me, he loved only me but, when he was away, he was busy making sure he reached his target of a thousand women in a lifetime.

CHAPTER NINE

Under My Thumb

By July 1985, everyone had accepted that Bill and I were a couple. Everyone, that is, except me. He was attentive and loving enough when we were together, but my newly growing woman's intuition told me that when I was not around, Bill had another life.

Many signs stared me in the face and any woman who has ever been cheated on would recognise them a mile off but I was still only fourteen and my trust in Bill was so immense that I did not dare question it. Yet, the evidence was mounting and the first inkling I had arose on our first anniversary.

Knowing that I was sentimental about the date, Bill flew me over to Paris to be with him on Valentine's Day and then insisted that I stay for the week so that we could celebrate our anniversary together on the 21st.

He spent most of his nights in the recording studio but our days were filled with lovemaking in that most romantic of cities. Even on rain-sodden and foggy February days, Paris casts a magic spell over lovers. I was so deliriously happy that my joy was practically infectious.

Mum, on the other end of the phone in England, finally conceded that Bill was good for me. She had never known me happier or more secure. After all her immense misgivings, Bill had, indeed, been as good as his word. He was looking after me.

Little did I realise that Mum, too, was preoccupied by a new man in her life. By one of the most bizarre twists of fate that life can offer, she had found herself increasingly drawn to an unlikely suitor – Bill's own son, Stephen. He was twenty years her junior.

After their initial meeting at Gedding Hall over Christmas, an intense friendship was developing that would one day blossom into love. At that point, however, she did not even dare contemplate the prospect. Her ten-year illness was only now beginning to fade away thanks to a strict controlled diet.

Ever cautious, she said nothing of this to me at that time – or, indeed, for many months. All Mum knew was that the fragmented pieces of our lives seemed to be coming together. She was flattered by a young man's friendship and was gaining strength. Above all, she was happy for me. I was flushed with love for a man who was taking care of me.

It was a different story the day after our anniversary. Woken suddenly in the middle of the night by a raging thirst and a deep, burning sensation in my throat, I reached out for Bill. His side of the bed was empty. From the desk on the other side of the room, I could hear the familiar tap-tapping of Bill at his beloved computer.

My head seemed to be on fire and a sudden wave of nausea floored my attempt to clamber out of bed. The room was spinning and my arms and legs were turning to jelly. 'Bill,' I croaked, 'I feel terrible. I think I'm going to be sick.'

He paused, a look of annoyance momentarily crossing his face at this unexpected disturbance. He turned in the half-light that glimmered across the room from his desk lamp, and could see I was not joking. The sweat was now standing in beads on my brow and I was shivering uncontrollably.

'Must have been those prawns you had for dinner,' he said. 'Dead dodgy, shellfish. Expect you've got a bit of food-poisoning.'

I flopped back on the pillow, too weak to move. 'Can you call the doctor, Bill?' I pleaded. 'I need help.'

'Aw, Mandy,' he moaned. 'You know I can't do that. They'll find out how old you are. Can't you just go and be sick? You'll feel better after you've thrown up. Honestly, I've had food-poisoning before. It's pretty grim for a few hours but it'll be gone by tomorrow.'

I was in no fit state to argue. I lay there in a sweat-bath, drifting in and out of delirium for the rest of the night, while Bill carried on working.

In the morning, when I awoke, he was fast asleep on the chaise longue, obviously perturbed enough by my writhing, dripping body not to want to share a bed with it.

I was covered with red spots.

'Oh my God,' he groaned when I woke him in a panic. 'You've got the measles.'

Had I not been nurturing a temperature of 103 degrees, it would have been funny. Bill was concerned all right, but for himself.

'Gawd, measles are OK when you're a child,' he grumbled, 'but I can't afford to catch them. Don't they make men sterile if you get them when you're an adult?'

Relegated to the dubious status of a nuisance child with a nasty disease, I was duly dispatched home to London on the first available flight, wearing three layers of foundation to cover my spotty complexion. I was too ill to challenge Bill's decision. I had to go home straightaway, spots or not.

Days later, as I languished at home in my sick bed, while Mum ferried in gallons of Lucozade and calamine lotion, I would wonder at Bill's hostile bedside manner. If you love someone and they become ill, you look after them. It is one of life's natural equations. Obviously not for Bill.

Karen, who had flown home with me, was totally sympathetic. We had become good friends over the months. In my double life, when I had no friends at school in whom to confide and none of the other Stones women on whom to lean, Karen stepped into the breach and took me under her wing. She genuinely liked me and we would spend happy hours in her office, giggling over Bill's peculiar old bachelor ways.

In Paris, while Bill slept late, we had gone window-shopping together, scouring the boutiques for bargains and the French street cafés for gorgeous young hunks. For our eyes only, of course. We had a competition going to see who could spot the cutest bum on the sexiest man and we would regularly collapse in fits of giggles when some bemused Frenchman swept up with talk of *l'amour* after being eyed up by two lascivious-looking English girls.

I did not know it but Karen was also drawn to me out of a sense of protection. As my friend, she felt shamed by Bill's secret – he was cheating on me once again.

My peremptory dismissal from Paris was not simply because I was spotty and contagious. Bill had two French models waiting in the wings. He wanted a bit of variety and he needed me out of the way for that.

His return to England in June should have been a joyful

reunion. After all those months of flying backwards and forwards to Paris, we could relax at home once again.

It was Karen who suggested we take a break together, she and I. Bill, she conceded, was neglecting both of us so we would go on holiday together, just the two of us, to Marbella. That would teach Bill he couldn't do without the two main women in his life. Unfortunately, that was not quite the way it worked out . . .

Perhaps Bill's guilt was getting to him. By buying me off with an expensive holiday, he could salve his conscience over his infidelity. More likely, he reasoned that, with me out of the way, he would have an opportunity to catch up on his other London girlfriends, whom he had long neglected since he met me. Whatever his rationale, when Karen suggested he should treat us to a holiday together, he leapt at the chance and so, in my blissful ignorance, I happily agreed to leave him for a ten-day trip to Marbella in July.

It was not the first time I had been to Spain. Many years before, during one of her periods of remission from illness, Mum had packed up her young brood and driven down to Spain for a summer of sand, sunshine, seafood and the carefree bliss of travellers on the road with only a few quid in their pocket but a whole lot of optimism.

I had been too young to remember much of our summer in the sun but, as soon as we hit the tarmac at Malaga, all the once-forgotten sensations stirred again. The dry, balmy heat, the smell of palm trees and the sound of cicadas clicking away in the parched long grass . . . it was paradise.

Karen had rented an apartment in Marbella. Bill might have paid for the holiday but, typically, it was a cut-price deal. No five-star treatment for us. This one was completely devoid of stars – a basic two-bed apartment only a stone's throw from the main street, but, what the heck! The sun was shining and the beefcake was out in force. Our biggest problem was going to be carrying on our competition to spot the sexiest bot. There were so many of them and plenty of them right off the scale. We were going to have fun!

That summer in Marbella, I remembered how to flirt. I had skipped several stages in my development by leaping from kiss-chase games straight into an intense sexual relationship at thirteen but now, just one week short of my fifteenth birthday, I began to regain a little of that lost ground.

Bill's obsessive jealousy prevented me from ever looking at another guy. Now, with Karen, I was free to look, see, smile at and even talk to more gorgeous guys than I had ever seen. By day we languished sunbathing on the sand and the beachboys were like the proverbial bees round a honeypot. We lapped up the attention but, at the end of the day, we rolled up our beachmats and headed back to the apartment – and the phone. I was in daily contact with Bill. He missed me. His avowals of love down a crackly phone line confirmed my feeling for him too. I missed him, but not *that* much.

By night we headed for the nightclubs that littered every Marbella sidestreet and glittered like so many baubles on a Christmas tree. One, Cuba, became our regular haunt. The music was hipper, the dancing hotter and the DJ had a bum we rated at least 17 out of 10. His name was Keith Daley.

Keith had spotted us on the beach while distributing cards for the club. His chat-up line had been no better than that of any of the other hunks in trunks who approached us all day long but his eyes were cheeky and appealing and his Scots accent left me weak at the knees. 'What's a gorgeous girl like you doing wasting her time here? I could get you on the stage, you know.' And so he did – the dance stage at his club.

Keith and his gang of fellow Glaswegians were regular Marbella-goers. They worked the season and played the punters for all they were worth. They were a laugh, easy-going, affable and great company to be in. By the end of our ten days, I was considered one of their gang. We swapped home addresses and phone numbers and vowed to keep in touch.

As we left for the airport, we saw Keith in the street. He grabbed my arm, kissed me on the cheek and made me promise to write. I promised. There had been no holiday romance. The only man on my mind was Bill, but there was definitely something about Keith Daley that made me want to know more.

As it transpired, I was to return to Marbella sooner than I had anticipated.

I flew back to London in time for my fifteenth birthday on 17 July. Bill sent me a beautiful bouquet of two dozen red roses but he could not see me; he was too busy working on the Poor

Boys' music. I had to wait a further two days before he took me out as a late birthday treat – to Tramp.

He seemed distant and distracted and blamed it on the pressures of work. However, there were symptoms of a much deeper malaise. I, too, was feeling the mounting pressure. Some deep-seated anxiety had begun churning away inside me. There were times, now, that I would literally feel sick with nerves before a phone call from Bill. Would he or would he not be able to spare some precious time to see me?

We still dined regularly at Tramp but my appetite suddenly decreased. I felt queasy and sometimes nauseous as we sat there at our dinner table, unable to put my finger on exactly how I was feeling or why I was feeling that way. I was with the man I loved but some nagging worm of suspicion and fear was gnawing away inside me.

Bill did not take my new nervousness in good part. It would infuriate him that he had to pick up the tab for an expensive meal when I had barely picked at it. There were other times when I would feel squeamish and have to adjourn to the Ladies room for a few minutes while we were out at a restaurant. That irritated him immensely. He wanted me by his side at all times. As with the time I had been stricken down with measles, he never showed the slightest bit of concern when I felt unwell. If I suddenly paled and took slow steady sips of water to curtail the feeling of sickness that welled up inside me, the most sympathy I would ever get from him would be a curt: 'You all right yet?'

I was determined not to let these strange symptoms of illness show but trying to disguise them and appear the life and soul of the dinner party while nursing a violent stomach cramp simply added to my mounting nervous pressure. All the time, in the back of my mind, I was thinking, 'Oh God, don't let me be struck down by the same illness that Mum had.'

I did not seek sympathy from Bill. I did not want to draw attention to my predicament. At the same time, I was aware of the irony of the situation because Bill was the biggest hypochondriac I had ever met. He was always convinced he was seriously ill. At the slightest hint of a cold, he would freak out and send Karen off to the chemist for all sorts of anti-flu pills and potions. He only had to sneeze and he would dash off to the doctor's, convinced he had some dreadful lurgy that would lay him low for weeks. He was forever going off to bed claiming he was 'going down with something' and he had started to have panic attacks, which would leave him gasping for breath and complaining of severe pains in his shoulder. He was convinced that these were early warning signs – he was going to have a heart attack.

His doctor, Georges Kaye, diagnosed them as stress attacks and told Bill he was taking on too much and had to learn how to relax. Bill was a born worrier and a lifetime of nitpicking over small details and brooding over past slights had left him heavily burdened. He had to unwind and take things more in his stride.

In fact, I dared to disagree with the doctor's diagnosis. My years of experience with Mum's illness had made me aware of the chronic allergies generated by various foodstuffs. Bill did not eat a healthy diet. He might dine in some of the most exclusive restaurants around the world but, given the choice, he would plump for a takeaway burger or a slab of pizza. Years on the road with the Stones, scoffing junk food at erratic hours of the day and night, had left him with a dietary problem.

Like me, he was simply allergic to certain foods. Dairy products, in particular, would spark off these attacks. The first one I ever witnessed, at his flat, was a mild one. Crouched over his computer one evening, there had been a flurry of phone calls which distracted him from his work. I could see he was getting uptight, so I adjourned to the kitchen to make him some supper.

I was chopping the lettuce for a side salad when I heard a strangulated cry from the living room. I rushed through to find Bill on his knees, clutching his chest. He could barely speak, so I helped him on to the settee where he lay down. Immediately, his breathing reverted to normal and he sighed. 'Christ, I thought I was a gonner, there, Mandy. The pain in my shoulder was crucifying.'

Dr Kaye checked him out. There was no sign of any muscular strain or injury, no indication of heart problems. The doctor said it was a stress attack.

Bill remained unconvinced and he began having stress attacks with increasing regularity.

On one occasion, he had gone down to Gedding on his own for the weekend to complete some work. I was at home with Mum when the phone rang. It was Bill, gasping down the phone that he was having a really severe attack. 'Get down here now,' he wheezed. 'I'm on my own. There's no one here.'

Mum and I rushed downstairs, hailed a cab and leapt on the first train down there. We were so concerned for Bill that we didn't even stop to think of calling an ambulance. By the time we got to the house, it was an hour and a half since the call. We barged through the doors, yelling his name, and a faint cry came back. 'In here.'

Bill was stretched out on the floor of the library, limp and motionless but very much alive. He was babbling away about pains in his back, his shoulder, his chest. Mum immediately called for a doctor who was by Bill's side in twenty minutes. He gave him the once-over and, yet again, could find nothing physically wrong with him. Prescribing some heavy-duty tranquillisers, he told Bill to take it easy for a few days. Maybe, he suggested, a holiday was in order?

Bill got even more uptight. He was due to go off to Venice for some more recording work. Worse than that, he had to fly there. His phobia about flying might well have been what triggered off this particular attack.

Then he had a sudden spark of inspiration. The work schedule meant that he had to fly over there but he did not necessarily have to fly back. I could join him out there; we could have a romantic break for a few days, then a slow, leisurely journey back home to London on the *Orient Express*.

I thought at first that it was a wonderful idea. I had not seen the Agatha Christie movie *Murder on the Orient Express* but, by the time Bill and I had done the trip, I could have written the script, with myself in the role of murderer. It was a 100-mph nightmare, completely off the rails.

The first problem was my passport. I had previously used it on many occasions to travel to Paris and Vence but then I had been travelling independently of Bill. There was no suggestion that we were a couple. Now we intended to travel together, sharing the same compartment. It would be obvious to rail guards, ticket collectors, passport control and border officials exactly what we were up to. Bill was instantly recognisable to older people wherever he went. He would have been caught bang to rights.

I'd never even thought about this prospective problem but Bill had and he had come up with a solution. I would have to pinch

Nicola's passport and pass myself off as my sister.

Nic was seventeen, only just over the age of consent but safe and, as I was later to discover, a favourite age for Bill's girls. I could not let Nic or Mum in on the switch. They were still unaware that I was having sex with Bill on a regular basis. The incident a year before had been consigned to the memory banks. Perhaps they did not care to admit the possibility, as I was still only fifteen, but I did not dare rock the boat again so I furtively raided Nic's cupboards one night, filched her passport and masqueraded as my own sister.

I did not feel particularly honorable about this, but need is must and Bill was firm. No grown-up passport, no go.

I managed to bluff it through passport control at Heathrow and again at the other side in Venice, although I was sure I had the guilty, sweating look of a traveller with half a hundredweight of cocaine concealed in my intestines. The worst part was checking into the hotel, wondering if they would play spot the difference between me and the passport photo. They did not. So long as no one called me Nicola, I was going to get away with it. If anyone shouted 'Mandy' at me in the foyer, however, the game would have been up.

It was still a bit tricky. Bill often forgot I was masquerading under a false identity, and kept calling me Mandy all the time, but our luck was in and either nobody twigged or they were simply much too discreet in that kind of hotel to bat an eyelid at the goings-on of their well-heeled customers.

Out greater concern was the paparazzi, who had apparently clocked on to the fact Bill was in Venice and had staked him out at the hotel. As we walked out one morning, we were met by a snapper clicking away at full speed like his life depended on it. Bill was furious but, frankly, I did not care whether the press were on to us or not.

Eighteen months on in our illicit romance and I was still not sure where I stood with Bill. Perhaps if a picture appeared in the paper, with my true identity, it would galvanise him into making the final commitment to me. I was tired of playing cat and mouse. I was tired of the lies and deceit. I wanted our love affair out in the open, ackowledged – most of all by Bill himself. I did not want to feel like his little teen-queen, locked away in her ivory tower, forbidden to be gazed upon by the rest of the world – far less his little sex slave – but I was beginning to wonder if, to Bill, I was a bit of both. He was constantly saying he wanted me to be his wife and the mother of his children but what was he actually *doing* about it? Nothing.

The worst of it was that I could never actually discuss these misgivings with Bill. He would never talk about emotions – his or mine. He might appear to be listening to me, to pander to my whims, but his eyes would glaze over and I would give up in despair. Bill was neither a talker nor a listener. I knew that by now. He was wrapped up in his work and his own little world – at the centre of which was Bill. I was an adjunct to that world – a vital one, a loved one but still only a satellite.

All this was made abundantly clear in Venice, surely, after Paris, the next most beautiful city in the world – the centre of love and art and romance.

Bill worked from midday to midnight and slept the rest of the time. I was left alone in our hotel room all day long, every day, watching Italian cable television which did not even have bloody subtitles. It was a joke. On the last day he capitulated and took me for a ride in a gondola, but that was it.

I pleaded with him to come with me to visit the Doge's Palace, the Bridge of Sighs, the art galleries – I felt it would be a major mistake for a fifteen-year-old English blonde with no Italian other than 'Just one Cornetto' to do the tourist trail in Venice on her own, but Bill said he wasn't interested in sight-seeing.

I was so bored, I just ate the whole time. It was only a five-day trip but I put on half a stone. I kept stuffing myself with pastries and cream all day long. The best was yet to come. The train journey was the lowlight in a week full of rock-bottom lows.

Quite simply, I was bored walking endlessly up and down those aisles, going from one meal to the next. Breakfast, lunch, tea, dinner. There was nothing to do.

Our actual compartment was tiny. Bill was never one to splash out on five-star hotels when a discreet three-star would do but even in one of those you got an ensuite bathroom twice the size of an *Orient Express* compartment. Maybe Bill was cutting costs here too. Maybe they had state suites tucked away on some other carriage, but ours was the size of a broom cupboard. I did not dare turn sideways in it with all the extra baggage I had put on after stuffing my face with Venetian pastries.

The sleeping arrangement was novel, too. There were two narrow couchettes – single bunk beds – to sleep on. Unless you were a contortionist, this did not lend itself to a very satisfactory lovelife.

Mind you, Bill was intent on having a go. Phobic about flying, he only ever felt safe on road or rail. With a bottle of Chablis to wash down his dinner, he was raring to go. We managed it somehow, although I had to suppress the ultimate insult – laughing at our performance. It was hilarious. There we were, squashed up together in this couchette, bobbing around, threatening to fall off with every twist and turn of the train.

It certainly wasn't the world's greatest sexual experience. I alternated between stuffing the sheet in my mouth to stop myself giggling and stuffing the sheet in my mouth to stop myself yelping with fear. It was quite scary because the train was rocking all over the place picking up speed through the long tunnels of Italy and Switzerland.

I can remember lying there, thinking quite clearly, 'I wish I was doing this trip with someone else.' It was a thought that had never entered my head while making love to Bill before and it shocked me because, with sudden clarity, I realised that I had pulled away from him.

Whether it was in self-defence as a result of his recent lack of care, or self-protection in case my misgivings about other women were to prove true, I did not know. What I did know at that moment was that I could now detach myself from Bill without breaking my heart. The balance of power was shifting again.

On our return home, I gave myself a few days to take stock of this new twist in our relationship. I began to notice things about the way Bill treated me that I had never paid much heed to before. I was suddenly aware of how he would sometimes relegate me to second place when he was in company, even with his own staff. In a discussion, a debate, or simply when ordering a communal dish off a menu, Bill would never, ever agree with me. If I volunteered a different opinion or ordered a vegetarian dish, Bill would always settle for the mainstream voice or the lamb bhuna gosht. In other words, he always sided with everyone else, against me.

Beyond that, he had lately begun to pick me up all the time over the tiniest little thing. He had slipped into a kind of parenting role; an irate father with a wayward teenage daughter. He'd pull me up if I discarded any of my clothes on the floor, no matter if I had carelessly tossed them to one side as a precursor to lovemaking. In his eyes, that was untidy – a crime – even though I only had a chair to put them on. What was I supposed to do with them? Bill had never volunteered me a bit of his precious wardrobe space. That was his own, neat, precise, orderly and totally bachelor-orientated. Yet if the staff left their jackets or coats draped around the kitchen, or left piles of laundry in the washroom, he'd never pick them up over it.

It seemed there was one rule for me and another for anyone else, yet the great paradox was that it was he who had insisted on drawing me into his life, he who had pledged undying love and refused to let me go. I began to wonder if Bill knew who the hell he was or what he really wanted from life.

He loved me because I was different, unaffected and under-awed by his celebrity status. Yet, clearly, he wanted to mould me. He was confused? I was confused by his confusion.

Then, as if to confirm his strict patriarchal stance, he insisted I accompany him to Ringwood in Surrey to visit his old friend Dave Burningham for the weekend. I wondered if his insistence was based on the fact that I had pulled away from him in the month following our farcical Venice trip. I did not consider the reaction my own body would have to the endless ebb and flow of our affair.

We drove down to Ringwood and spent a pleasant day with Dave and a few friends. Bill was relaxed and confident. The gulf between us had been bridged. We made love that night like newlyweds, keen to explore each other with a new-found enthusiasm after our weeks of separation.

The next day, however, when I woke, I was doubled up in agony. There were shooting pains, like red hot rods of steel, traversing my guts. I had been sick with tummy pains and nausea many times before but always managed to control my reaction to them. This time, I was strait-jacketed by pain. There could be no cover-up.

Desperate not to wake Bill, I stumbled, clutching my stomach, down to the swimming pool where I dived into the warm water in a bid to ease the pain. No chance. Every stroke, every ripple of the water against my extended belly was like being ripped apart by jagged spears. I was in agony.

Bill had to take me home. Deeply displeased at the way I had disrupted his weekend, he refused to talk to me throughout the drive home. I did not care. I crouched in the back seat, gripping my stomach and praying my insides would spill out there and then – anything to ease the pain.

To Bill's chagrin, I was desperately sick all through the night and, in the end, he had to call Dr Kaye next morning. On his advice, Bill took me straight to the Cromwell Hospital where they ran a battery of tests on me and found no explanation for my crippling pains. I almost wept. I was not a fraud. My pains were agonisingly real. Then it hit me. If there was no medical reason, then there must be a digestive one.

What had I eaten that could have caused such uproar in my body? Nothing, but I had drunk something – freshly squeezed orange juice – pints of it. They were serving it like it was on tap and, because the others had been knocking back booze like it was going out of fashion, I, a non-drinker, had kept pace with them on orange juice.

The suggestion from the doctors, to whom Bill listened avidly, was that it was all psychosomatic. I was in no fit state to defend myself – I'd never even heard of Pre Menstrual Syndrome.

It was a further twenty-four hours before I began to feel part of the human race again. Several days later, when I felt sound enough in body again, I tested my theory. I pressed half a dozen oranges through the squeezer and tentatively knocked back a reasonable cupful of the juice. The result was the same, although, thankfully to a lesser degree.

Bill would have none of it. He had made the supreme effort of mucking up his plans and ferrying me to hospital but I was to look no further than that. I could most certainly not expect any tender loving care nor understanding. He was not capable of it.

It was a lesson learned – sadly, by both of us. On many occasions later in our relationship when I would be doubled up in pain, sobbing, Bill would just shrug and say, 'It's all in your mind, Mandy.'

However, my emergency visit to the Cromwell hospital had obviously triggered off some other thought process in Bill. Just days later, he suggested I pay another visit to Dr Kaye, only, this time, it had nothing whatsoever to do with my stomach pains, real or imaginary. Dr Kaye was being called upon to sort out our lovelife.

Bill and I had been making love regularly since that first night in Paris the previous October. When we were together, Bill regarded it as his right, morning and night. More than that, he needed it. Sex was like his life's blood. He needed a twice-daily dose simply to function. Forget drugs and booze, Bill was a sex addict.

At that time, I had never heard of the phrase. I was happy just to be in bed with him. He made no kinky demands. He simply made me feel secure. He did not take me to the heights of ecstasy with his five-minute performances but he made me melt when he wrapped his arms around me, promising he would look after me always and forever.

There was only one problem and that was the issue of contraception. Bill had told me right from the beginning that he would not wear condoms because he was allergic to the rubber. He relied on the withdrawal method and, every month, I would spend days sick with worry, waiting for my period to arrive. Ever since I had read how unreliable the withdrawal method was, I could not relax. Bill, too, was not a hundred per cent scrupulous in pulling out in time. Sometimes he would just grin and say, 'Sorry, Mandy, Wicked Willie just got carried away.'

Half of me, carried away with the romantic notion of marriage and motherhood and happy ever after, said it was OK. Even if I fell pregnant, things would work out. With every orgasm, Bill told me he loved me. I had heard those words every day we had been together for nearly two years now.

I certainly wouldn't consider any other option. I didn't believe in abortion. The Roman Catholic tenets of life were bred deep in me. After all, had we not often spoken, long into the night, about the family we would have one day? Bill told me he planned a whole brood of baby-Bills and mini-Mandys. The only proviso, he said, was that, obviously, we had to wait until I was older.

The other half of me said, yes, that's the sensible thing. It would be a disaster to get pregnant now, at fourteen or fifteen. There were too many things for Bill and me to do together first, places to see, love to share exclusively before sharing it with another.

So, on the occasions I thought I was pregnant, I worried

myself sick. Bill, however, was completely blasé about the whole thing. He dismissed my fears, saying it was pointless to worry about anything until it happened. I did not share his confidence. I took to keeping a fastidious diary, noting down the date, time and duration of each period and the occasions on which we had sex. I read up about ovulation and tried to dissuade Bill from sex on those two or three days mid-cycle when I was at my most fertile. He never listened. His sexual urges took priority over reason and rationale every time.

I became increasingly paranoid. Sometimes, when I was a day or two late, I would be totally convinced I was pregnant. I'd start having pains in my womb, tingling nipples and feeling nauseous. I knew that worrying could delay my cycle and also that the tension could make me feel sick and that simply being late made your breasts and womb ache. It did not matter. Suddenly I was seeing babies everywhere. The worst of it was that there was absolutely no one in the world in whom I could confide. I had cut myself off from my mum, my sister and my friends to be with Bill and Bill simply didn't want to know ... until out of the blue one day, he turned to me over supper in front of the video and said, apropos of absolutely nothing, 'We'd better get you on the pill. Better see Dr Kaye.' He had already made an appointment for the following day.

So that was it. The decision was made. I wish now that I had not allowed myself to be steam-rollered into taking the pill.

My mother's illness had evolved shortly after a sterilisation op, made necessary because she was allergic to the pill. Two of her sisters suffered from chronic reactive allergies when prescribed the pill.

But Bill wanted his sex and wanted not to have to withdraw. He wanted to go all the way, all the time. The onus, naturally, had to fall on me. I wrote the date of my appointment in my diary and noticed that it marked the anniversary of another landmark in our love affair. Dr Georges Kaye would prescribe my contraceptive pills on 16 October 1985. It was a year to the day that Bill took my virginity.

CHAPTER TEN

Hey, Little Schoolgirl

For some peculiar reason, being on the pill made me more cautious about having sex with Bill. This, naturally enough, was the exact opposite of the purpose that had prompted him into frogmarching me to Dr Kaye. I could not exactly fathom why I felt more reticent about sleeping with him. He loved me, I loved him. What was the problem?

The problem was that I was growing up. I was no longer the thirteen-year-old nymph he had lured into his bed, no longer the fourteen-year-old adolescent he had initiated into full sexual intercourse. Now I was fifteen and beginning to face my premature womanhood with a list of questions that Bill would not answer.

Why did we always make love when he demanded it, not when I desired it? Why was it always at morning and night, never the spontaneous culmination of romance and affection? Why was his lovemaking – and lovetalk – always confined to the bedroom? Why was I taking the pill? What exactly were the effects of an allergy to condoms? Was there indeed such a thing?

Bill would answer none of those questions. By now I knew him well enough not even to bother asking. He was the most non-confrontational man I had ever encountered and, these days, I was meeting quite a few.

I met most of them when I was with Bill – his peers, his cohorts, his cronies, whatever they were, they were all men, and I began to look at them with the more discerning eye that comes with heightened sexual awareness. Even if my awareness was precocious, I had been with Bill long enough to start looking at him in the context of other men and I began to see that the way Bill treated me was not tantamount to a reciprocal loving relationship between equals.

I was not about to start banging some feminist drum about women's rights and him doing the washing up while I studied but, on an emotional level, there was clearly something lacking and it was not on my side.

I had fallen in love with Bill as an emotional, not a sexual nor physical, response. He filled a need in me. I, too, filled a need in him – the desire for a daughter to call his own. But how did that fit with his overwhelming sexual desires? And why, when he was so keen to look after me, did that desire not stretch to fulfilling my emotional needs?

When it came to confronting his emotions, Bill was a closed book. I had not been perceptive enough to recognise this at thirteen or fourteen. Name me a girl who can understand her own emotions at that age, never mind those of a man she is physically and psychologically bound to.

Now, however, I was becoming increasingly aware that Bill never took the time to think about me when it mattered. He was too wrapped up in himself and there were deeply buried reasons for him being that way. His own childhood was regarded by Bill as a depressing experience of abject poverty and deprivation. But was this really the case?

I had, by now, met Bill's parents. I knew Bill Senior and Molly Perks to be honest, hardworking folk who, because of the politics of the post-war era, had not been able to give Bill what he now considered to be his by right – money, privilege and an education. I surmised that Bill had only adopted this stance when he started rubbing shoulders with the rich and famous. He had measured himself against them and found himself lacking. He was wealthy and successful simply through being a Rolling Stone but he still did not equate with the cultured classes whose tables he now shared in the best restaurants in the world.

Hence his desperate quest to acquire status symbols like Gedding Hall, the holiday home in the South of France, the Mercedes and an antique collection to make Lovejoy turn weak at the knees. Also his compulsion for books, so neatly stacked on the shelves of his impressive library, and most of them unread. At least he could appear erudite. Even if he did not actually comprehend much of those mighty tomes, he could still read a title and memorise its author; at least he could claim that he was aquainted with the world's major writers.

Being a Rolling Stone brought with it its own traumas. Fame, fortune and adulation might be his but he was still just the bass player, the moody one in the background, hiding behind shades and a sombre expression.

I knew by now that that was Bill's backseat way of trying desperately to carve himself a niche as different, special, worthy of attention, but it did not really work. Mick and Keith received the front-line status he craved. They called the shots. No matter how mean and moody and intelligent Bill hoped he looked, he was not going to be the Main Man. No way, never.

So his professional resentment spilled over into his lovelife. He was greedy in relationships; he wanted to be in charge. He wanted to bully and to impress. He wanted adulation. Yet, still buried deep inside him was the little boy lost, the child who had called out to me and won me over, disguised in the mature man of the world whom I had subconsciously sought ever since my own fatherless childhood. What a mess!

The more I became aware of the ties that bound us, the less Bill wanted to know. He refused to acknowledge that a relationship could be founded on more than sex and avowals of love. But words are just that – words. What people do and what people say are two entirely different things.

Bill maintained that he loved me but his gestures sometimes said differently. He would climb into bed beside me at night and lower himself on to me without the luscious foreplay that had characterised our first two years together. He wanted to relieve himself with my body. There were times, when he was heaving on top of me, that I felt like a sex aid. I might as well have been a blow-up doll for all the attention that was given to *my* sexual needs.

Now, increasingly, his perfunctory lovemaking was for his benefit, not mine, although at least he gave me what I craved along with the act – the words of love. He was always vocal during sex; that never changed. He liked to talk and would list the things he was doing to me with relish. The sexy words turned him on, driving his passion to a greater frenzy until he culminated, gasping 'I love you Biscuit.' Hearing those words, I would be at peace. Anything was bearable, so long as I knew I was loved. His little girl. His baby.

He still kept me tucked away in his London flat, a separate entity from the rest of his life. Gaining strength, I confronted him with this anomaly.

'Mandy,' he would say, 'You know I can't. You're only fifteen. It would get me into trouble. It would wreck my career. It would ruin my life.'

'So what, Bill,' I countered, with what must have seemed to him boring monotony, 'do you think it's doing to mine? I'm only fifteen. I deserve a life, not just being holed up in your flat, waiting for you to come home from some press reception where you've been photographed with some twenty-one-year-old on your arm. So what makes that so respectable?'

Stuck for words, Bill would put his arms round me and try to win the day with a cuddle.

I had bought that line for two years. I was not having it any more. I began, sometimes, to turn my back on him. On occasions, I would go to sleep, ferociously turned away from him, refusing all his sexual advances. This was not a two-way thing any more. I was giving all the time; he was taking. It couldn't be right. Having weighed up the prospect of flitting around town in public with a succession of sexually permissible lovelies, while getting the cold shoulder from the under-age lover he purported to love above all, Bill finally capitulated. He started to take me out – to film previews, to concerts, to restaurants like Langans where the paparazzi would practically fall into our soup to get a picture of us together.

Photographs of us began to grace the gossip columns of all the tabloids but they still did not know my identity or, if they did, they did not dare pursue it any further. Without a signed affidavit that I was having a sexual relationship with Bill, they were powerless to print any allusion to it.

Bill assiduously collated these cuttings of us together, and filed details of them in his computer dossier. Again, it was his lust for publicity, not his love for me that had won the day. I had scored a point but at what cost? Emotionally, Bill was just as far away from me as ever.

In stark contrast, the friends I had made in Marbella were a siren song to my youth. Now the summer season was over, they had all retreated to Glasgow for the winter and the whole gang, headed by the irrepressible Keith, kept in regular contact with me. The phone lines were hot with the typical inane banter of teenagers chattering about the latest chart hit and who was hot and who was not.

We had an empathy among us that Bill and I could never reproduce – the empathy of a peer group, drawn together by age, no more, no less. Having been deprived of communication with my peer group since I was thirteen, due to my involvement with Bill, I slipped naturally into place with the Glasgow Gang, as I called them. Our closeness was further enhanced by the distance in miles between us. How easy to make best friends among people you have met only briefly, in halcyon days of sun and fun, then to continue, courtesy of the phone, with no irritating habits, no enmity, no petty jealousies or other teen disruptions to intrude on what is, logistically, a long-distance friendship. I was ripe for it.

In November, nearly four months after I had last danced the night away with them at the Cuba Club, I took the train up to Glasgow to meet up once more with my summertime pals. Keith met me at the station. As I climbed down on to the platform with my weekend bag, he raced up and threw his arms around me in a spontaneous, loving hug. 'You look wonderful,' he smiled. 'Even without a tan!'

It was like a meeting of long-lost chums. Freed from the confines and restrictions of London life with a Rolling Stone, I dropped into the student lifestyle of my Scottish mates. Sleeping on a friend's floor, our summer friendships were renewed in the bleak, dank surroundings of Glasgow in winter. I had a ball.

There were to be several more trips to Glasgow over the winter months. They were totally innocent. Although Keith and I were deeply attracted to one another, he knew my commitment to Bill would not let me become involved with anyone else. Instead, I turned Keith into my confidante, talking to him until the small hours about my relationship with Bill and my fears that we were pulling apart.

'That's what happens in love,' Keith told me sagely. 'It goes in phases. You can't sustain the highs of passion forever. At some point you have to have rows and confrontations. Then you slip into the comfort of love and friendship. That's the best possible combination. When you lust after someone you love as a friend.' He looked at me meaningfully.

'But that's how Bill and I began. I loved him as a friend and it grew from there,' I said, totally missing the point Keith was

137

trying to make. 'The problem now is that he's not being a friend to me. Sometimes he makes me feel like a sex object,' I moaned. 'We just don't seem to communicate any more.'

Keith put his arm round my shoulders. 'Well, you can always come up and see me for that. I'll communicate with you until the cows come home!'

Dear sweet Keith. Tanned and beautiful, young and fun-loving and free. What a wonderful, desirable contrast he was to staid and stuffy Bill, so set in his ways and so ungiving in his demands. Yet it was still Bill whom I loved.

My weekend retreats to Scotland were giving Bill food for thought. He began suffering from increasingly violent stress attacks, invariably in my absence. Alarmed, he consulted Dr Kaye who admitted him to the Cromwell Hospital on 26 January for four days of exhaustive tests. According to Bill, he was given a clean bill of health after this but he had had plenty of time, while in the clinic, to take stock of his life – and mine. When, after his hospitalisation, we were lying tucked up in bed one night, he said solemnly, 'I'm worried about all the school you've been missing, Mandy. You need an education. It's the most important thing in life.'

This was an about-face. This was the man who had told me for the last two years that I did not have to bother my pretty little head about exams; that I should bunk off school to spend my days in bed with him instead. He would take care of my future. I would be his wife and you did not need a university degree for that.

'I think,' he went on, 'you should go to a new school. There's a private college not far from here, in Kensington. If you went there, you could spend more time here with me. It's only ten minutes up the road.'

I looked at him in some surprise.

'I'll pay for it,' he added hastily. 'I just think we'd be able to see more of each other if you went to a school on the doorstep.'

I wondered if this was Bill's roundabout way of saying 'I want you to live with me and this will make it official. You stay here, you go to school, you come home here afterwards. And no more weekends in Scotland.'

'Are you suggesting that we live together?' I asked, knowing that to be a huge step for a man so protective of his bachelor life that he had not yet awarded me my own space in his wardrobe.

'I thought we already did,' he grinned, avoiding a direct answer as usual.

But it was enough. It was more of a commitment. It was a real move. Not just the continual promises that had bound me to him for so long. I rang Mum and told her what Bill had suggested. At first she was adamant that I should stay at my old school. She had no inkling that my attendance there had been so sporadic for so long that they had probably taken me off the school register.

'You can't let Bill pay for your schooling. It's not right. I've always managed to pay your fees so far. I can manage for another year more.' Mum's pride had been wounded. It seemed to her like an accusation that she was incapable of looking after her own children.

'Mum,' I cajoled. 'Just think of Bill as my best friend. He's looking after me now. Besides,' I added, 'he's promised me we'll get engaged as soon as I'm sixteen.'

It was a long-kept secret between Bill and me that we planned to marry. I had never breathed a word of it to a soul, fearful that it would alert Mum to the fact that we were, indeed, having a sexual relationship. I had preferred her to labour under the delusion – whether it was hers or mine – that he was my kindly benefactor, my father figure. I could not have anticipated her reaction. There was a stuned silence at the other end of the line. Then she said, 'I know you love Bill. I know he's looking after you. But be careful, Mandy. At the end of the day we all have to look after ourselves. Don't let him hurt you.'

I nearly cried. My poor mum. All this time she had known what was going on and, knowing me, had forced herself to stand back in the wings. Only if Bill was ever to hurt me would she swoop in to protect her young. I had no doubt in my mind that if Bill ever tried to do the dirty on me, he would have my mother to answer to and it would not be a clean fight.

I felt so humbled by this revelation that guilt once more engulfed me. 'I can't do it, Bill. I want to go back to my old school, I want to go back to my family,' I sniffed. 'I want to go home to my mum.'

The surging hormones of adolescence engulfed me in a wave of conflicting emotions. A child of fifteen should not have to be torn between schools, lovers and parents. It was all too much. I burst into ready sobs and Bill tried to comfort me.

'I don't know what's the matter with you these days,' he said. 'You don't seem to know what you want or who you want to be with. Haring off to Scotland every five minutes...' he paused and let the unspoken accusation hang heavy in the air. I knew Bill's jealousy, it was a foe of old, but he dared not lend weight to his suspicion by couching it in words. Instead, 'You've changed,' he said accusingly.

I had tearful moods, I sometimes refused to submit to his sexual demands – in Bill's eyes that could only mean the ultimate threat to his masculinity – I must have another man.

'There is no one else, Bill. I promise you that. I just don't know how I feel any more. Yes, I've changed. I'm changing all the time. I am fifteen, for heaven's sake. I haven't stopped growing yet!'

In my petulant mood, I could not begin to see through the fog of my confusion that the radical swings in my emotions coincided with something else, something vital that we never considered for a moment. I had changed when I started taking the pill.

Within two weeks, I had enrolled at the Mander Portman Private Tutorial College in Kensington. I liked the atmosphere. The teachers were sympathetic and encouraging. Best of all, there was no uniform. Now I was officially a student, no longer a schoolgirl. I immediately felt grown up.

There was, however, still plenty of homework and I had a great deal of lost time to catch up on.

I was due to recommence my studies at the beginning of the summer term on 16 April. Bill paid my fees in advance and by way of a celebration (for our new living-together status? For me renewing my studies? For his final victory in separating me from my family? Probably all three!), he suggested an Easter break. Just the two of us, on a driving holiday down in the West Country. 'Like a honeymoon?' I teased him.

He just smiled and enfolded me in his arms again.

The holiday was, indeed, like a honeymoon. Left entirely to our own devices, we walked, talked and shared more moments of genuine intimacy than we had done for six months. It was lovely to switch off from London and the pressures of Bill's work. He left his blessed computer at home, he switched off the mobile phone, there were no distractions. Just Bill and me.

We headed first for Bath where we walked round the Georgian terraces and marvelled at the architectural glory. Then we went down to St Ives, its rugged windswept, coastal beauty standing in stark contrast to the bustling town centre with its narrow, winding streets and pretty harbour. Then on to Torquay for the glories of Devon cream teas before ending up once again at Dave Burningham's Ringwood home.

This time, I steered clear of the orange juice. I did not want a repeat performance of the stomach pains that had landed me in hospital last time, dismissed as a crank. However, Ringwood, and the memories of that episode, might have alerted me to another odd coincidence I had overlooked.

Just as my moods had altered radically since starting on the pill my dietary problems had also been exacerbated. Previously, when I had felt insecure about Bill's affections and wondered about his fidelity to me, I had suffered a loss of appetite and felt sick when faced with certain foods. Now a pattern of low tolerance to some foods was beginning to emerge. I could not digest anything fried or greasy. Oily dressings on salads and dairy produce made my stomach churn and gave me headaches.

On one occasion, just prior to our 'honeymoon', I had had to rush from the dinner table at Tramp to be sick in the Ladies loo. Bill had to take me, pale, shaking and shivering, back to the flat and put me to bed.

Strange things were happening to me. Feelings of anxiety, panic and confusion plus physical agonies like painful swollen breasts and breathing problems. But then, in 1986, little was known about the effects of PMS.

Had I not been so engrossed in Bill and our honeymoon period, I might have noticed that I was becoming physically ill in response to more and more things and that the illness had started in earnest when I went on the pill.

When we got back to London, things between us settled into a comfortable pattern. I went dutifully off to school in the morning and worked diligently at my studies, gaining, to my astonishment, straight As in many subjects, like English, history and French, and upper Bs in most of the others.

Then I would go home to the flat and do the housework. Even though Bill was infallibly tidy, he baulked when it came to

141

washing the floor and cleaning behind cupboards, something I, with my years of expertise in house cleaning, could never let pass.

Then I would pop out to do some food shopping and cook dinner.

All the while, Bill would be welded to his computer, jotting down every detail of his day. Bill made a note of all the minutiae that most of us would never blink at. When he stopped working, however, then it was time for play and Bill had a little friend who always wanted playing with. Big Bill and Wicked Little Willie needed constant attention. Yet it was then that I had to sit down and do my homework. 'Mandy,' he would whisper seductively into my ear as I pored over my schoolbooks. 'Let's do something. Something really naughty.'

The sight of me bent studiously over my homework turned him on hugely. He would start to kiss the back of my neck and, encircling me with his arms, cup my breasts in his hands.

'Bill,' I protested, night after night. 'I've got work to do. You were the one who encouraged me to concentrate on my studies. Now will you please let me get on with them?'

But his hands would continue their exploratory path down inside my blouse, rubbing and tweaking my nipples gently, while his tongue slid down my neck to lick along the length of my shoulder. 'I love your breasts,' he would moan. 'So small, so firm, such tiny pink nipples.'

He would press himself into me so that I could feel the hardness of him in the small of my back as I sat hunched over, then he would take my hand in his, lift the pencil from it and place it, still firmly in his, on the growing sign of his ardour. My studies would have to be abandoned again.

I was half-housewife, half-whore. How had this happened to me? I wanted us to be just Mandy and Bill, friends and lovers, simple and genuine, like it was in the beginning, but things had moved on too far.

The husband-wife set-up was having an adverse effect on Bill. He began, noticeably, to let himself go. When he got up in the mornings now, he did not bother to get dressed for ages. He would slop about the flat in his dressing-gown, unshaven and unkempt with his hair unbrushed. For the first time, he looked like an old man sitting at the breakfast table reading the paper, his white roots showing. He had always taken great pride in his appearance before, although he was not too vain to let me know, from the start, that he dyed his hair. Naturally, it was a shock of pure white. He had gone prematurely grey, he had explained to me on the first occasion when I had caught him with his head over the bath, rubber gloves on and a tube of auburn dye in his hand.

I had laughed and told him I did not mind. In fact, ever the hair expert, I would help him with his monthly treatments. Thereafter, I had assumed the role of his personal hair-dyer. Karen and I had even flown over to Paris once, at his emergency request, just to do his roots and bring him fresh supplies of dye as his had run out. Now, however, Bill did not seem to care what he looked like. When he could be bothered getting dressed, he simply grabbed whatever was to hand. He started to wear old clothes, horrible trousers that were too short for him and tatty old slippers. He just didn't seem to care about his appearance when he was with me. He stopped brushing his hair and shaving. He was even worse when we left London for Gedding. He would slouch around in ancient bomber jackets he had bought back in the early seventies, with huge collars and giant, deep, knitted ribs. His jeans were still flared, although, to be fair, not massively so, because, in having them taken up to fit his short legs, much of the flare had been diminshed. They were all old hippy rejects that anyone else would have consigned to Oxfam. Instead, Bill had relegated them to Gedding Hall where everyone was a country bumpkin and he cared not one whit how he appeared.

Even when we went into town for a meal, he would dress like Old Farmer Joe. All that was missing was a straw sticking out of his mouth. Not to put too fine a point on it, he looked a mess, and eventually I told him so. Straight in, with all the tact and finesse of youth.

'Bill, you look awful. I thought it was supposed to be women who went to seed once they got married and settled down? Well, we're not even married yet and look at the state of you. I make an effort all the time to look nice for you.'

He grunted. 'Everyone likes to relax, Mandy.'

The truth was that if he did not care enough to make an effort for me, then he obviously did not have sufficient respect for my feelings. Seeing him like that was like a smack in the face. 'He doesn't care about me if he's not trying any more,' I thought.

As usual, I took all the guilt and blame upon myself. That

was my main problem. Raised a Catholic, my guilt-potential was vast, a veritable reservoir of angst, ready and waiting for all-comers to dive in and absolve themselves of their sins – leaving the tidemark of guilt in me instead. Bill milked this for all it was worth.

After my personal assault on his appearance, he was well primed to stage his *pièce de résistance*. He felt he had something to get back at me for. He did not care about being scruffy but he did care that I had had the temerity to comment on it. He seethed over this slight and waited for his moment to wreak some kind of revenge. When it came, it was utterly devastating.

Mum rang me. 'I need to see you, Mandy,' was all she would say. 'It's important.'

She came round to the flat that afternoon and, when I got in from school, I found her sitting in the kitchen, awaiting my arrival. Bill was out. He had gone off early in the day to discuss some business deal and had told me he would not be back until late. I had not seen Mum for several days, although we kept in daily contact via the phone. She looked radiant. Much later I discovered that her blossoming love affair with Bill's son Stephen was the reason for the gleam in her eye and the lift in her step, but, right now, she looked gravely concerned.

'What is it, Mum? What's happened?'

'It's Bill,' she said quietly. 'He rang me yesterday.'

Memories of the treacherous phone call he had made to Mum two years earlier, after he had taken my virginity, came flooding back. What had he said and done this time?

'He said', Mum faltered, 'that you had given him something.'

What? A jumper? His dinner? A new teapot? What?

'Little animals. Those were his exact words.'

Animals? From the look on Mum's face it was obvious we were not talking hamsters here.

'He said,' she took a deep breath to compose herself, 'Patsy, Mandy has bought a pair of second-hand Levis down Portobello market and I think she has caught something off them which she has passed to me. I said, "What kind of something?" and he replied, "Er . . . little animals". I couldn't believe what I was hearing.'

Sitting there, listening to what my mum was saying, neither could I. It took a second for comprehension to filter through.

144

Mum stepped into the breach. 'What he was inferring, Mandy, is that you gave him crabs. Pubic lice.'

Surely it was not true. Unbelievable. I couldn't have. *He* couldn't have.

Then, above the rising panic, shock and disbelief, my thoughts began to collect themselves. I had been itching in the genital area for some days but I was beset by so many physical and psychological problems since I had started on the pill, that I never questioned the odd itch. Why should I entertain even a vestige of suspicion about a venereal infection? I had never had sex with anyone but Bill. The penny dropped – but he might have had sex with someone other than me.

'Did you buy some old jeans?' Mum's voice was saying through the fog.

'Yes, I did, a couple of weeks ago. But they were clean, Mum. Anyway, I washed them first before I wore them. You know what I'm like, I'm obsessed with cleanliness.'

'I don't believe you can catch these things off clothes,' she said slowly, and sadly.

This was simply too big a revelation for me even to begin to comprehend. Bill had crabs. Bill had rung Mum. Bill had tried to blame it on me. What did all this make Bill? And where did it leave me? As I sat there, I felt the subliminal itch in my crotch start up again. There was nothing imaginary about it. It was real.

'I have to go to the bathroom, Mum,' I said with what must have been a noticeable catch in my voice. Mum hugged me. She would never let me down. She would support me in everything.

'Your father did the same thing to me, Mandy, on the night you were conceived but at least he had the decency not to try to dump the blame on me and the dignity not to try to embroil the rest of the family in it.'

I knew what she was trying to say.

'Don't ever think it is your fault.'

After she had gone, I sat like a zombie, trying to put off going to the bathroom, unable to face the evidence that would substantiate this appalling scenario. I don't know how long I sat there, nursing a cold cup of coffee, until my bladder told me I could no longer put off the evil moment. I went to the bathroom. I looked down and, with trembling fingers, examined myself. My heart plummeted. Sure enough, there was a minute midge-like insect clinging to me.

I suppressed the scream that was building up in my throat. The room spun. I flopped back down on to the toilet and began to weep tears of rage, frustration, repulsion – and most of all loss. What had I left now that Bill had done this to me?

Then I got angry. How dare he hit me with this double blow? First, his infidelity. Second, and even worse, his deceitful, back-stabbing betrayal of me to my own mother. It was the lowest, most despicable act I had ever heard of. And I loved this man? Man? What man – he was a worm, a snake, a side-shuffling, sneaky crab, that was what he was. He was no better than a pubic louse himself.

At that precise moment, I hated him with a vengeance and a loathing I had never suspected I was capable of, for abusing my body and, far, far worse, my trust in him.

Exhausted from the shock and my distress, I fell on to the bed and lost my misery in the deep sleep of the truly unhappy. When I awoke, there was no sign of Bill. He had called while I was asleep and left a brief message on the answerphone. He had had to go down to Suffolk on business. He would be back in a day or so. How very convenient. How totally fore-planned.

As ever, unable to face a confrontation or a sticky situation, he had run away, hoping that things would have blown over by the time he came home, but this time he had gone too far.

I needed time and space to sort myself out but, first of all, I needed to get myself to an STD clinic. The man I had loved with all my heart had used me, abused me and now given me a sexually transmitted infection, but the blow I could not handle was his final act of treason in trying to dump the blame on me. To avoid telling me the truth, he had gone to my mother. The ultimate ignominy was that he was trying to paint me as an irresponsible child yet he had been bedding this child for two years.

The only question that remained was simple. Where did I go from here? Taking one last look around the flat that had been my home from home for two years, I picked up my bag and walked out.

CHAPTER ELEVEN

Walking Back ... to Happiness?

It was my own fault, really. I had finally walked out on Bill. I had scraped together all my courage and what was left of my dignity and tried to start my life over without the man who had dominated my formative years. Then I let him back in.

For endless days and nights, I shut myself away in my room, reliving every moment of our years together, wondering where it had all gone wrong and trying to sort out my feelings. At just fifteen, I had experienced more love and lust, more pain and heartache than anyone else I knew, whether they were fifteen or, like Bill, fifty. It was all charted, every last high and low, from first kiss to last row, in babyish scrawl in my diaries.

I scattered them now over my bed, a carrier bag full of school jotters, message pads, the pink-velvet-covered diaries I had received as a Christmas present and the odd scraps of hotel notepaper that were all I had to hand on some occasions when Bill and I were away on holiday.

There, too, were the holiday snaps: Bill and me sunbathing by the pool in the South of France, shivering in the March wind outside a pretty pub in the West Country. Another of Bill sitting up in bed, smoking a cigarette, looking secretly very pleased with himself. I felt a pang of remembered love. I recognised the setting straightaway. It was at the Hotel le Warwick, just after we had had sex for the very first time. A stabbing pain shot through my heart. These pictures, each just a fleeting moment in time, were all I had left of our love and our life together.

When we had posed so happily for the camera, just like young lovers, who would ever have anticipated that, one day, it would all end in tears and acrimony? A tear splashed on to one Polaroid, a snap of us dining together at San Lorenzo, me blonde and tanned from my recent holiday in Spain, laughing and care-free. Bill beside me, pensive and distracted, an ever-present cigarette in his hand, his eyes on me. He looked like a man very much in love. How had it all gone so horribly wrong?

Out fluttered all his little love notes, scribbled and left on my pillow when he had rushed off to recording sessions, leaving me, sleepy and replete from his lovemaking, in our bed. 'Dearest Mandy. How much I love you.' How much now, Bill? That you could do this to me.

A Victorian card peeped out from one of my jotters. A sweet, handpainted posy of old red roses and Bill's spidery handwriting. 'Darling Mandy. This card is nearly as old as I am!'

The tears were flowing freely now. If Bill's notes could devastate me in this way, what would my diaries do? Fearfully, almost as if it was a timebomb ticking away, set to explode in my face, I reached out for my first diary, a black Lett's school booklet, bought for my first year at secondary school. It charted my transition from a child of twelve to a brand-new teenager.

The first months, I knew from memory, bare but for the odd reminder – dentist today – yuk. Maths today – double yuk. Then I had met Bill and the pages spilled over with the thrill of my first love.

I had picked up the diary habit from Bill, partly because in that, as in so many other ways, I had used him as my role model but also because I had so often found myself at a loose end, stuck alone in the flat when Bill was working and I should have been at school. At the time, writing all about our life together had helped me to make sense of the overpowering feelings I had for, and about, him. Perhaps they would help me to make sense of my life now. It was time, I knew, to expiate all the pain and guilt. To get Bill out of my system. To rebuild my life and all those shattered dreams.

Pulling the security blanket of my bedcover around me, I snuggled into my pillow and began to read. As I walked through the pages recalling our life together, I wept. My scribbles breathlessly recounted those blissful early days when Bill had swept me off my feet, the father figure and friend I had longed for all my life. My heart still ached for him the way he was then.

Now, as I read on, I could see, with hindsight and the advantage of my two and a half years' growth, that it was not I who had changed so much as Bill. Even from the start, he had rarely shown me any respect, and even less real love. What there was in plenty was lust and infatuation.

As I read on, it became clearer and clearer that the person

148

Bill held in the highest regard was... Bill.

Aged just thirteen, I had written in a fit of childish pique: 'Bill's just incapable of loving in the daytime or outside of the bedroom. He never shows me any real affection during a normal day at home. Bill spent all today at the computer. Again.'

Now I saw that this was his means of defence – and a weapon. I had lost count of the number of times I had tried to confront him about some problem and he would just walk off and start working at his computer.

Here they all were, those innumerable times, all listed in my diaries.

That was Bill's other major distraction. His own painstakingly detailed diary. Every day, he poured his life into a hand-written log. He would enter the details of every phone call he made or received, noting the exact time and the details of every conversation and meeting. Then, later, it would all be entered into the computer – twice the effort, twice the time.

I recalled, with a hot flush of guilt, how I had, on occasion, stooped to sneaking a look in his diary, driven by insecurity and the now wholly justified fear that he was being unfaithful. I had written: 'Bill is seeing other women! He has made a full note of their names and the times he has seen them. Times that just happened to slot in around the times he did not see me. Just who the hell are these tarts? But when I tried to talk to him about it, he just said they were old friends and turned back to the computer. Sometimes he makes me want to scream. But what can I do?'

There, too, was Astrid Lundstrom, his girlfriend before me. I had never seen her as a threat but I realised now, through the notes in my diary, just how regular her appearances were in Bill's life. She had been with him from the age of about seventeen and he had always claimed that she would not let him go.

I had written: 'Astrid was on the phone to Bill again, looking for money. He is buying her a flat for 200,000 pounds, the silly bugger. He told me she could not handle losing him and turned to drink and drugs, so he feels guilty about her. Bill is so soft.' Now I could see that that was exactly what Bill had wanted me to think.

The truth was that he hated to part on bad terms with any woman. It was too much aggro. He would pay any price to keep

149

them sweet so he kept them all dangling, tied to him in one way or another. With Astrid, the tie was financial; with me, it was emotional.

I had always been adamant about never taking money from Bill. Here, in my diaries, was the confirmation of my financial independence – the details of my pocket money and wage packets from Tip Toe Shoes, the outlay on presents for Bill, food for the King's Road flat and flowers for Gedding Hall. There, too, was the stark contrast with Bill's tight hand on his own cash. He never lavished gifts on me. Now that I had ended the relationship, I had gained nothing material from it, nor did I want anything. There was no wardrobe full of designer clothes nor a jewellery box full of gems. I never asked for any of that and I didn't expect it. I was with Bill because I loved him.

He had, however, tried to buy his way into my affections – although not on the same scale as with Astrid. Instead, he treated me as the child I was. I wrote: 'Bill wants to give me pocket money every week. I said no. But he says I can use it to buy food from Marks and Spencers instead of using my own money for our teatime meal every day. He says 50 pounds a week. End of cheese on toast and lettuce salad, hooray!' I had also noted: 'Bill says he will take account of this extra 50 pounds a week in his ledgers. Maybe he can get back the tax on it.'

(Every monetary outgoing was religiously logged in his accounting system.)

I wrote: 'Bill is worried about his finances. He says he will be in deep trouble with the bank unless the Stones go on tour soon. But he doesn't want me to know more, in case I worry too much.'

I was a bit gullible in buying than one. The bottom line was that Bill was secretive about his money. He was terrified of another woman ripping him off. During all that time I was with him, he never gave me any indication of how much he was truly worth. He was forever bemoaning the cost of meals, phone bills and taxi fares, just like any working man would.

The message now came across loud and clear. He did not trust me. He did not trust anyone. I thought that after we had been together for a couple of years he would have started to confide in me. That's what couples were all about, caring, sharing and supporting one another but, no, Bill always kept everything to himself.

All the pieces of the jigsaw were falling into place. I realised with sudden clarity that, for much of the time, I had felt shut out of huge chunks of Bill's life. Ours was not togetherness in the true sense of the word.

Then there was a litany of his obsessive jealousy. From incidents at Tramp, when he would repeatedly glare at me while I danced and even, on occasion, freeze me out when a man had looked at me, believing I had sent some furtive, flirtatious message to him with my eyes.

More serious was his determination not to let me have a career of my own. I had to be totally dependent on him. I wrote: 'Bill wanted me to stay at home again today, to be with him and forget about school. He says exams are stupid. He will educate me about life and my job will be to be his wife and love him. Suits me!'

Foolish first love. Now I could see that he was deeply insecure. He couldn't handle the thought of me making a life away from him. The message I was getting now was that Bill was uptight about money, women and relationships. Almost as uptight as he was about his emotions. I had long felt that the only time Bill ever revealed any genuine emotion was in bed but there was once, just one single occasion in all our time together, that he finally cracked and revealed his true feelings. I scoured my diaries for the entry I was looking for. There it was, one weekend in 1985, at Gedding Hall. I had not spared the detail on this entry. It had stunned me so much.

'Something weird happened last night. We were having dinner at Gedding. Mum and Nicola were there, one of Bill's friends, Terry Taylor, and the staff, Monique and Louis. Bill said something sarcastic to me – I can't remember exactly what – but I was furious. He's always putting me down in front of other people and usually I just take it. But this time I turned on him and, for a couple of minutes, just shouted and screamed at him – telling him exactly what I thought about him. I didn't hold back and of course everyone was shocked into silence.

'Bill said something like, "Don't embarrass me, Mandy."

'I screamed: "I don't care who's listening."

'His friend tried to interrupt and I told him to mind his own business and shut up! I was sick of keeping quiet while Bill took the mickey out of me in front of his oh-so clever mates. I really went to town.

'And then Bill did the weirdest thing. He burst into tears. I couldn't believe what I was seeing. I felt terrible but at the same time it was amazing to see him actually respond. Then he got up from the table and ran straight up to his bedroom. I followed him and he was sitting on the bed sobbing his heart out. He kept repeating himself: "I just can't take it any more. I've been holding so much in, Mandy, for so long. Everything is building up inside me."

'I put my arms around him and tried to reassure him. Poor Bill. But I knew this was good for him. Finally, he had broken down the walls he's been hiding behind for years. I was thinking: "At last he's opened up. At last I am going to find out what's really going on in his head." But I was wrong. Bill got up this morning and it was like nothing had ever happened. Once his tears had dried and he'd pulled himself together, he was exactly the same as before. I tried to talk to him about it later today and he said: "Oh that was nothing, don't worry about it." We're back to square one.

'Sometimes I despair. Bill just won't let down his barriers for a moment. If only he would let me – or anybody – in.'

No, I realised, reading those incredible words, it was not I who had the problems. It was Bill.

Reading those diaries was like going through intensive therapy. With no one to turn to or confide in, I had poured my innermost thoughts and feelings out on paper. My diaries had been my friend and confidante and now, as in all true friendships, my diaries had come to the rescue, whispering in my ear that here was the evidence; I was not to blame for the way things had turned out. I had been a pawn in the game. I had lost my heart, my innocence, my schooling and almost my family but I had gained knowledge of pure, unconditional love. Bill was the ultimate loser.

Yet, while my brain and my powers of reasoning told me one thing, my heart told me another. I was inextricably bound to Bill, as only first love can bind you. No matter what he did or said, no matter how much water flowed under the bridge, the memories of our affair would linger on, shaping me as a person, affecting my every future relationship.

Mum knocked on my door, intruding into my melancholy. 'Just thought you might like a cuppa, chicken. You've been shut away in here for hours. I was getting worried about you.'

Now there was another iron in the fire, another tie that bound us all together. By some perverse twist of fate, Mum and Stephen had hitched their wagons together, too, and were fast rolling down the rocky road to everlasting love. Their affair was the antithesis of Bill's and mine – daughter and father-figure; son and mother-figure. Funny old thing, life.

How on earth had this tangle arisen? Again, it was my fault. Had I not met Bill, Mum would never have met Stephen. I tried to recall how it had all started. Having just reaquainted myself with my diaries, it was not difficult.

I remembered Mum, bristling with disapproval, yet invited to chaperone me, had accompanied me to Gedding one weekend in mid-1984, before Bill and I started sleeping together. She did not spot the signs of love and carnal knowledge because, at that time, there were none. At least none that were mutually reciprocated. Then, while she had gone to keep a watchful eye, she had lost her own heart. She had met Bill's only son Stephen.

Casting my mind back now, I could recall that fateful first meeting with total clarity.

Mum was in her natural habitat, the kitchen, sorting out some fresh salad and vegetables for dinner, knowing that she was, if she was lucky, undergoing a temporary reprieve from her illness that might last the weekend, just so long as she was careful to eat nothing that would throw her digestive system into an uproar. Ever careful not to offend the delightful French couple, Monique and Louis, who ran Gedding Hall for Bill, she had suggested that she help them by preparing a large salad. As she was standing over the sink, up to her elbows in vegetables, with a paring knife in her hand, Stephen had walked in.

An unexpected visitor, he had popped down to Gedding simply because he was at a loose end that Saturday afternoon. Surprised to find this strange woman in an apron at the kitchen sink, preparing vegetables, he had assumed she was a new member of staff. He wanted to make a cup of coffee and, out of politeness, he offered Mum one, too.

They sat at the kichen table and chatted, as strangers do, about this and that and everything but themselves for half an hour before Stephen got round to introducing himself and then Mum revealed that she was my mother. They had both been as shocked as each other. If Stephen had supposed Mum to be a new kitchen-maid, she had assumed that he was a friend of Bill's. She was astounded to find that he had a son who was so grown up and, further, that they were so very different.

Where Bill was diffident and withdrawn, Stephen was bright and sparky. Over six foot tall and well built, he looked physically nothing like his small, slight father.

That day, Mum and Stephen had set the seal on a friendship that, over months and years, was to develop into a powerful and long-lasting love affair – again, the opposite of Bill and me, who had dived headfirst into the grand passion of love and sex with such alacrity.

Mum had great misgivings about getting involved with a man so much younger than herself. She was forty-one; he just twenty-one but Stephen had never seemed his age. He was old beyond his years, serious, intense and very deep. He was intellectual, too, in a way that Bill secretly resented. Stephen had gone on to further education and had graduated successfully from college. Intellectually, physically and emotionally, he was light years in advance of his father. At the same time, he had developed an air of self-sufficiency and independence that made him mature and responsible beyond his youth. In many ways, Bill was the child in the family, with his puerile demands and his petulance.

Brought up by his father, Stephen had known a life only as the son of a Rolling Stone – and the most cool, detached, self-orientated Stone at that (and that was saying something!). Raised without a mother and with a father incapable of giving him much time, and even less overt affection, Stephen had known no real love, no security, no home to call his own. Brought up in the 'care' of a succession of nannies and left largely to fend for himself, it was inevitable that, one day, he would seek out the mother love he had never known.

Then there was Mum, warm, loving, affectionate and totally selfless. Being one of ten children herself, having a family had brought the greatest meaning to her life. She had relinquished her own career to be a mother.

Having been hurt and deserted by her husband, being a woman who knew pain and a sense of loss, it was natural that the love in her should reach out to Stephen and touch him in a way that no one ever had before. Just as I needed an older man because I had had no father, so Stephen responded to a mature woman because he had known no mother.

It was the perfect equation, based on genuine emotional response and need. Over the years, many outsiders would raise their hands in horror at such an apparently bizarre foursome. To all of us, there was nothing more natural in the world.

Problems had only arisen between Bill and me when I had eventually grown up to understand my needs and see that Bill actually fell short of fulfilling them. Of all of us, he had the least maturity in examining his own emotions.

For Stephen, however, Mum would never fall short. She helped him to grow and, in turn, he helped her on the way to health and happiness. Theirs was holistic love, shared in every way. Bill was incapable of that.

At first, however, I had problems in accepting the situation that was plainly evolving between Mum and Stephen and so did Nicola. It was some time into their relationship before I actually cottoned on to what was happening. When you have grown up with a mother who has remained resolutely single in order to bring up her family, the last thing you expect is for her to have an affair with your boyfriend's son! I never suspected that anything was going on between them until I walked into the library at Gedding one night and caught Stephen with his hand on Mum's knee. That gesture in itself was not out of the ordinary, but the way in which they suddenly sprang apart with a guilty look spoke volumes.

I said, 'What the heck is going on?' I was very taken aback – and extremely annoyed – to see this young man making overtures to my mother.

Neither of them spoke but guilt pervaded the air. I felt quite disgusted and turned on my heel and walked off.

To a teenager, the mere thought of your mother in a sexual encounter is totally repugnant but when it is with someone to whom you are practically related, and he happens to be twenty years younger than her, then the repugnance factor shoots right off the scale. I targeted my disgust at Stephen. Up until then I had liked him immensely but after that night I refused to speak to him for weeks. Mum, ever conscious of the delicacy of the situation, made sure that she and Stephen were never caught *in flagrante* again.

Their affair was conducted with the utmost caution, but their genuine love for one another was too strong to walk away from altogether. As it was to transpire, theirs was a love that would withstand the test of time and, seemingly insurmountable, obstacles.

Ultimately, and much later, on learning of their illicit love, Bill would give Stephen the ultimatum: 'It's either Patsy or me,' and dear, sweet, loyal Stephen, forced to choose between his father and his lover, would stand by Mum.

At this juncture, however, in their early years together, Mum and Stephen kept themselves to themselves. I never once saw them kiss or even touch in front of me. While they behaved honourably, I misbehaved abominably, in true miscreant teenage fashion. I mercilessly took the wee out of Stephen at every given opportunity. I wanted desperately to embarrass him, to humiliate him for his audacity in daring to make advances to my mother. Nicola and I would plot our put-down lines together. Neither of us could stand the thought of them as a couple.

As time went by, however, we got used to seeing them together in the context of friends and, as they were so unobtrusive about their love, there was nothing we could malign them for. Eventually, as we calmed down, we came to realise that Mum had never been happier or healthier. If Stephen was responsible for that, it would be churlish in the extreme to try to deprive her of it.

In him, she found a man who, for the first time, was sympathetic about her poor health. Instead of moaning, 'It's all in your head,' as Bill did with me, Stephen would always be at Mum's side when she had a bad turn, ministering to her with mugs of hot tea and his own cup of kindness.

Bill must have been aware, too, of what was going on, but, typically, he refused to acknowledge it. He never talked about them. Only once did he ever mention the possibility that they were lovers and even that was in his usual oblique fashion. Watching them out on the lawn playing croquet and falling about with laughter as Bill's two dogs tried to scamper off with the croquet ball, he said, 'Patsy and Stephen seem happy together.'

I felt quite sure that he never voiced his opinion to Stephen on the subject. As father and only son, they were remarkably distant with one another. Bill would exercise his authority over Stephen by telling him to fetch things from the kitchen or the library, silly little things that he could quite easily have gone for himself, but it reinforced his status as boss. Stephen, in contrast, was only too happy to help anyone and he came into his own when Mum, Nic and I were all down at Gedding.

We would all sit around the kitchen table, chatting for hours, and Stephen positively glowed. He felt he had finally come home. At last he had a family.

Now, I thought to myself, as I sat on my bed, listening to the comforting, familiar sounds of Mum pottering about in the kitchen, making a cup of tea for us, all that was over. Bill's selfish acts had torn us all asunder. What a mess!

For several days, I stayed cocooned in my misery. No amount of exhortation from Nicola or Mum could drag me out of my torpor. I just wanted to be left alone to mourn the passing of my love affair.

Bill was not willing to let me go so easily, however. He rang incessantly. At first, I took the phone off the hook but, at Mum's behest, replaced it after the first couple of days. She persuaded me that no one ever achieved anything by running away from an issue and, anyway, that had always been Bill's tactic. If necessary, she would stonewall him until I felt strong enough to tell him myself that what he had done was unforgivable and that it was over between us.

For several days, unfailingly polite and restraining her natural anger, she simply told Bill that I was not available or that I did not want to speak to him.

He sent flowers, a large bouquet that, if one flower says a thousand words, spoke volumes. However, the only two words I wanted from him were, 'I'm sorry.' That would have conceded his guilt. They were not forthcoming.

Still he rang. Still I refused to speak to him.

Mum was becoming ever more anxious about my continuing gloom and my refusal to rejoin the world, and also about how long she could continue to put up with these incessant phone calls. It wasn't fair on her. I had to be strong. I had to tell him I never wanted to see him again. I bit the bullet.

Late one evening, the phone rang and we all knew it was

Bill. I ventured downstairs and intercepted Mum just as she was about to pick up the receiver. 'I'll take it, Mum,' I said.

With some hesitation, she picked it up and handed it over to me. Then she turned and walked into the living room, closing the door firmly behind her.

I heard his voice, those familiar tones I had not heard now for over a week. Only a short week, but it seemed like a life-time. 'Patsy?' he said, 'It's Bill.' A lump rose in my throat. I could not speak. How could it be that, after all he had done to me, I still trembled when I heard his voice? 'Patsy, are you there?'

I bit my lip. 'It's me, Bill,' I said, desperately trying to conceal any sign of emotion in my voice.

'Mandy,' he breathed. The pleasure and relief in his voice were unmistakable. 'Mandy, how have you been? I've been worried sick about you. Nothing, not a note, not a word, and your mum won't tell me anything. I've been going out of my mind . . .'

His voice seemed to be coming from a million miles away, yet I could practically feel his presence next to me. Clutching the phone, I could see him in front of me, sitting on the sofa at the flat, cradling the receiver next to his ear.

I swallowed hard but still I couldn't speak. I did not know where to begin, what to say.

'Mandy, I have to see you. I need you.'

The silence between us now was like a bond, stretching from Chelsea to north London, reaching out along the phone lines to bind us inextricably together. How much silence had there been between us over the years? So many things left unsaid, so much pain glossed over and walked away from. Still I could say nothing.

'Mandy, we must talk, but not like this, not over the phone. I have to see you. Please come home, Mandy.'

But where was home? I stood in the darkening hallway of my mum's Muswell Hill flat, looking at the frayed seam of the carpet by the door and remembering all the times I had lain in Bill's arms. This flat was no longer my home. I had left it behind when I fell in love with Bill.

'Come home, Mandy,' he said again, softly, pleading.

'I'll be there,' I said and put the phone gently down.

Like a battered wife, hooked on the mental anguish. I knew I had to go back.

With trembling fingers, I dialled the cab firm. 'Taxi from Muswell Hill, please,' I said. 'Going to Chelsea.' I hesitated for a second. Then I answered the cabbie's inevitable question. 'Right away.'

CHAPTER TWELVE

Happy Birthday, Sweet Sixteen

He was waiting for me at the door. I walked up the stairs to the flat and he stood at the top, watching me ascend.

'Hello, Mandy,' he said, but there was no accompanying smile, no sign of relief or gratitude or love or loss in his expression.

My head pounded, my chest felt like it had an iron band compressing it. There was a lump in my throat. I had needed, wanted, to see Bill again, but now, confronted by him, I was unsure. How could we cross this yawning chasm of recrimination and pain that lay between us? What words were big enough to describe the emotional turmoil that Bill had put me through – not just in the last days and weeks, but in the two and a half years of our affair?

Bill had no words either. His vocabulary had never extended to discussing his feelings, other than perfunctory words of love. Nor was he able to start now. We looked at each other in silence for a moment, searching for the right thing to say. Then he said, 'I've missed you, you know.' I did know. What I knew there and then was that he had won.

He might have missed me but not in the way that I had missed him. He had not plumbed the depths of his soul in a desperate search for the true meaning of our love. He had not wept and raged and been forced to walk away from our affair then, in a tumultuous about-turn, walk back again. For Bill, it was, once again, just as before. I had come back. He had won.

My heart sank. We sat down together on the settee, my silence announcing his victory as clearly as if it were pealed out by church bells. I shook my head sadly at the enormity of the realisation that I could never change him, never make him see me differently, never get him to look on me as anything other than his little girl – sweet, silly, juvenile Mandy. Now, I knew he was thinking, she has come to her senses.

I turned to face him and there could only be one question.

The question he assumed I would never ask – my prodigal return meant that I no longer considered it of vital importance. Oh, but I did.

'How could you lie to me, Bill?'

Silence. A quizzical look momentarily crossed his face. Then it was quickly replaced by one of annoyance. 'Don't start, Mandy,' he snapped. 'What's past is past. You're here, I'm here. Can't we put all that behind us?' If only it were that easy.

'Bill, I catch a sexually transmitted infection and you tell my mother I gave it to you? Where is the sense in any of that? If I had caught it, I could only have caught it from you. I don't have sex with anyone else to get sexual infections from. And why my mother? Why not tell me? Am I such a child, you still have to go running to my mother to smack me?'

'Mandy,' he sighed, 'what is important is that you are here and I love you. We've survived this, now let's forget it.'

I kicked myself. I had steered him away from the issue in hand, which was his infidelity. When it came to slipping his way out of a tight corner, Bill was a veteran. I was a complete novice in this kind of confrontation. 'But I could not have caught anything unless you gave it to me, Bill.'

He reached across and tried to stroke my hair. I brushed his hand away brusquely and looked down at my own hands, nervously twiddling the ring on my wedding finger. I had never yet been able to take it off, no matter how monumental the rows between us. It was now part of the fabric of my life, a daily habit that had evolved following the incident when the newspaper reporter almost caught me wearing it that day two years before. Every day was the same. In public, I wore it on my right hand but, at the end of every day, I replaced it on my wedding-ring finger and went to sleep, dreaming my childish dreams of being together with Bill forever. Now, I slowly removed it from my finger and turned it over and over in my hand.

'Mandy,' he said, 'I told you not to buy second-hand jeans.' It was no use. No matter what I said, Bill would always follow his own course, do his own thing, even believe his own lies.

I took his hand and spread his fingers out in mine, his neat little hand, no bigger than my own, and placed my ring in his palm. 'I love you, Bill,' I said, 'but I can't live with you. At least not right now. I think,' I took a deep breath before saying

162

the words, 'we need more time apart. Maybe put a bit of distance between us. We both need to clear our heads and see how much we really do mean to each other.'

'What are you saying, Mandy? That it's all over between us? You don't mean that.'

'No, Bill, that's not what I'm saying. All I am saying is that we need to be apart for a while. I don't know how long. Maybe a month, maybe a year. Maybe even longer. We'll just have to see. But what I do know is that we are not good for each other right now.'

'So, we've split up and you've come back just to tell me we're splitting up. Why did you bother coming back in the first place?'

'Oh God, it's like talking to a brick wall. Bill, can't you see that everything is not always black and white. There are shades of grey in between. 'I love you but I don't know if I love you enough and I no longer know if you really do love me. I don't know if you ever really did, not in the way I loved you.'

'God, Mandy, what do you want as proof? A Porsche? A diamond ring? Red roses every day?'

'Respect,' I said quietly. 'Just your respect for me as a person.'

He looked at me blankly. He opened his mouth to remonstrate but I rose from the settee and turned to the door. 'And a holiday,' I said. 'That's what I really want more than anything right now. A real break. To lie in the sun, empty my head and just toast.'

'Jesus,' he broke into a big grin. 'If that's all it takes, we'll go. Great idea. Barbados, just the two of us. But in a few weeks' time. I've got some deals to tie up first.'

I shook my head in silent exasperation. 'Bill, why won't you listen to what I am saying? You just sweep in and assume you can have and do anything you want. Well, I want something for me for a change. Space. I'm going to Marbella. Alone. But don't you worry about me. I'll be fine. I've got some friends there. They'll put me up for a few weeks.'

'Oh yeah, Keith Daley and co, is it?' he smirked. 'The DJ you've been flying up and down to Scotland to see on a weekly basis?'

'Don't try and turn this back on me, Bill. There's nothing

between me and Keith. I've got nothing to be ashamed of. But if it suits your suspicious mind to try and wriggle out of this by imagining Keith and I have slept together, then you just have to live with that. I don't, because it's simply not true.'

But Bill was not yet beaten. 'If you go, Mandy,' he said very slowly, 'then that's it between us. Not for just a few weeks or months. Forever. You go and we're finished.' The ultimate threat.

'I don't want that, Bill. You know I don't, but I'm still going to Marbella. As it happens, it's Nicola's birthday next week. We can go together. Be sisters again.'

Bill suddenly saw that, this time, I meant business. If I walked away from him now, it would be forever, because he himself was dictating those terms. He rose from the settee and crossed the floor quickly, stopping me in my tracks at the door. He put one hand firmly on the door handle and the other, more gently, on my arm. 'OK,' he said softly. 'Go then. But do one thing for me. Let me pay for the tickets.'

I gaped at him. After all this, he was still playing his games. Before I could open my mouth, he added, 'As a birthday present to Nicola.'

'I'll suggest it to her, Bill. But whether or not she accepts is up to her. I'm going anyway.'

'I wish you'd stay. Just for one night. Tonight,' he wheedled.

There it was, the blackmail for the price of a plane ticket. I was not that cheap.

'No, Bill. I have to go home.'

'I'll ring you tomorrow,' he said. 'Promise me at least you won't go without saying goodbye.'

'I promise, Bill,' I said.

His grip on me softened. He knew I was as good as my word. I always kept my promises.

Later in our relationship Bill was to pass on other sexually transmitted infections to me, namely candida, better known as thrush, and also *Chlamydia*.

*   *   *   *   *

Within the week, Nicola and I had flown to Marbella where we were met by Keith, Colin and the others. They had offered to put us up in their rented flats for the fortnight, sleeping on floors but who cared? We knew we would not be doing much sleeping anyway.

It was the beginning of the season for our Glaswegian friends. Everyone was happy, glad to be back in the Spanish sun after the dreariness of a Glasgow winter, all of us young teenagers, freewheeling, footloose and fancy free.

Summer time and, as the song goes, the livin' was easy. I freed myself from thoughts of Bill and simply soaked up the sun and fun. Dancing until dawn, playing childish games on each other, in those short two weeks I recouped so much of my lost teen years.

My stolen weekends in Glasgow had built a firm foundation for some true friendships with kids my own age but especially with Keith.

I saw the way the holidaymaking girls looked longingly, lasciviously at him, taking in every inch of him, savouring his hair, already streaked blond from the sun, his body slim and tanned and rippling with young muscles. Most of all, however, it was his laughter, his easy-going good humour that captivated them. We would walk down the beach distributing leaflets for Cuba, and, while all male eyes would turn to Nicola and me as we skipped along, so all young female eyes were fixed on Keith.

Curiously, he had abandoned his old flirtatious style. If he turned on the charm these days, it was purely for business, to pull in gorgeous young female punters to the club. Something had got to Keith and, one moonlit night, our last on this holiday in Marbella, I found out what, or who, it was. It was me.

We'd had a night like any other at Cuba, bopping until we dropped, giggling and gossiping about who were the hunkiest holidaymakers that week and who were the girls and guys most likely to end up falling into each other's arms and beds. In the days – and nights – of 1986, before AIDS became the global threat it is now, summer holidays meant sun, sea, sand and sex, sex, sex.

Only Keith and I had stood back and let the traffic pass, as it were. Nothing had been said between us. There was no sign that he felt the same way about me as I was very strongly beginning to feel about him. Until this, our last night together.

Normally, after the club had closed, we would all stagger

back to the flat a few streets away, exhausted but happy. On this night, however, Keith had taken my arm and led me down to walk alongside the beach. 'You're going home tomorrow,' he had whispered as I gathered my bag and prepared to set off with Nic, Colin and the others. 'Walk with me.'

I had not needed to be asked twice. We walked along the silver sands and I was suddenly aware of the closeness of him. It struck me that, in all the year I had know him, in all the weekends we had passed together in Glasgow, we had never been alone together. Why? What had we been running away from? It was time to stop running.

I could feel the magnetism between us, binding us together without the need for words or gestures. Then Keith stopped by the seafront, the water lapping round our feet. Afraid to face the truth of the moment, I bent down and removed my sandals, feeling the coolness of the wet sand under my toes.

'Have you finished with Bill?' he asked hesitantly, looking down at me as I crouched at his feet.

I turned and looked up to meet his gaze. He was nervous. Fearful of my reply? I rose and stood to face him, eye to eye. 'No,' I said truthfully.

His gaze dropped for a moment then Keith smiled and pulled me to him. 'When you do,' he said quietly, 'I'll be waiting.' Then he lowered his face to mine and kissed me with a tenderness I had never known before.

* * * * *

I loved Spain. I adored the balmy heat and the crazy people. I loved the *mañana* mood. If it couldn't be done today, what the heck, tomorrow's another day. Everything and everyone was laissez-faire. I had never felt so relaxed, so fit and happy. As a parting shot, as he drove us to the airport on our last day, Keith had offered me a summer job doing promotion for Cuba. He knew that Nic and I had pulled in more men to the club than the other girl promoters put together. I thought of nothing else all the way home. Why not? I was almost sixteen. I was free to do what I wanted. It was time to take a sabbatical from Britain and from Bill.

By the time we landed at Heathrow, I was ready to turn

around and take the first flight back but if I were to leave London for the summer, there were things to be done first.

I rang Bill and told him I was back. He was playing it very cool. If I could leave him for two weeks, he would do the same. He invited me to dinner at Tramp the following week. He was busy until then – games, games...

So we found ourselves meeting, awkwardly, both of us on edge, a week later. Bill was unfailingly polite – always a bad sign. I dutifully answered all his questions. Yes, I had had a lovely time. Yes, the weather had been fantastic. Yes, my Glaswegian mates were all out there, yes, including Keith Daley. I answered the unspoken accusation hanging between us. No, there was nothing between us at all. No, I had not sorted out my feelings. No, I did not want to finish with Bill but nor did I want us to get back together again. Not yet.

I was going back to Spain. Not on holiday this time. To work.

Bill hit the roof. 'We've been through all this bloody routine a month ago. You wanted a holiday, you got a bloody holiday. And I paid for it, too.'

I refused to lower my dignity to respond to that. It was despicable. He had paid for Nicola's flight, no more no less.

He went on, carried along on the tide of his rage. 'What more do you bloody want? You're just taking liberties, Mandy. No, it's more than that. You're taking the piss!'

I said nothing. There was no point in any rejoinder.

Warming to his theme, he ranted, 'You go and we are finished. This time I really mean it. Over, the end. In fact, don't bloody bother coming back.'

That was it decided, then. The next day I started to make my plans to go over to Marbella for the duration of the summer season. Mum was perturbed but I was set to turn sixteen in a few days and she knew I had been well looked after by the Glasgow Gang.

I booked my flight for ten days' time, on 27 June. There was no looking back.

Despite his threats, Bill had backtracked. We were in daily contact by phone. My lack of resistance to his demands made him believe he could still dissuade me from going, still persuade me to come back to him as his lover, his child-wife. He had changed his tactics. He was warmer, more mellow, trying to charm me where force had failed. He thought I would change my mind at the last minute. Typical Mandy, bloody obstinate, stubborn to the end. Or so he thought.

In fact, I had never felt more unsure of myself. I was taking a quantum leap – away from him. Yet I still cared about him more than anyone in the world.

On my last night in London, he took me out to dinner and I went back with him to the flat. I wanted to say goodbye properly. I wanted no acrimony. I wanted him to know I loved him – but as a friend, right now. He was up for that. We fell into each other's arms in a farewell cuddle and, exhausted by the emotions of our parting, both fell asleep. When we awoke, we were snuggled together, my arms around Bill's back, my face nestled into his back, protected, secure, without the heavy burden of sex hanging over us. It was as it had been in the beginning, all those years ago. It could be like this again. I knew I was doing the right thing.

I crept silently from the bed and over to his desk where I wrote him a letter. The words came easily. Watching him sleep so peacefully, all the old feelings of love and affection swept over me. He had not tried to pressure me into sex, he had not tried to brow-beat, bully or humiliate me into staying.

'Dear Bill,' I wrote, 'Thank you for giving me my freedom. I love you and need you and always will. Mandy.'

As I signed off, I could hear him stirring in the bedroom. I tiptoed to the bathroom, quickly splashed my face and brushed my teeth and went back into the sitting room to pick up my bag and jacket.

Then I heard it. The low, mechanical tap-tap-tapping that meant Bill was at his computer. Doubtless logging the contents of my love letter. I turned on my heel and walked out of the door.

*　　*　　*　　*　　*

The first phone call I made from Spain a few days later was to Mum. 'I'm here, I'm fine and everything is brilliant. Just to put your mind at rest, Mum.'

However, there was something in her voice as she gamely tried to assure me that London was grey and cold and much the same as normal, that prompted me to ask her, 'What's happened?

What's wrong?' A sixth sense of warning sent a chill through me. Had Bill said or done something to Mum in order to wreak revenge for me leaving him this way? The scars from the STD syndrome were a long way from fading yet.

'Have you seen Bill?' I asked, straight to the point.

'Umm,' she replied hesitantly. She was obviously trying to protect me by covering something up but to no avail. I knew when Mum was pulling that nesting-bird-with-her-fledgling-young stunt.

'And? Mum, what is it? What has he done?' panic rising in me now. What could be worse than the tricks he had pulled on me and Mum before? I knew of nothing but then I did not operate like Bill. Who knew what he was capable of?

'I popped into the office', she said, 'to have lunch with Karen.' Suddenly there was a note of courage in her voice. She had decided to play this one with a bold front. Anger was always better than pity. 'And why not? It's weeks since we've been out for a meal together.'

Karen and Mum had become good friends, too. More Mum's age than mine, Karen and she had slipped into an easy friendship while staying at Gedding Hall together.

'Get to the point, Mum.'

'You'll never believe this Mandy but Bill had completely changed the office around.'

Uh-huh. Nothing too devastating in that, itself.

'In what way?'

'Well, when I walked in, I got the shock of my life. There was all your stuff, Mandy, all your clothes and things, packed up and stacked in binbags and suitcases in the corner of the office. It looked like they were waiting for the binman to call, Mandy. I think they were going to throw them out. Your big Mickey Mouse was sticking out of the corner of one bag and there was no disguising they were your things. Karen looked terribly embarrassed, like she had just been caught in the act. Well, I looked at her and then I noticed. The walls were different. There were big empty spaces where pictures had been taken down.' She paused. There was a silence that Pinter would have been proud of.

'Go on, Mum,' I said.

'Your pictures, Mandy. All those lovely photos of you and

Bill together at Gedding and in France. And that smashing one of you two at his birthday dinner, where you've got your arms round each other. All gone. Remember that big one of you he had in pride of place on the mantlepiece? Well, that was taken down, too. And in its place was one of Bill with Stephen. Every trace of you was gone. It was like you had ceased to exist.

'I was standing there with my mouth open and Karen said a bit apologetically, "Can you take these things away, Patsy?" I was so stunned. I thought, "They're all completely off their trolley." I wasn't going to say anything, Mandy, I didn't want to upset you. But now I've thought about it, you're better off without him. You are, really. He's a very bitter man, Mandy. He can't deal with the fact that you left him to go to Spain. He doesn't want you to have any independence, or any life of your own. These are not the actions of a sensible, sane man, Mandy.'

I counted out a handful of pesetas. Yes, I had enough to make one more call to London. 'Got to go, Mum. Money is running out. Don't worry about Bill. Maybe it's just too painful for him to have these constant reminders of me around the place when I am hundreds of miles away, having the time of my life. Look, I'll speak to you in a couple of days. Look after yourself and give my love to Nic. I love you. 'Bye.'

Then I picked up the receiver again and steadily, determinedly, dialled Bill's number. There was no answer. No matter. There would be another time. The pictures might be gone, so were my clothes and so was I, but the anger lingered on. I would have to deal with that one when I had calmed down myself...

* * * * *

I rang him on my birthday. Sweet sixteen and never been missed. He knew it was my birthday, he had always sent flowers and a card before. It would be noted in his computer diary so that, when he logged on the day before, a timely reminder would pop up on his screen before his eyes. 'Mandy's birthday. Order flowers.'

Of course, he might have scrubbed that reference, just as he had tried to eliminate the last vestiges of me from the flat and the office.

The massive display of exotic tropical blooms I had received that morning from Keith had only served to bring home the contrast with Bill.

I stood in the café bar and dialled his number. He answered immediately. It struck me that he might have been waiting for my call, hanging about by the phone like I had done so many times for him. I told myself not to be so naive. Bill did not do things like that. It was 6.30 pm, he was always home at that time, relaxing prior to going out for dinner or to another mega showbiz bash, with the inevitable blonde on his arm, no doubt. Why should he wait in for me?

'Happy birthday, Mandy,' he said, disarmingly.

Although it was long distance, his voice was so clear that I could hear every inflection. He sounded like he was only around the corner. There was sarcasm in his tone. 'You'll have to excuse the fact I didn't send you a present. You neglected to leave me your exotic forwarding address.'

That was palpable nonsense. Karen had been left explicit details of my whereabouts, including the international post code and phone number of the club.

Bill was gunning for a row but I did not want to pick a fight. It was my birthday. The irony of this particular birthday's significance had not escaped me. Finally, I had reached the age of consent and my long-time lover and I were half a continent apart.

I half-laughed to myself at this quirk of fate.

'Is there something funny?' demanded Bill, defensively. I remembered how Bill hated not to be in on anyone else's laughter. Years of being the butt of Jagger's jokes had made him completely paranoid that everyone was laughing at him. 'Or is someone making you laugh, Mandy? Eh? Like I couldn't lately. Is that it?'

'Oh, for heaven's sake, Bill, stop being so paranoid. I'm on my own here.'

'What, no Keith then?'

'Oh, grow up, Bill.'

'No, you grow up. You're the bloody child who wants one thing one minute and another the next. Your problem is you don't know what you want.'

'A bit of peace from you, basically. I go out of the way to phone you on my birthday and all I get is hassled. Bill, some things never change.'

171

'No, but you do, Mandy. You change with the wind. Well, so far as I'm concerned you're blown away.'

'I beg your pardon?'

'You heard.'

'What are you saying, Bill?'

'Nothing you don't already know. We're finished. I really don't want to see or hear from you again. Get out of my life, Mandy.'

He was bluffing so I called his hand. "We're through Bill. This time I mean it"

As I slammed the phone down I felt a curious sense of relief. This row was unlike all the others. This row had about it the ring of truth. I had had enough. Bill wanted to hurt me, genuinely hurt me as much as possible. What better time to pick than on my sixteenth birthday? The day on which he had always promised me we would get engaged. Dreams, so many dreams. All dead now.

*　*　*　*　*

But the nightmare was only about to begin.

I returned, heavy-hearted and with a face as long as a wet weekend in Glasgow, to the flat I was sharing with the other girls. 'Bad news, huh?' said Kelly as I walked through the door.

I nodded glumly.

'On yer bike, pal,' she suddenly yelled. 'It's your birthday and we are goin' to seriously P–A–R–T–Y! Bugger Bill Wyman. Live a little, Mandy. You're free of him, now.' And they swept me out of the flat to join up with the rest of the gang at Cuba.

As we roared up the road, I did not have time to ponder on the consequences of what Kelly had actually said. How did she know about Bill? I had said nothing to anyone about him, other than that we were friends and that only because photos of me with Bill had been published in the papers occasionally. To protect Bill, I had confessed to him being an old family friend.

Obviously, shrewd Glaswegian heads had been put together and come up with the theory that where Bill and I were concerned, two and two made five. 'Well, what the heck,' I thought now as I prepared to down a glass of champagne. They were all wrong anyway. For Bill and me now, two and two made nothing. Of course, I was quite, quite wrong... For some people, Bill and me together made a very large sum, with several noughts on the end of it.

Within a couple of days the whisper was out around Marbella that I had been out with Bill Wyman. Being a newcomer to Spain, I did not realise that Marbella is really a very small place where everyone knows everyone else and they love nothing more than a juicy bit of local gossip.

Then it caught alight. After the Glasgow Gang surmised that something had been on the cards between Bill and me, the rumour went round like wildfire. No one actually confronted me with any of this speculation but I knew by the hushed tones when I walked in a bar and when they played a Stones record at Cuba that all eyes were on me.

Well, I figured, people just talk. I was used to that, coming from a north London council estate where people had small minds to match the small doilies they put out for you to rest your cuppa on. So what? Nobody could prove anything so long as I said nothing. However, there was one person to whom I had turned. One pair of broad, muscular shoulders on which I had cried. Keith had stepped into the breach and helped to heal the hurt over Bill and Keith had introduced me to Maurice Boland.

A bit of an Irish wide boy, Maurice was the archetypal wheeler-dealer who was inevitably bound to ship up in Marbella one day, eyes fixed on the good life and feet stealthily planted on any path that would take him there.

Keith had introduced me to him as someone who had a financial stake in the Cuba Club, although I was never quite sure of what his exact connection was. Maurice was always there, spinning apocryphal tales of his business coups and name-dropping like crazy. He loved to think he was a friend of the stars but, frankly, Marbella was full of showbiz people and even if you were a washer-up in a restaurant, you could claim to rub shoulders with the likes of Shirley Bassey and Sean Connery.

Everyone knew Maurice was a bit of a wide-boy but he was good company and always had a grin on his face. In true Irish tradition, he certainly had the gift of the gab and could convince you he could walk on water if he felt like it.

One day, Maurice invited Keith and me round to dinner at his home with his wife Wendy. It was not for a convivial meal, though, as I had expected. Maurice wanted to talk business.

He had had a sniff of what had happened between Bill and me and, no slouch when it came to spotting big bucks a mile away, realised he had a big story on his hands. He did not beat about the bush. He suggested outright that I do a kiss and tell series of revelations about our love affair.

'To be sure, Mandy, it will make you a fortune. You need never work again,' he cajoled. His plausible Irish charm was wasted on me. Back then no amount of money in the world was going to persuade me to spill the beans on Bill. I loved him. It was as simple as that. I simply couldn't live with him, that was all.

I politely declined Maurice's offer and he accepted my decision with good grace – or so I thought.

A week or so later, Keith and I were again invited over to Maurice's home for a meal. There, we were introduced to a couple of old friends of Maurice and Wendy's. The man was short and dumpy and walked with a noticeable limp. I noticed he wore a surgical boot with a very high, built-up sole. Middle-aged and bespectacled, he looked like a jovial bank manager who had enjoyed a few expense account meals too many.

His wife, small and plump, blonde and very tanned, was dressed in a flowing kaftan. Looking more like a leftover hippy chick from the seventies than a bank manager's wife, she revealed a vast cleavage and an equally vast smile as we were introduced.

'Mandy,' said Maurice, 'I want you to meet two very dear mates of mine. Pat and Barrie. They've lived in Marbella for years.'

They seemed nice enough. Like Maurice, they were extremely convivial and appeared terribly interested in everything I had to say. They were surprised I was just sixteen and still at school. Did I want to carry on with my studies? I said I did not know, I was taking this break in Marbella to consider my future. They suggested I should try modelling. They knew people in the fashion business who could give me advice, probably get me started. Or had I thought of an acting career? They knew people in showbusiness and with looks like mine...

Then the subject of Bill came up. I must have looked a little suspicious because Maurice interjected, 'Don't worry, Mandy, Pat and Barrie are absolutely sweet. You can trust them with your life.'

Politely, I confirmed that, yes, I did know Bill, and, yes, we had gone out together for some time. Then I changed the subject, but Pat and Barrie kept alluding to Bill and, suddenly, I twigged.

I looked accusingly at Maurice. He caught my glare and was forced to admit it. Barrie and Pat were reporters but, not to worry, they wouldn't say anything. Nor could they, I figured. I had given them nothing and I made sure I stayed deep in an inane conversation with Wendy about interior decorating for the remainder of the meal.

However, it was going to take more than a gallon of white-wash to cover over the stitch-up job that had just been perpetrated on me. The jolly meal with 'old friends' Pat and Barrie was a set-up from start to finish. They had come to get a story, wearing hidden wires in their clothing. The whole dinner conversation had been taped – and they went straight to Fleet Street.

The *News Of The World*, Britain's biggest-selling Sunday newspaper, had gone absolutely mad for it. They were set to splash on it. They were calling it the scandal of the year. Within twenty-four hours, the story of Bill Wyman and his lover, aged thirteen, was set to blow sky high.

CHAPTER THIRTEEN

Scandal!

It was Maurice who broke the news.

'Mandy,' he said, 'I've got some good news and some bad news. It just depends on the way you look at things.'

I had just woken up to find Maurice knocking on the door of my room. 'What are you on about, Maurice? It's a bit early to be talking in riddles, isn't it?' I said sleepily.

What he said next woke me as effectively as being thrown into a vat of ice cubes.

'The *News Of The World* has got hold of your story. They're going to run it on Sunday.'

I leapt out of bed and rushed to the door where Maurice was standing, looking concerned. 'Tell me you're joking. This is just one of your little tricks. Please, Maurice.'

'I'm sorry, Mandy. It's the truth. Pat and Barrie went straight to the papers. I think they were just trying to find out if anyone was interested and then they were going to come back to you with a deal. But the papers are going to expose it anyway. They say it's a scandal, what with you being only thirteen an' all. And, you know, Mandy, it *is* a scandal. A man of his age taking advantage of a little schoolgirl like you.'

I wasn't hearing Maurice any more. I was in a daze, too shocked to comprehend it all fully. I just went to pieces. I was in bits. I was shaking with fear, literally shaking.

Maurice put his arm around me and said softly, 'Don't you worry, Mandy. It's for the best, truly it is. It wasn't natural, what Bill Wyman did to you. You had to break free from him – that's what you're doing here, isn't it? In your heart of hearts, you knew it had to end. He's taken everything from you for years, well now it's your turn to do something for yourself.

'Look at it this way, it could open doors for your own career as a model. Your name will be on everyone's lips, your face in all the papers. We can make you a star, Mandy.'

'Oh shut up, Maurice,' I screamed. 'What do you know about

anything? There's one thing that seems to have escaped your notice. I loved Bill. I didn't ever want to hurt him. I don't care about a bloody modelling career. *His* career will be in ruins now. Oh my God, what am I going to do?'

I started to cry then, real tears of fear and distress but there was one thing I knew I had to do. Phone Bill and let him know what had happened. Give him time to prepare himself for the avalanche that was bound to follow the publication of the story.

I threw on some clothes and dashed to the phone. With a trembling hand, I called Bill at his King's Road flat. No reply. I was so distracted, I couldn't remember the phone number at Gedding Hall. I fumbled through my address book and found the number. No reply. Struggling to hold on to some composure, I tried his office. I had not wanted to call Karen. I wanted no one to get an inkling of what was about to erupt until I spoke to Bill himself, but what option was there now?

Karen picked up the phone. 'Hello, Bill Wyman's office.'

'Karen,' I said, trying desperately to keep the tremor from my voice. 'It's Mandy. I need to speak to Bill urgently. Is he around?'

'Mandy, he's in Vence. Have you tried him there? He should be in at this time of day. Better give him an hour or so to wake up, though. Anyway, how are you? How's Marbella? Missing me?'

She sounded so cheerful, so efficient, so normal. I thought of her reaction in a few hours' time when she discovered the real reason for my call. Then the shit would really hit the fan. This was no time for idle chat.

'Can't talk, Karen, got to dash. Speak to you soon.'

Then, shaking with terror, I called Bill in Vence.

'Hello,' his voice was the catalyst. I started to sob again, hot tears running down my cheeks.

'Bill, it's me, Mandy.'

'What's the matter, Mandy? Are you crying?'

'Bill,' I choked, 'Bill, something terrible has happened.'

'What? What is it, Mandy?'

'The papers have got hold of our story. They're going to print it on Sunday.'

There was total silence on the other end of the line.

'Bill, are you there, Bill? It wasn't me, I promise you. I didn't tell them anything.'

'Well.'

That was all. Just one word. I did not know what reaction I had expected, but this forbidding one-word censure was not it.

'Honestly, Bill, please believe me. I never wanted this to happen. That's why I'm ringing. I had to warn you.'

'Bit late for that now, isn't it? You'd better leave me to deal with this.' His response staggered me. He was totally cool, his tone was distant, not shocked or surprised at all. There was absolutely no sign of any feeling in his voice. I knew then that he thought I *had* done it. I had let the cat out of the bag. I was responsible for all this. I had betrayed him.

Then he hung up on me.

Dazed, I could not quite take in what had just happened. This was a double blow. The situation was horrendous in itself, but Bill's negative reaction to it – and me – was far, far worse. I slumped down on a chair, still clutching the receiver, the noise of the disconnected tone buzzing through my head. What now, Mandy? Where do you go from here? I had no answers.

Alone, hundreds of miles from home, in an inconceivably awful mess, I did not know where to turn nor who to turn to. I had never felt so alone in my life.

However, I didn't have much time to think about it because then the whole Stones machine rolled into action and swept me along with it . . .

When I rang Mum, a few hours later, Bill had already been in touch with her. He had told her to get herself and Nicola out to Marbella straightaway, to be with me. He said none of us were to do anything at all. Someone would be in touch to look after us. Above all, we were not to talk to any newspapers.

Later, in the cool light of hindsight, we realised that Bill had used Mum, forcing her into a situation where she could cover for him. He could not come to Marbella, for obvious reasons. He could not afford to be seen with me, it would corroborate the whole story. So he did the next best thing. He sent my own mother to make sure I spoke to no one. It never crossed his mind that perhaps I needed him with me. Perhaps, together, we could be strong. Perhaps, at last, we could face the world and confirm that, yes, we were lovers. That was not Bill's style. He had, at all costs, to protect himself first and foremost – and himself only.

I was not happy about Mum coming out to Marbella. I did not want to embroil her in all this. By the time I called her, I had pulled myself together a bit and told myself, 'You can deal with this, Mandy. You got yourself into it, now get yourself out.' I had to cope on my own and, I rationalised, I could. After all, I had been living away from my family since I was fourteen.

Mum was insistent. Bill had convinced her I needed her by my side. As ever, she was prepared to drop everything for me. She flew out immediately, accompanied by Nicola and a Stones minder, Arnold Dunn.

He had given them explicit instructions that they were to talk to no one and he would go along with them, just to make sure they didn't. Dunn had also arranged a 'safe house' for us, high in the mountains outside Marbella. Secluded and remote, it was a safe haven from the prying eyes of the press, who had descended on Marbella in hordes the minute the story broke. I could not bring myself to read the papers. I wanted to shut out the horror of it all and pretend it wasn't happening. Perhaps if I closed my eyes, all this nightmare would go away.

Mum's arrival brought with it a new set of problems. Keith came with us to the house in the mountains. I felt, initially, that he was my only ally in all this. We had grown inseparable throughout the crisis, but Mum was instantly wary of him. The minute she clapped eyes on him, she said she felt he was bad news. She had an intuitive and instant sense of distrust. It made the atmosphere very tense among us all.

Cooped up inside the house, shut off from the outside world and constantly under the watchful eye of the burly Stones minders, nerves were stretched to breaking point. I began to feel like a prisoner – if not of the media, who were by now crawling all over Marbella like a rash – then of the Rolling Stones.

It was ironic. For years Bill had kept me imprisoned in an ivory tower of his own making, sheltered from the world, his little sex slave, tied to him by the bonds of sex and emotion. Now here I was, free of the affair, but quite literally incarcerated in a refuge in the mountains.

Bill, however, was no longer my main worry. He had, as good as his word, had everything 'taken care of'. His money and position meant that all he had to do was pick up the phone and tap into the vast network of highly paid and super-efficient Stones staff who would act on his behalf.

He had often told me that one of the dubious privileges of being a Rolling Stone meant that, if ever he screwed up, the Stones entourage would silently slip into place and sweep up the pieces without anyone being any the wiser. Well, here was the proof. Except I was the one in pieces, being swept under the carpet. As yet, however, my experience of the Stones machine was just the tip of the iceberg.

The minders were the drones – all menial domestic jobs a speciality. I was about to meet the Big Boys, the professionals who meant business...

The lawyer appeared early the next morning. He walked in unannounced and my first impression was how huge he was, and scary. Extremely tall, dark and well built, he had a menacing air as he stood there in his navy cashmere coat and Armani suit.

He introduced himself as a lawyer and I thought, 'Why is he here? What's going to happen?' Up until that moment we'd been kept completely in the dark. So far as I was concerned, providing I kept a low profile for a few weeks, and spoke to no one, the whole thing would blow over. Bill and I would be able to resume our lives as before. So why the lawyer?

He took charge immediately, in that authoritative way that those steeped in the law assume like a natural birthright. Ushering Mum and me into a side room that had previously been locked but which I now saw was an office, he indicated to us that we should sit down on two leather armchairs facing a large oak desk.

He deposited his coat and briefcase on the desk and turned to face us, not sitting down, but standing, leaning against the desk, looking solemnly from one of us to the other, as we tried desperately to feel as comfortable as possible in his unnerving presence. There was no opening chit-chat. He went straight to the point.

'Look, I have to spell out the very severe possible consequences of this situation. Mandy was under age when she had a sexual relationship with Bill. That means, Mandy,' he turned his steely-eyed gaze on to me, 'you've broken the law and the law, I have to tell you, takes a very dim view of sexual offences like this. Your mother, who is responsible for you, has broken the law too. If you are found guilty, Mandy, you could be put in care, and your mother could be sent to prison.'

I was too stunned to speak. Nobody had ever spelt out that our love affair could lead to prison. Bill had certainly never mentioned it. All he ever said would be harmed were his reputation and his career. I had truly never stopped to think about it being illegal. In the typical blinkered way that lovers do, I had closed my eyes to the consequences and let myself be swept along on the tide of love. Anyway, who ever said that thirteen-year-olds were supposed to be responsible or adult in their behaviour? And my poor mum, what did she have to do with any of this? I had rebelled against her and now she was to pay the price? It was all crazy, but here was this man, stern, official and terrifying, telling us that what I had done could put my blameless mum behind bars. I burst into tears.

Surprisingly, the lawyer had a soft spot buried deep inside somewhere. He relaxed a bit when he saw me sobbing. His voice became less severe as he said, 'Look, it needn't be as bad as that but it's my duty to tell you the worst possible outcome as well as the best. At its best, if you keep quiet, we can make sure you are all right. You will probably have to go to Scotland Yard on these charges. Your best bet is to say, quite simply, "No comment" to every question. Say absolutely nothing.'

He had our full and undivided attention. Anything that could get us through this nightmare and keep my mum out of prison, was all right by me. I would have jumped over Niagara Falls in a barrel at that moment if he'd asked me to, so long as it got Mum off the hook. The lawyer, knowing full well by now that he had a rapt audience, walked us through his recommended legal procedure. We trusted him. We had to. The options, as he had spelt them out, were simply too terrible to contemplate.

He was with us for about an hour and his message was quite clear. Do as he said with no questions asked.

We were shipped out of Spain thirty-six hours later. Obviously, the sudden appearance of Mandy Smith and family at Malaga airport generated a huge furore among the press, who had been encamped there for days. They knew, with that sixth sense that Fleet Street has, that I would have to be flushed out of hiding at some point and would more than likely turn up there for a flight home. Now, it had proved well worth the wait.

They clamoured around us like a baying pack of newshounds, cameras flashing and shouting all sorts of questions. We marched on, eyes straight ahead and said nothing, just as the lawyer had told us. Flanked on either side by a mountainous Stones minder, there was no way the press could get close to us.

Shrewdly, the second they were alerted to our presence, they had all booked seats on our flight. The plane was full, packed to the hilt with news reporters, TV journalists and photographers. Gingerly, I boarded and took my seat, feeling grateful that the sixteen-stone bruiser seated next to me had only one goal in mind – to deck anyone who came within six feet of me.

The plane's engines roared into life and we took off, surrounded on all sides by members of the press who were frantically filing their copy, aware by now that there was no way they could elicit a single quote from me.

I had settled into a kind of quasi-trance, suspended half-way between shock and disbelief, when suddenly an announcement came over the plane's broadcast system. 'Could Miss Mandy Smith please come to the front of the aircraft and make herself known to flight staff?'

I sat bolt upright. Was this some kind of press tactic to separate me from my minders? Everyone knew who I was. In every seat, heads turned and all eyes were on me. My legs turned to jelly. There was nowhere to run, nowhere to hide.

The announcement came again. I nudged my minder who nodded. 'Better see what they're after. I'll be right behind you.'

I rose unsteadily to my feet and teetered down the aisle to the front of the plane. There, waiting for me, stood a uniformed policeman and a WPC. My heart seemed to plummet into the pit of my stomach. I could feel the blood drain from my face. I thought, 'This is it. They're going to arrest me. I'm going to be taken to a police cell and charged as soon as we land.' My knees buckled under me and the WPC reached out to grab my arm.

'Mandy Smith?' said her colleague, 'We've been instructed to tell you to make an appointment and report to Scotland Yard within the next few days.'

'You're not putting me under arrest, then?' I stuttered.

'No, there are no charges at the moment. But you must report to Scotland Yard.'

A wave of relief swept over me. At least I was not going to be dragged off the plane in handcuffs.

However, I still had to run the gauntlet of the press all the way back to my seat. The double gins had been put to one side again and they were scribbling away about this latest development. I was mortified. I felt the raging flush of embarrassment turning my face puce as I stumbled back down the aisle. When was this nightmare going to end?

*   *   *   *   *

We had to report to the lawyer's office in the morning, before going to Scotland Yard.

Transposed from the Marbella setting where he had first confronted us, he was no less threatening on home ground. His message was the same: say nothing and we might get you out of this mess. I had never dealt with a lawyer in my life before. Were they all this intimidating? Weren't lawyers supposed to be acting in defence of their clients? It fleetingly crossed my mind that I was not really sure whose side this guy was on. He was so forbidding, so censorious of what Mum and I had done.

Hill Street Blues had a lot to answer for, deluding us into believing the legal profession were normal human beings like the rest of us, I thought wryly.

Then we set off in a cab for Scotland Yard, Mum and me huddled together, holding one another's hand for comfort. I had never known nerves like it. My stomach was churning up inside and I was in a state of complete confusion. Panic, fear and anxiety all vied with each other for prominence. I felt sick.

Mum, realising my terror, smiled wanly. 'Don't you worry, Mandy. They can't do anything to me that I can't handle. We'll get through this together.'

Together, yes, but who was it who had been together with me during all those years of duplicity when Mum knew nothing of what was going on? Who had really got me into this mess? Bill. Where the hell was he now?

Suddenly, a wave of anger washed away all the other confused emotions. If I was guilty of having under-age sex, and Mum was guilty of collusion by not preventing it, what the hell did that make Bill? In a flash, I saw that my intuition about the lawyer had been spot on. It all fell into place. He was *not* on our side. He was acting for Bill.

I looked at him as he sat upright, superior, motionless, opposite Mum but his expression, as ever, revealed nothing.

The sudden realisation that we were pawns in a game designed to get Bill off the hook was of little comfort as we walked into Scotland Yard. Two policemen approached us and immediately separated us, which put the fear of death into me.

'Would you accompany my colleague, Mrs Smith,' said the taller of the two, 'and,' he turned to me, 'would you walk this way please, Miss Smith?'

Nausea bubbled up inside me. I thought, 'It's over now. They're taking me to a cell, they're going to lock me up.' Then he and another policemen led me down the corridor into a side room. I held my breath as I walked in, expecting to see barred windows, a bare single bed and a lavatory in the corner, but it was merely an office, empty of all furniture save a desk and three wooden chairs.

Behind the desk sat a senior policeman. Severe and unsmiling, he indicated that I should sit opposite him. The lawyer sat down next to me. I did not feel at all comforted by his presence. I had no confidence in this lawyer. Rolling Stones money was pulling his strings. He was as much of a puppet in this as I was but it wasn't him in the dock, it was me.

Two other officers entered the room and stood on either side of us while the seated one started to grill me. He had a list of questions in front of him and he started to read. His tone of voice and his manner were aggressive. Looking me straight in the eye, he banged off questions one after the other.

'Name? Age? Address? Did you have a relationship with Mr Wyman? Did you have under-age sex with Mr Wyman? Is it true about these allegations in the press?'

He was like a tape recorder, repeating his questions over and over, one after the other.

I did as I had been told. My answer was the same every time. 'No comment. No comment.' On a superficial level, I must have appeared really cool and calm, but on the inside my heart was beating fit to bust. My forehead was pounding with tension and I thought my temples would explode from the pressure.

Curiously, the interrogating officer then sat back and didn't try to pump me any further. He was not giving me the third degree like I had anticipated. He was just asking questions. And I was refusing to answer. Impasse.

Then, suddenly, after about fifteen minutes of this perfunctory questioning, he stood up and picked up the papers from the desk. As he shuffled them into order, I almost dissolved in tears of relief. It had not been as awful as I had expected. Then it struck me, 'This has all been too easy. Now they're going to arrest me and charge me.'

But, no, the lawyer stood up then and motioned for me to do the same. 'You may leave now,' he said.

I hated him at that moment. He had done nothing for me. What really bugged me most of all, though, was my over-riding fury that Bill was not there to answer any charges nor to support me. Where was he? He was in the South of France, lying low, with his ex-girlfriend Astrid as the perfect cover. She had been called on to slip back neatly into place as Bill's regular girlfriend, all above board and, more important, above the age of sexual consent. To all intents and purposes, it looked as if Bill had been ensconced in a steady relationship with Astrid for several years. If there had been any dalliance with me, all record of it was now scrubbed. The police could prove nothing against Bill.

Bill and Astrid would deny it utterly and provide affidavits from countless friends and allies that they were madly in love, totally inseparable and had been for years. The Stones machine was omnipotent. It had covered Bill's tracks as he had always said it would. Mandy who? So long as I continued to say, 'No comment,' he was home and dry.

My anger knew no bounds. I couldn't believe my life had changed so much. I'd left behind my family, my childhood and everything I had known for Bill. I was with him for two and a half years. A fifth of my entire life. Two and a half years during which he had totally consumed me, body and soul. Then I left *him* to give us both a breather and get ourselves sorted out. Now suddenly everything was gone and I stood accused of having under-age sex with a man who had run off out of the country to save his neck. How chivalrous!

And this was the man I loved? The awful truth was that he still *was* that man. There was simply too much between us for me to turn my back on, although that is exactly what he had done to me.

I met up with Mum in the entrance to Scotland Yard. She, too, had been grilled and given nothing away. She, too, was shattered by this turn of events, torn apart by the ordeal that I was going through, as I was for her. She, too, was cognisant of the fact that the lawyer – and the law – seemed stacked in Bill's favour. The bottom line for her, as for me, was the eternal question: where the hell was Bill in all this?

We went home and cried in each other's arms.

* * * * *

The days passed and stretched into weeks. Mum, Nic and I stumbled blindly on, not knowing what was going on beyond the four walls of our flat. Our case was up before the Director of Public Prosecutions, who was studying the legal notes and the Scotland Yard interrogation and deciding whether or not to prosecute. It was like being out on bail, pending sentencing. Would we, or would we not be banged up when he had made his decision? The Sword of Damocles hung over us and one day blurred into the next.

Throughout the whole episode, Bill was noticeable by his total absence. There were no letters, no phone calls, no messages of support. Not a cheep.

My pride refused to let me call him. It was he, after all, who had led us blindfolded into this appalling set of circumstances. It was our necks on the line, not his. He knew it, too. He knew exactly what was going on. He knew all about my interrogation at Scotland Yard, all about how the DPP was considering the case – after all it was *his* lawyer who was briefing me.

Only once, when the black hours of night, the fear, worry and loneliness all seemed impossible to bear, did I succumb to my need for him. I called him just that once. All I wanted, all I needed, was simply to hear his voice.

The conversation was extremely short. Bill made it quite clear that he didn't want to know. He was perfectly polite but he might have been a million miles away, he was so cold and distant.

I decided, there and then, never to call him again. It was too painful. It confirmed my worst fears – that, scratch the surface, and Bill really, truly did not care about me. I could not live with that knowledge. I would rather nurture the memories of our lost love.

The next two months were hell. I kept waiting for the knock on the door, the looming figure of a policeman to say, 'Mandy Smith, we arrest you...' I jumped out of my skin every time I heard police sirens in the street.

The lawyer had warned us that it might take weeks, even months, before the DPP decided whether or not to prosecute, but, as with everything else, not knowing is worse than knowing even the worst. Left in limbo, life lost all direction, all meaning. I was lost in a wilderness. Bill had gone to ground. The mainstay of my life had collapsed. What was the point in any of it?

Then, after nearly three months had elapsed, Mum came roaring in from shopping one morning, brandishing a fistful of newspapers. 'They're not going to prosecute!' she burbled gleefully. 'Look, it says it in the papers.'

Sure enough, there were the reports: 'No prosecution decision by DPP on Wyman case.'

The relief was like bathing in warm milk. Finally, Mum and I could breathe again.

But I couldn't forget. How nice of the lawyers to let us know we were in the clear. Bill, too, would have known before it hit the press. The lawyers would undoubtedly have kept him informed every step of the way. They were *his* lawyers after all. However, there was no space in my life for bitterness. The nightmare was over, consigned forever to that part of my psyche that was labelled 'Lessons Learned. Do Not Repeat.' My self-defence mechanism leapt into play. It was as if I had been watching some incredible fantasy film. Maybe this had not actually happened to me at all? However, as I soon discovered, it wasn't over yet, not by a long chalk.

As soon as he thought the coast was clear, that his name was safe and no charges would be pressed, Bill was back on the scene, just like nothing had ever happened...

CHAPTER FOURTEEN

Miss You

A chapter of my life was over but a new one was just beginning. Maurice Boland had been right about one thing. When the legal furore over Bill's alleged affair with an under-age girl had all died down, the whole world wanted to know more. I was the name on everyone's lips. Who was this creature Mandy Smith? And what was she?

Bill had come out of the affair triumphant. The speculation merely enhanced his reputation as a Lothario. My reputation, however, was somewhat different. I was the subject of miles of column inches in the media, virtually all of them vicious. Fingers of accusation were universally pointed at me and Mum.

It was just like the old days when the local scandal merchants had a field day over Mum, an attractive single woman bringing up two kids on her own. This gossip, however, was on a global scale. I couldn't just hear the whispers as I walked down the street, I could see them, writ large in black and white, in every newspaper.

The press really went to town. While Bill basked in the limelight he had sought all his life – publicly proclaimed a super-stud – I was made out to look like some trashy teen nymphet, some sultry Lolita with dubious morals, a seducer of older men. Worst of all, a girl who used her sexual charms to get what she wanted – money.

Mum was painted unsparingly as the ambitious Svengali who had manipulated the situation. She had encouraged her daughter to bed a Rolling Stone to get a slice of his fortune.

Bill, of course, was the innocent prey, ensnared in this vipers' nest.

The female columnists were the worst. They spared no savagery as they tore into us. It was heartbreaking to read the spite and venom that was poured over us. Somehow, somewhere, the press had lost sight of the facts: man, forty-seven, seduces girl, thirteen. However, Mum held on firmly to the dictat by

189

which she had always lived her life. 'Be true to ourselves. Let them think what they will. We, at least, know the truth.' We had survived worse.

We soon learned how to handle the universal condemnation. We simply stopped reading the papers. It was too painful. Far better, Mum kept reminding us, to hold on to our dignity by not responding.

The name of Mandy Smith spelt money to a whole host of other people who suddenly came creeping out of the woodwork. Not least of all Maurice Boland.

Realising that, in the right business hands, Mandy Smith was set to be a nice little earner, he became my manager. 'Mandy,' he told me, 'I'm gonna make you a star.' Whether he did or not is a moot point. The offers were already coming through the letterbox in droves.

The modelling career I had set my childhood sights on suddenly beckoned. There were offers from top designers, fashion houses, mass-market clothing companies. There were chat show invitations, TV and radio interviews, even offers of acting parts. There was interest from the music business, too. Stock, Aitken and Waterman, a small, private record label that was guaranteed gold in the record industry, with a chain of formula Top Ten hits behind them, wanted to sign me up. It was all deeply flattering but, more important, it was a fresh start.

I believed I could model successfully; I knew I could sing. Maurice negotiated the deals.

However, what I could not, and would not, do was talk.

There was an ulterior motive behind all the offers. The interviewers, fashion editors and chat show hosts all wanted one thing from me – to get me to spill the beans on my life with Bill. I flatly refused. Wild horses would not have dragged the story from me. Despite the fact that Bill had unceremoniously dumped me while the prosecution was under review, I could not do the same to him. He simply meant too much to me. He had been my life for too long, no matter how ungallant his exit. Only a woman could understand how that depth of emotion can conquer everything.

No amount of money could compensate for what I had lost, and no amount of pain would motivate me to seek revenge. All

I wanted was to start over. To put Bill behind me. If the chance of a career in modelling or music was the way forward, then my feet were already on that road.

I left everything to Maurice. After all, I was a novice, a complete ingénue. I had to trust someone with my business affairs. However, I stipulated one thing in every deal that Maurice tied up. I would never, ever speak about my love affair with Bill and that was to be specified in the contracts – no Bill questions, or no deal.

Things started to move very quickly. I did several fashion photo sessions for newspapers. I signed a promotional deal with Brutus jeans to relaunch their label in a blaze of publicity. I signed up with the PWL record label and recorded my first single, 'I Just Can't Wait'. Life suddenly zoomed into the fast lane.

I felt like some kind of whirling dervish, hurtling at breakneck speed between business meetings, photocalls and recording sessions, swerving like mad to avoid the persistent questions from the media about Bill. Maybe someone should have said, 'Hold on, Mandy. Time to put the brakes on.' I was doing too much at once, but there was a reason driving me on. I was racing away from the past and forging a future for myself. If Bill had promised me a secure future, then stolen it away from me, here was my chance to do it for myself. I would prove myself – to him, to everyone. I could make it on my own.

Mum and Nic were by my side, the three of us united again and strong. They had stood by me during those long months of fear, worry and distress and never once uttered a recriminatory word. There was no 'I told you so' admonishment from Mum. She was simply there for me, as she had always been. And from big sis Nic, who had always harboured a desire to break into modelling, who also had a singing talent, there was never the slightest nuance of jealousy as she watched my ascent to success. They had walked through the valley of darkness with me. All they wanted was for me, finally, to be happy.

The only shadow in the sunshine of our lives now was Keith. Keith worried me. When he first declared his love for me in Marbella, I had thought he was the answer to all my prayers, that the firm foundations of our year-long friendship had paved the way for a beautiful summer romance.

However, Keith had acted very strangely during our time in

the Stones' capitivity in Spain and afterwards, when we had flown to London. Instead of being concerned about me, he seemed to be positively revelling in the media attention. It was as if he was actually enjoying all the limelight that was causing me so much discomfort. He was advocating that we should go out, hit the town, be seen at venues where the paparazzi would be hanging out. Get our pictures in the papers – all this with the threat of a prosecution and possible jail sentence hanging over Mum and me.

I was not so blindly in love with him that I could not see that this was at odds with a genuine concern for my plight. I began to wonder if maybe romance was taking a back seat to greed. I could not bear to think it but maybe Keith was using me as a means to an end?

The unthinkable soon became the undoubtable. In those late autumn months of 1986, as my fledgling career began to take off apace, Keith returned to London to join me. 'Gonna put my career on hold to help you with yours,' he told me breezily. Oh really, Keith?

Now we were on my home ground and I had Mum and Nic for emotional support, I had begun to see Keith in a different light to the incandescent Marbella sunshine. The carefree, spontaneous suitor I had known in Spain had done a disappearing trick.

In his place was a guy who wanted to live with me, live off me and steer me into corners where I did not want to be.

In Glasgow, he had been different again. There, too, he had been kingpin of the social crowd, liked and respected by a gang of acolytes. I had fallen for his easy, Scottish charm, been flattered by the attention and affection he had showered on me. Now, in London, his tan and his charm were fading fast.

Keith wanted to call the shots, mastermind my career, pick and choose which deals I accepted and accompany me to all the attendant celebrity razzmatazz. I noticed he was no longer happy just to be with me, at home, relaxing in front of the TV. He was happiest at a showbiz thrash, knocking back champagne like it was going out of fashion, rubbing shoulders with the rich and famous. He did not want me, he wanted the package that went with me.

Keith wanted to go to Tramp, Keith wanted to go to the

Hard Rock Café, Keith wanted to go to PWL studios and offer advice on the production of my records. Keith wanted the world and I was the key to it, but, as the scales fell from my eyes, this lady was no longer for turning. If Keith wanted me to open showbiz doors for him, he was going to have a long wait.

Mum's intuition about him had been spot on. Keith, too, was a user and I, on the rebound from Bill, had fallen hook, line and sinker for a holiday romance.

I came to this slow, painful realisation myself after our every date for weeks seemed to degenerate into argument. Still, I could not bring myself to believe the worst. I longed to believe that Keith loved me. I had just extricated myself from one emotional disaster – surely I could not have let the same thing happen twice?

As I was to learn, however, patterns are hard to break. I had set an emotional precedent with Bill, where I saw our love through rose-tinted glasses and thereby walked the thorny road to disaster. I was still on that road, now letting someone else bleed me dry.

The rows went on but I could not break away or admit to myself that I had picked another man who would use and abuse me. Then, one night, we had been out for dinner at a beautiful little Italian restaurant in north London. We had bickered throughout the meal – pointless arguing, based on nothing other than irritation in each other's company.

The bill arrived. Keith, tight as always, made a show of searching for his wallet. 'Damn,' he said, 'I must have left my credit cards at home. Can you pick up the tab on this one, love? I'll pay you back later.'

If I had had a pound coin for every time he had thrown that line at me, I would have been rich, but it was not so much him living off me as the arrogance of this pathetic ruse that was so deeply insulting. As I paid the bill, I looked at Keith sitting, smug and satisfied, opposite me, and I knew I no longer had it in me to love him.

I could no longer kiss him. When he came to reach out for me as we parted that night, I turned my head away from him. Even then, the words were too hard to say. 'I'm tired, Keith,' I offered lamely, with a heavy heart but he knew, just as I did, that it was over.

He left me, on my doorstep and drove off to the flat where he was staying with friends – in my brand new Astra car – I never saw either of them again.

Although I was not yet seventeen, I had bought the car with my first earnings, vowing to pass my test as soon as my birthday came up. In the interim, Keith had been driving it, swearing he would get round to giving me lessons very soon. Only weeks before, I had handed over the money to pay for it, my pride and joy, my first, my lovely, gleaming little white car.

Ah well, I let it go. It was a small price to pay and I couldn't have cared less, but Keith still had to have the last word. Just weeks later, he wreaked his revenge with a kiss and tell saga in the *News Of The World*. It was a sad and sorry end to something I had once thought was precious.

He painted me as a pathetic bimbo who had exploited Bill and had attempted to do the same to him. It was, in fact, a complete reversal of the truth but there was no need for a rejoinder in my defence; there was no need to talk to another newspaper to set the record straight because the whole sordid episode proved I was right about Keith; I was better off, by far, without him.

I would not be hurt again. Twice, now, I had had my fingers burned. There was no room for a man in my life. I threw myself into my work instead. The modelling was lucrative, but the music business was the most fun.

To my astonishment, my first single was a massive hit overseas, soaring to the top of the charts in Italy, Spain, Greece, Germany and Japan and selling in vast quantities elsewhere. PWL, realising the potential of their latest signing, hastily organised a promotional tour.

First, however, they had to try me out. They had taken a gamble with this little girl. They already knew I could sing but whether I could perform was another matter altogether.

My first public performance as Mandy Smith, pop artiste was at the Hippodrome in London. The date was 17 January 1987. It is etched in my memory as if carved in tablets of stone. I was petrified. I had to perform before the massed ranks of London clubbers, miming to my own record, which, thus far, the UK record-buying public had not rushed out in droves to buy. Teetering around the Number 70 mark in the charts, it was not guaranteed to make my performance go down a storm. I would have to make my debut on merit alone.

Mum, Nic and a gang of aides from the PWL camp accompanied me to lend moral support. I stood shaking underneath the stage, ready to be propelled through the Hippodrome trapdoor, as the DJ announced my name. My legs turned to jelly, my knees threatened to give way. I wanted a hole in the ground to swallow me up. Whatever had convinced me that I could stand up in front of all those people and actually sing?

Then, suddenly, it was too late to run. I was on and someone else took over. Quivering, quaking Mandy Smith was submerged in Mandy pop star. I went out there and belted out the lyrics with the best of them. I lost myself in the music and it was only when I'd finished that I noticed the sea of faces in front of me, all smiling and cheering and singing along. I had made it.

That night, I was on a high that I never wanted to come down from. I understood then what Bill had told me about the rush of adrenalin that engulfs you after a live performance. You are buzzing, you are fired up, you can conquer the world. I was hooked.

PWL were thrilled. They wasted no time in fixing up dates for a world tour. First Europe, then America. Mandy Smith was going to take 'em by storm.

My first TV appearance was in Holland where pop compere Adam Curry introduced me as 'The latest chart sensation from London.' I secretly hoped that I would live up to all this hype but, what the heck, I was having fun for the first time in years.

The *Sun* newspaper asked me to participate in a rush-release single they were bringing out to raise funds for the survivors of the Zeebrugge ferry disaster. There, I met singer Ben Volpeliere-Pierrot, lead singer of Curiosity Killed the Cat. Now, they really *were* the biggest chart sensation in London. Everything Curiosity did at that time went gold. They were the darlings of the press and the hottest, hunkiest heart-throbs around.

Ben immediately asked me for a date. Deeply flattered, I went out with him several times but on a purely platonic basis. There was no way I was going to stroll into another relationship after my past two experiences. I was still walking wounded.

Ben, bless him, respected my bizarre instructions to keep his hands off, although he was a bit bemused by me.

'Mandy,' he told me, 'you are a complete contradiction in terms. You come across as the sexiest thing that ever walked on mile-long legs. Yet, you're not interested in sex at all are you?'

Well, I wouldn't have said that exactly, Ben. It is just that, so far as I was – and still am – concerned, sex without the attendant love and emotion is purely an act. I was not ready to be that actress.

The funny thing is that, when you switch off from men, they turn on to you in droves. Any woman who has ever been on a desperate quest for love knows that the chances of finding it are in inverse proportion to your needs. You want a man? They can sense it at fifty paces and back off. You don't want a man? They reckon you most certainly do and they go to determined lengths to prove it to you.

I had never been so popular. Whenever I went out, some bit of beefcake would approach me with a view to persuading me I needed him in my life. However, I always had a sneaking suspicion that sex with a sultry starlet of dubious repute was all they were after. They did not get it.

The only one who came close to romance was Mark Shaw, singer with another chart-topping band of the time, Then Jerico.

We dated a couple of times and I liked him very much, but there was something I could not quite put my finger on, that stopped me from placing implicit trust in him. Then I found out what it was – he was married. Thanks, but no thanks, Mark.

Throughout all these months, Ben remained my one true and constant flirtation. The press picked up on our friendship and immediately had us practically married off, or at least living together. It was nonsense. In fact, Ben and I never progressed beyond the snogging stage.

We finally pulled apart when he started spending rather too much time with a crowd of clubbers who were into designer drugs. Ben was a lovely boy but I didn't want to get involved in that scene.

If I was out with a group of people I always made it clear that I wasn't interested in any kind of drugs. I stood out from the rest of the young hip London scene like a sore thumb. The dealers gave me a wide berth. The word was out that Mandy Smith always said NO to drugs – and loudly.

That apart, it was a brilliant time to be involved in music.

My years with Bill had introduced me to the music business – but his crowd had their heydays in the sixties and seventies. They were old-timers. In the late eighties London was buzzing with young faces and alive with young energy.

I became good friends with these new music upstarts – Mel and Kim, Climie Fisher, Kim Wilde, Bros, Jason Donovan, Rick Astley, Kylie Minogue.

Rick, especially, was a delight. When I started out, he was just the tea boy at PWL. Then he had his first hit, 'Never Gonna Give You Up', then another and suddenly he was the most bankable newcomer in pop, with every new release destined to make it to the top.

Sweet-natured Rick never let any of his momentous success go to his head. We celebrated his first Number One at PWL with a pot of tea and cream cakes all round. A lovely, lovely guy. He was also on hand to give me advice for the next nerve-wracking step in my putative pop career. I had done live appearances, now I had to perform on TV. The first time I had to sing on camera was for a German TV show. I was more hyped up than nervous but, again, as I had found that night at the Hippodrome, the anticipation was far worse than the event. The minute the cameras started rolling for real, a star was born.

After that first TV performance, I was completely addicted. I adored the thrill and buzz of it all. It freed me to be someone else, that star of my dreams. It was far easier to be that than to be little old me with my problems in real life.

As my confidence grew, so did my voice. I didn't sing live at first. I'd mime until I got my confidence and then I would sing with an open mike over the backing tape. That was no problem. My biggest fear was that I would pop out of my dress in the middle of a number!

My friend Kim Wilde had recently been caught by the cameras as her left breast made a bold bid for stardom all of its own while she performed live on stage in front of a TV audience of millions. She was mortified. I felt so much for her and was petrified thereafter that the same thing might happen to me. Instead of biting my nails nervously before a performance, I was like a woman possessed, checking and double-checking my dress to make sure that I was inextricably bound in. Then, when the lights went up and the music from my backing tapes blared out, I completely and utterly lost myself in the performance.

I played in some fantastic stadiums in Italy and Japan. One of the best gigs was the San Remo Festival in Italy where I sang in front of 40,000 people. My other mates, Kylie, Kim Wilde and Climie Fisher were also on the bill and we had a riot, taking off after each gig to go clubbing together.

However, as Bill had so often told me, life on the road was incredibly draining. All the non-stop travelling was exhausting, even for a sixteen-year-old with indefatigible enthusiasm. I noticed – as did others around me – that I became irascible if I didn't get six or seven hours' sleep at night. There were times when I felt I could sleep round the clock. Instead of tucking into sustaining meals to give me energy, I found I had no appetite. During one tour of Germany, I became very ill after drinking some polluted water which knocked me for six. I lay there in my hotel bed, fighting a temperature of 103 degrees, dehydrated and desperately sick. In my delirium, I thought of Bill. How lonely it must have been for him, the relentless tours, the endless succession of hotel rooms and airport lounges. Then I thought, 'But hold on, that was always his excuse for going to bed with groupies. Now *I'm* living that life and I haven't needed to resort to those tactics.'

My resolve was strengthened, but it came and went in waves. There were still times when I missed him desperately.

Some of the solo promotion trips were pretty lonely. I'd finish a job at some unspecified little German town that seemed to be interchangeable with a dozen others, go back to the hotel and spend the rest of the night on the phone to Mum or Nic.

Initially, my sole companion on these trips had been Maurice but, gradually, as we spent more time in each other's company under the pressure of touring, I began to see that he, too, was not the face he presented to the world.

'Sure Mandy,' Maurice would ooze when I confronted him over these sudden bookings, 'You agreed to do it weeks ago. I told you all about it.'

Exhausted by my already punishing schedule, I would shrug gamely and make a tired vow to myself not to take on quite so much. However, Maurice had a vested interest in seeing to it that I took as much as came my way. After all, he was on a minimum 20 per cent of my earnings and the money was rolling in. As long as I continued to get up at dawn, sing, dance and pose prettily for the cameras all day, we would both be rich.

Increasingly, Maurice was also failing to prevent practised interviewers from asking me loaded questions about Bill. I was forever being put on the spot in front of a TV camera by being asked to give details of my love affair with a Rolling Stone. It is very difficult to wriggle out of a direct attack like that on screen without looking guilty, like you have something to hide.

Maurice was not being selective; he wanted me here, there and everywhere but, without selective marketing, I was being projected as a blonde bimbo who would do anything for big bucks. I felt he was beginning to give me a bad name.

In the the spring of 1987 I finally decided to tell him that I wanted a new manager. Maurice was an expert opportunist but as a manager I believed he was an amateur.

'Oh Mandy,' I thought to myself, 'time to get off this merry-go-round.' Time to find someone who would not misinterpret my love and devotion.

Martin Potter stepped into the breach as my new manager.

I broke it to Maurice gently. He took it extremely badly and stormed off home to Spain in high dudgeon. I had expected him to ply me with that ineffable Irish charm in an attempt to dissuade me from our split but, no, he had simply walked out.

I soon found out why. He had a final ace up his sleeve. He walked straight into the waiting arms of Fleet Street and, as he had done before, at the beginning of all of this, coughed the lot. Within two months both he and his wife Wendy had sold stories about me to the papers. They betrayed me, just like Keith. Climbing into the realms of interplanetary fantasy, Wendy even claimed that I had stolen Maurice from her and that we had an affair. That was so ridiculous, it was risible. Had Maurice been the last man on earth, or even in the solar system, I would not have found him marginally as attractive as an astronaut's faecal bag.

There was no point in retaliation. What goes around, comes around. I knew there would be retribution, divine or otherwise, at the end of the day. I had not stooped to belittle myself thus far; I was not starting now.

Sure enough, my recompense for all the years of pain and

confusion with Bill seemed to be finally coming to fruition. I was having a ball. I travelled the globe on modelling assignments. In particular, one glorious, glamorous, sunsoaked session for an upmarket glossy mag left memories that will never fade. They were great days, basking in the sun on silver sands, the beauty of it only slightly marred by the way that, as the sun set, everyone else on the crew turned to drugs to get their highs. I was on a natural high just from the beauty of the scenery.

It seemed the media and I were destined never to get along, whichever side of the fence I was on. Even with my professional hat on, as a working model, the lifestyle, with its ever-present drink, drugs and sex, was so far removed from my own that I could not relate to it.

Having exhausted themselves over my affair with Bill, the press were now focusing on my purported affairs with any and every man that came within a five-hundred-yard radius of me.

This time, it was the American actor Robert Rusler. While he was in London promoting his film *Shag*, I met him in Browns nightclub and we went out a few times. It was as boringly innocent as that. I was not remotely interested in a heavy romance. The papers, however, decided I was, so let them get on with it.

If I clung to anyone in those days, I clung to PWL. At their HQ, in Borough, south London, there was a real family atmosphere. PWL had formula hits down to a fine art. They took unknown acts and gave them the PWL treatment – hey presto, a surefire Top Ten success. The only thing we all had in common was the floggability factor.

Kylie was cute and squeaky-clean, Rick was sweet and even squeakier-clean, Mel and Kim were 'gorgeous nice girls'. Don't ask where I fitted in, but hey, we were all nice people, and we greeted each other's individual success with a resounding cheer.

Bar mine, that is. I was a singular UK failure for PWL. My singles were selling like hot cakes in Europe, but somehow I could not crack the UK market. My ubiquitous presence in the media, tarred as teen nymphet, ex-lover of Bill Wyman may have had something to do with it. It did not matter. I was happy in what I was doing. That was enough. There was only the odd occasion when my press and the reputation it had earned me actually got to me.

Sometimes I wished I had better songs but then I knew

I didn't have the right kind of image for the bouncy, upbeat numbers. They, the surefire winners, went to Kylie, Number One in the PWL stable.

I recorded a song called 'Got To Be Certain' and I remember coming out of the studio, resignedly telling everyone, 'That's not for me.'

Sure enough, it was handed to Kylie instead and it went straight to Number One like an arrow.

However, there was monetary compensation for the odd disappointment. No doubt about it, my music and modelling career were astonishingly lucrative. During 1987 and 1988, I was that rarest of creatures, a truly marketable commodity. I earned around £200,000 – big money for a little girl.

Never having been money-motivated, this burgeoning bank balance came as a shock to the system. I did the obvious thing – I blew it. Well, put yourself in the same position. Seventeen years old and suddenly a top flight earner. Would you hole it away for a rainy day?

I became, albeit briefly, a shopaholic. Boy, was it fun. The whole world was a jeweller's emporium but no longer was I just window-shopping. Step aside Imelda Marcos, I was going for gold with a major spend, spend, spend, but at least I had a bit of class. I did not blow my wages on baubles. I plumped for a gold Rolex – a mere £8,000 to you, Modom. A Cartier bracelet? Certainly, Miss Smith.

Of course, I did not blitz it all on myself. I sent my Nan and Grandad on a cruise around the Mediterranean. They had never been out of Britain in their lives before. Mum, too, became a beneficiary, much against her wishes. She had finally moved from Morant Place, driven out by the barrage of press habitually encamped on her doorstep, and had moved to another flat in Muswell Hill. It was sparse and in serious need of redecoration. She refused all financial help from me and was prepared to set about her new home with a vat of white emulsion when I swept in. We spent a fortune decorating the place. So what? Nothing was too good for my mum.

With hindsight, I can now admit that, yes, I was a complete klutz with my hard-earned wages but you're only young once.

It taught me a lesson more valuable than the mound of cash I had briefly stashed. It taught me to be prudent with money.

Not miserly, not profligate, just sensible.

Much later, I would be grilled in a court of law over exactly what had happened to the massive income I had generated in my career. The judiciary, the legal profession and the press were all deeply sceptical and believed I must have salted it away in a Swiss bank account. I have to put my hands up and say, 'It's a fair cop, your Honour. I blew it and loved every last penny of it.'

In a way, it was my reaction against those years with Bill. His Scrooge-like precision with pounds and pence had left a lasting effect on me. I wanted to rebel against his rules, his meanness and his lifestyle. In other words, he was still with me, in everything I said and did. I missed him but, dammit, I was going to carry on kicking against it.

There were some things, however, that were hurtling on out of my control, principally my health. No matter how dogmatic I was about what I thought, what I actually felt was another thing altogether and what I felt was increasingly more and more ill. I knew I was pushing myself too hard. I knew I was not getting enough sleep. I knew, for sure, that I was not eating enough. All those factors were to erupt together in February 1989.

Following the success of my European tour, I was set to embark on a US blitz. A round of promotional interviews would precede a concert tour. It meant worldwide record sales, a higher profile, increased revenue . . . the sky was the limit.

But I was shattered. As the date, 22 February, grew closer, I grew weaker. I could not do it, I could not go.

I told Sally Atkins from the record company, that I just couldn't face it. Both she and PWL were aghast. They knew this was the last step in my path to big-time pop success. I could not possibly back out now. They cajoled and coaxed. They kept insisting that I should go and, in the end, I gave in. I knew as soon as I set foot on the plane that it was a mistake. Throughout the flight, I felt terrible. Weak and dizzy, I began to feel palpitations in my chest and, for the first time in two years, I could feel that old familiar tightening in my lungs that spelled an impending asthma attack.

The plane landed in Miami for the first leg of the tour and we were ferried to our hotel. I went straight to bed, although there was a scheduled meeting with the US record company executives in two hours' time. I fell into a semi-conscious state and Sally, thinking I was asleep, jetlagged, went on her own.

It was pitch dark when I awoke a few hours later. I was alone, in a strange hotel room, in a country I had never visited before. Waves of nausea rushed over me. I had never felt so panic-stricken. I fumbled blindly for the phone by my bedside and, hardly able to breathe, asked the operator to put me through to London, England. I heard the number ring, far in the distance, and then the blessed relief of Mum's voice. I could barely speak but Mum, recognising the symptoms of a severe asthma attack, immediately instructed me to ring off. Then she redialled my hotel and informed the medical officer to rush to my room immediately with an oxygen mask.

The next thing I knew, a team of medics had barged into my room with more breathing apparatus. 'Don't you worry, Miss Smith,' they were soothing me, 'We can deal with this. You'll be fine. Just breathe deeply and relax. You're not alone. Just take it easy and breathe and we'll have you fit in no time.'

As I lay there, fighting for breath with the men in white coats all around me, Sally returned with the record company execs. 'Oh my God,' she gasped. 'Don't die on us, Mandy. We'll get you well again. I promise, I'll take you home. We'll find out what the problem is.'

The problem was that I could tell no one what the problem was. Given the US time differential, it was five years to the day, almost to the hour, that I had met Bill Wyman and, unbeknown to anyone in that room, Bill had already walked back into my life.

CHAPTER FIFTEEN

Together Again –
This Could be the Last Time

Why did we get back together? A million reasons.

I thought he would change. I thought he would show his feelings more. I knew he could no longer accuse me of being a child and bully me into submission. I had proved myself – to me, to him and to everyone – that I could make it on my own. I was so tired of all the travelling and being all things to all people. Model, singer, dancer with an entourage that demanded I do this, do that, do everything to keep them in paypackets. I was debilitated and demeaned by the continual press depiction of me as a wild child. I was sick of guys coming on to me and turning out to be shallow, feckless, young and silly. I was ready to settle down. I had had my flings and my freedom and my space – and it was a sham. There was no depth or meaning to any of it. I was seventeen. I wanted to feel secure and Bill was the only man who had ever made me feel that way.

Most of all, it was because he came back to me and told me he loved me. He missed me. This time, he promised, it would be different.

We had been in contact for months. He had rung me out of the blue and I had melted at the sound of his voice. He had congratulated me on my successes, seen my pictures in the glossy mags, heard my single on the radio, watched me perform on TV. I had lapped up his praise and the dice started tumbling again. I started calling him for advice, on my career, on my management, on my accounts. His was the voice of authority but this time we were on different ground. I had earned his respect as a woman. Then we met.

It had taken me many months to pluck up the courage to return to our old haunt, Tramp, for fear of bumping into him there; for fear of the emotions it might stir up. Not that I would admit it, even to myself. I reasoned that I had no time for clubbing. I had busied myself by concentrating on my career.

'All work and no play', said Nic, 'makes Mandy a dull girl.' Point taken, dear. Repeatedly. Until, finally, one night, cajoled by Nicola, I donned my dancing gear and took the plunge. I could always turn and run if I spotted Bill.

Johnny Gold, the owner and Bill's old friend, greeted me with an ecstatic hug. 'It's been far too long, Mandy. Great to have you back,' he enthused and ordered champagne on the house.

'Is Bill here?' I asked hesitantly, prepared to grab my coat and go should there be any chance of a confrontation.

'No,' said Johnny. 'He's been away in Suffolk for the past week, working on his book.'

I breathed a sigh of relief and set about enjoying myself in earnest. I danced until I dropped. It was a release from all the tension that had been building up over the weeks. Finally, I flopped on to a seat by the dance floor but Nic dragged me up again. 'On your feet, dearheart. You've got months of lost time to make up for,' she laughed.

Then it happened. As I danced alongside her, I could feel someone's eyes on me, boring into me, seizing me in their grip. The hairs on the back of my neck froze. I turned, as if in slow motion and searched through the throng of frenzied dancers crowding the floor. There he was. Framed in the entrance, a solitary figure all in black, his face expressionless, his eyes on mine. Time stood still.

Then there was a hand on my arm and I was jerked back to the heaving mass of bodies and the pulsating music. 'Dance,' hissed Nicola. 'Dance, damn you.' She whirled me round to face her and I knew what she meant. She would not have me run to him nor run away from him. She would show him I was made of stronger mettle. Was I?

I danced mechanically at first, then, as the music rose to a crescendo, risked a glimpse over her shoulder to where Bill had stood. He was gone.

The DJ switched tracks. On came the haunting guitar notes of a slow number. Time to give dancers a few minutes to catch their breath. Time for would-be lovers to pair off for the night. 'Time Waits For No One', by the Rolling Stones.

I fought back the tears and told Nicola it was time to go home.

* * * * *

It was 24 October 1988, Bill's fifty-second birthday.

I knew I should not go but I could not stop myself. The memories of that night at Tramp burned deep into my brain and seared my heart. If only he had not simply disappeared like that.

I needed to know. Were his feelings as deep as mine? Was he as unable to face me as I was him? Could time ever heal the pain? No phone call could ever bridge that gap. At some point, I had to meet up with him face to face. And tonight was the night.

I saw him the moment I walked in. Seated at his usual table, surrounded by acolytes and beautiful, simpering blondes. It was his birthday, after all. Now or never. Go, Mandy, go.

I strode up and caught his gaze. His mouth dropped open almost imperceptibly but I saw it.

'Mandy,' was all he said.

'Happy Birthday, Bill.' And I meant it.

He stood up, reached over the table, oblivious to all the cat-like glares from the other women and, taking my hand, kissed me gently on both cheeks. A friendly, continental hello but I knew his heart was thumping away as fast as mine. I could feel it.

'Best birthday present I ever had,' he whispered and his hand held mine just a moment longer.

Dazed, I turned away and made to rejoin my own group but, all night, I knew that Bill's mind was no longer on his birthday nor his party. His mind, and his sights, were fixed on me. This time, I could walk away, knowing I had won.

It was pathetic, really. Now I, too, was playing games but, then, I had learned from a master. I wanted him to realise the depth of his feelings for me. To feel the pain of seeing me, wanting me, missing me. He had told me of those feelings before but those were just words. Now I could see it and it was the truth.

We had given each other time. Now fate was drawing us back together. That, too, was only a matter of time.

Now the tables had been turned on Bill, for the first time ever, by a woman. He did not like it. He resisted it for as long as possible. Naturally, he did not chase me, pursue me or bombard me with calls. He was still far too cool for that. However, I had learned to be as cool as him and now it was a waiting game.

During our time apart, Bill had moved from his flat in the Kings Road to one round the corner in Evelyn Gardens. One evening, he invited me round to see it but this was no, 'Come up and see my etchings, little girl,' line.

He said: 'I'd like your opinion, Mandy. It needs a woman's touch. And you've always had good taste in furnishing and decor. You have an artistic flair for those things.' Well, well. Things had indeed progressed.

I went round the following week. There was no point in jumping the last gate too soon.

We both knew what we were there for. When he met me at the door, the whole charade disintegrated. He led me gently in by the hand and there was no need for words. Words had created walls between us years before. Words had been weapons to inflict pain and hurt, anger and sorrow. This time, he took me in his arms and said it all with a kiss. A kiss that told me, yes, he loved me. A kiss that said I loved him back. He did not attempt to take me into the bedroom. This was not about lust but love.

We stood together for a long time, locked in each other's arms, feeling the warmth and relief pass between us, as if by osmosis. Then finally he spoke.

'Can we get back together, Mandy?'

They were the only words I wanted to hear. I nodded, mute with delight, fearing that, if I spoke, the words would tumble out along with tears.

It was only much later, after hugging and holding for an eternity, that I told him, 'There have to be changes, Bill. If we're going to make this work between us, this time we are not going to destroy one another. This time there has to be commitment. Togetherness.' I paused. 'And no other women.'

A huge grin split his face. 'Blimey,' he laughed. 'Is that all? I thought you were going to ask for the moon.'

In the bad old days, asking Bill to stay faithful *would* have been asking for the moon – and the sun and the stars – but not now, he promised me. He said it had been me and no one but me all along but, before, I was too young to be in that sort of relationship. I had not known what I wanted. So he had availed himself of other women while I made up my mind.

Now I had grown – we both had. Now we could be a couple in every sense of the word. It felt like all the pieces of the jigsaw had finally slotted into place.

*   *   *   *   *

The Stones were preparing for their world tour. Bill had to fly out to Barbados for a recording session the following day.

I was so happy to be back with him at last, after two years apart, that I could not bear to be parted from him only hours later.

We were back to the interminable phone situation and words, words, words. On those long-distance calls over the first week or two, we covered all the ground since we had parted. All bar the Scotland Yard incident. We both avoided the topic like it was bubonic plague.

As the phone bills mounted, we re-established what we both knew was inevitable. We were together. We were in love. We would never be parted again.

Then Bill flew on to Antigua for the tour rehearsals. He was obviously missing me. He told me so repeatedly. He had missed me every second of every day that we had been apart. I wanted to believe that so much. This time around, he said, it was so different. This time, he was well and truly ready to make the commitment.

So I said, 'Well, where do we go from here.' Bill replied, 'We'll get engaged.' Not a question, not a request. A statement – we will get engaged.

I was fairly stunned but I was thrilled too. For him, this was a huge step. Was I hearing right?

I said, 'Bill, could you repeat that please? I think the line is a bit crackly.'

Slowly and solemnly, he repeated, 'You and me, Mandy, had better get engaged.'

I had heard right. He had said it. He meant it. At last, after five years, we were finally going to set off together on this wonderful dream life he had always promised me.

Naturally, however, the offer did not come without strings attached. Let's face it, the leopard was not changing his spots after fifty-two years in the camouflage game. He added the rider that he would discuss all the arrangements with Karen, his secretary. Ever the astute businessman.

However, no way was anyone coming between me and the man I loved at such a crucial juncture. This was *my* engagement, not a secretarial engagement.

I went straight out to Aspreys to look for a ring. I spotted the one I wanted – a beautiful band of gold and diamonds – and thought, 'Yes, I'm having that.' I was never that bold before but I had changed.

Bill was obviously in the same cavalier mood. I had spotted the ring. He wanted to name the day. During his next phone call, the following day, I told him I had found the most beautiful engagement ring. Without hesitation he replied, 'So when are we getting married then?'

I caught my breath. After six years of trauma together, this was hardly a whirlwind situation, but it still winded me. 'Hold on, Bill,' I said. 'Let's get real. You've got the tour coming up and we've only just got back together.'

'So?' his voice and the ensuing silence spoke volumes. 'So?' he repeated.

I said, almost apologetically, 'Well, with the tour coming up, it won't be for months.'

Another silence. Followed by a long, low, long-distance moan.

'OK,' I said, jumping into the breach. 'Let's do it right away.'

It was Bill's turn to be surprised. He said, 'Wha–at?' Articulate as ever but, when it came to emotions, Bill was never fully *compos mentis*. He stuttered, 'But are you well enough?'

I assured him that I was. Bill had been privy to my collapse in Miami. Via Stephen, Mum had let it be known that I was unwell. 'I'm not sick, Bill,' I said, caught on the hop by this oblique question.

'But, Mandy,' he said, 'You're so thin, you're working too hard.'

'Well, Bill,' I countered, 'Maybe it's time I devoted myself to something more worthwhile than the music business.'

He laughed. 'Marry me,' he said. 'Tomorrow if necessary.'

It was my turn to laugh. 'Soon, Bill,' I said. 'As soon as possible.'

210

He was right, however. I had, indeed, been ill, but he did not know the true extent of it.

Plagued with dietary and hormonal problems, I had barely managed to get through the working days but I let no one know how seriously my strength and stamina had been depleted. Only Mum and Nic, watching me grow thin and pale, had seen it and understood. I was beginning to suffer from the same symptoms that had kept Mum bedridden for all those years.

There was no firm diagnosis. There was no cure. Mum had just had to sit it out for years until, finally, she conquered it herself. I could not, I would not, let the same thing happen to me. I was going to fight this all the way.

At the back of my mind, I thought that being married to Bill would make me better, make me strong again. Everything would be all right then.

Like Mum, I had consulted several doctors over my condition. Like Mum, I had found them all dismissive, convinced it was all in my head. Until, finally, I had found one who seemed sympathetic. Unlike all the others, my new doctor saw that my ill health was not psychosomatic. She realised I was suffering from a combination of allergies that would have to be treated individually over a long-term period.

Naturally, having my health undermined meant that there was an attendant depression – mind and body work hand in hand – and the only cure for that was happiness.

My doctor was quite firm about this. She said all my worries would resolve themselves when I found peace of mind and security. Marrying Bill was just what the doctor ordered.

I thought it all through, long and hard. If I was to be absolutely honest, there were two vital reasons why I wanted to marry Bill. One, I loved him. Two, I wanted the respectability.

It sounds terrible, but I felt somehow tainted by the smears about our past relationship. I had been labelled a bimbo and a wild child. Mud sticks and there were odd moments when, undermined by illness, I almost began to believe it about myself. I had never spoken out, I had had no chance to remove that label. Bill knew it was not true but he had made no attempt to dispel the myth either and it hurt me.

I thought that, if we married, the whole world would stop vilifying me.

I would finally be free to be me, Mandy, Mrs Wyman, myself, not some idiot bimbo that people pointed accusing fingers at.

There was only one fly in the ointment. Bill was not quite ready to relinquish his bachelorhood freedom. Mum was in contact with Stephen in Barbados when I told her about the engagement and she was horrified. Stephen had seen Bill out there and she knew he had a girl with him called Melissa. She could not believe I would seriously consider marrying him when he had promised fidelity and yet was still playing around so she told me about Melissa, thinking it might make me see sense. I was furious, but I didn't have a chance to take him to task over it. After our phone call, Bill had announced we were engaged and promptly sent Melissa packing.

I knew Melissa. I'd had a confrontation with her some weeks before at Gedding when Bill had invited me down for the weekend and she was there too. I could not believe it. He was flaunting another woman before my very eyes. At least he had always managed to keep them out of my sight before. To give him credit, we were not actually a couple at that point; it was just before we got back together but that invitation to Gedding was one of the steps along the way to us finally becoming a couple once more. I went mad. I really saw red. I practically exploded. Bill told me there was no way out of it. Melissa's visit had all been pre-arranged months before and, anyway, she had just turned up, what could he do?

He could do nothing, that is the way he was, non-confront-ational to the bitter end. However, I could do something about this fiasco. I went storming up to Melissa's room and let rip. I told her how stupid she was. How could she put up with being treated this way? What kind of idiot was she? He was using her. Poor Melissa was left shaking by this tirade but it had the desired effect. She hid in her room for the rest of the weekend and fled at the first opportunity on Monday morning.

I did not feel sorry for her, nor ashamed of my outburst. I felt quite justified. Bill was not going to make a fool of *me* that way.

To cap it all, now Melissa had shipped up at Bill's side in Barbados. It should have been the final straw but, because he sent her packing, I let him off.

Bill was totally contrite. He promised me he had thrown away his address book and, like a fool, I believed him. Now, at Bill's insistence, it was all systems go. He suggested we should have our engagement party on 9 May, to coincide with the opening of his new London restaurant, Sticky Fingers.

It was perfect timing. It would announce to the world in one fell swoop that we were officially together and that Bill was a successful businessman. It crossed my mind that this was also a handy bit of publicity for his latest business venture but I dismissed this suspicion. He was my fiancé. He was not being anything other than entrepreneurial, I reasoned to myself.

There were occasions, however, when I arrived at the office to find Bill and Karen discussing the engagement publicity like it was some kind of business transaction, not one of the happiest days of our lives. I thought, 'Hold on, this is supposed to be an emotional investment, not a financial one.' Then I would put my naive head on and retreat into my fantasy world, thinking, 'Ah, but he loves me . . .' I was so blind!

I threw myself into the wedding preparations. There was so much to do and so little time. We had set the date for 2 June 1989.

Because Bill had been married before, we could only marry in a register office. With my religious beliefs, however, I desperately wanted a church wedding. So we compromised. We would have two ceremonies. The first, register ceremony would be followed, three days later, with a church blessing. It was double the work and only weeks to do it in but I had never been happier.

I organised the cars, the cake, the church, the guest list, the bridesmaids, the flowers, my outfit. With the help of some of my family, I made all the arrangements. It was my day, our day and I wanted it kept that way. I did not want it to be taken over and exploited by Bill's office. I threw myself into it and really exhausted myself over every tiny detail. It was my big quest.

Naturally, my health suffered. I was living off my nerves. My stomach was in knots. The weight dropped off. I lost over a stone in just a few weeks but the only problem that really presented itself was over my dress, which had to be altered and re-altered to keep pace with my diminishing waist.

I had found it in Harrods, in the Bridal Collection. I strolled in and there it was, my dream dress, just hanging there waiting for me. It was an exquisite concoction in ivory silk and antique lace. It was love at first sight.

I fingered it lovingly, picturing myself floating down the aisle in it when suddenly a voice behind me interrupted my fantasy. '*Would* you mind not fingering the merchandise, Madam?' intoned a severe voice with the kind of plummy accent only used by Harrods assistants and the Royal Family. I was quite taken aback.

'I beg your pardon,' I said. 'In fact, this merchandise is already in rather a grubby state.' As indeed it was. Obviously many before me had also examined it with tender, and dirty, fingers.

'The reason for that,' she sniffed, 'is that people like *you* keep handling it.'

'Actually,' I said, 'I was thinking of buying it.'

The assistant's face then registered a possible heart attack and she practically rose two feet in the air, she was so above herself.

I tried on this dream of a dress and that was it. I had to have it. It was around £5,000 and filthy but no matter. My mind was set on it. I got the name of the designer, Louise Hamlyn Wright, and contacted her immediately. She was thrilled that her beautiful creation was finally going to a good and loving home and happily offered to alter it to fit. Basically, she had to rip it apart and remake it from scratch.

She added masses of extra beading, pearls and sequins and made a train and shoes with matching butterflies. Her husband John, a jewellery designer, created matching earrings and a tiara.

Between them, they made a sensational job of the entire outfit. The only problem was that, as I continued to lose even more weight between the final fitting and the wedding day, it had to be taken in yet again. In the end it had reduced itself from a generous size ten to a wasp-waisted, tiny size eight.

The cost had risen accordingly. It had doubled in price by the end of the day but I had not the slightest regret. It was worth every penny. Anyway, what price happiness?

Unfortunately, Bill did not see money in quite the same light. He was not paying for my outfit, of course, but he did have to buy me a ring. He was not thrilled about this and flinched visibly when he saw the price tags on the pair I had finally chosen in the exclusive royal jewellers, Aspreys.

My divine engagement ring was £25,000 and the wedding ring was coming in at a bargain-basement £15,000. He tried the same old excuse he used on me all the time when I fancied something nice

'Mandy,' he said, 'I think it's too old for you. It's not your style. You're just a young girl, what d'you want with something so fancy? You should have nice sweet simple things.' In other words, cheaper. Ho-hum.

I said, 'Look Bill, it is only once in a lifetime and I'm going to be looking at it every day.'

It took a fair bit of convincing but, in the end, he relented and then I bought him his.

We were nearly there. As the big day drew ever closer, there were only two things left to do: organise our stag and hen night parties – and have an AIDS test.

I was rather taken aback when Bill suggested this but he said it was a symbol of putting his past behind him forever so that we could start our new life together with total peace of mind. I reflected silently that, given Bill's track record, perhaps it was not such a bad idea after all.

He did not seem to be wracked with nerves while waiting for the result, but he beamed a huge smile of what might have been relief when Dr Kaye rang to tell him the result. It was all clear.

Time, then, to set up the stag and hen parties. We arranged for them to be on the same evening, 26 May, leaving us a clear week to recover for the wedding. As I don't drink, it was not a problem for me but Bill anticipated nursing a major hangover. He was not giving away his bachelor status lightly.

I settled for a dinner at Sticky Fingers with Mum, all my cousins, Nicola, a varied gang of chums and two gay friends Colin and Tom who creased us all up when they arrived in full drag.

'Well, dear,' said Colin. 'It *is* a hen night. All us girlies together. Got to dress for the part.'

Bill went off with a few of his mates for a riotous meal at School Dinners and we arranged to meet up in Tramp later.

It was around midnight when, still giggling, we hens all descended on Tramp. Bill was already there with his fellow stags. We greeted one another with a hug but, as it was a bit unorthodox for the hen and stag parties to meet up and share festivities, I left the lads to it and rejoined my gaggle of girls at a different table on the other side of the club.

At the next table were John Taylor and Simon le Bon from Duran Duran. They, too, were on a boys' night out. They smiled and waved hello at me. We had met on several occasions before and I liked them both very much. I had never forgotten how I was a Duran Duran fan all those years before.

As soon as I got on the dance floor with my Aunt Adrian, John and Simon homed in on us and started to dance with us. They were in really high spirits, laughing and whooping it up all around us but then John did a strange thing. He grabbed me close and started nuzzling my neck.

This was no joke, I realised with a start. He was actually coming on to me and coming on strong. I gently pushed him away and held him at arm's length. 'Steady, John,' I told him. 'I'm on my hen night!'

He started to laugh. 'Well, we'd better get a move on, there's no time to waste,' he replied in earnest.

But I knew it was no laughing matter, not with Bill around. I'd always adored Duran Duran and Bill knew it. Whenever he saw them on TV he would grimace, 'Look at that good-looking sod. Who does he think he is?' and then glance at me to gauge my reaction.

Well, his stag night was ruined when he found out they were in the club on my hen night. He got the hump and pulled my mum to one side. He told her that he wanted to call off the wedding. Mum just ignored him and he stormed out of the club and went home, upset because I decided to have a good time with the girls in Tramp instead of spending the night next to him.

He didn't even need to see Adrian and me dancing with John and Simon. God knows how he would have reacted if he had seen John at the end of the evening, pressing his phone number into my hand and suggesting we should go out.

Bill never had any confidence in those situations. He just couldn't see that if it was him I wanted, then the sight of John Taylor wasn't going to change that. I could have rung John but, of course, I didn't. A few years earlier and I would have jumped at the chance.

I didn't even notice Bill leave the club. When Mum told me about it the next day, I couldn't believe it.

I rang him but everything was back to normal and the wedding went ahead as planned. It was just another one of Bill's tantrums.

CHAPTER SIXTEEN

The Wedding of the Year

As the big day grew closer, I grew increasingly more anxious. Life seemed to be conspiring against me, somehow. Everything that could go wrong, did.

Apart from the débâcle over the hen and stag parties, which had created an air of unspoken tension between Bill and me, there were problems at every turn.

For Bill, marriage was a huge step after thirty years of bachelorhood. He was not getting cold feet but he was certainly giving some people the cold shoulder. Mostly me. He was on edge all the time. I could not approach him about anything to do with the wedding. He would wave away any joint decision with a dismissive, 'Oh, just get on with it, Mandy. It's your day, isn't it?'

Instead of being thrilled and excited by the impending nuptials, it was as if he just wanted it to be over and done with so that he could get on with his life.

However, there was one issue he was adamant about. He called me to the flat one day and said there were some papers he needed my signature on. When I arrived, he gave me a kiss, sat me down and informed me that I had to sign some kind of pre-nuptial agreement waiving my rights as a wife to his fortune in the possible event that, one day, we might divorce.

It was a staggering proposal, completely out of the blue.

I knew only too well how tight-fisted Bill was; that was not a problem but this was a slap in the face. How could he think of divorce just days before getting married? I was insulted and incensed and, for once, lost for words.

As I sat there open-mouthed, Bill realised that perhaps, he might have been better off broaching this matter in a more subtle way, like maybe actually discussing it with me before having the documents drawn up. He sat there, shuffling a sheaf of papers and looking increasingly more discomfited as he realised his

gaffe. 'Look, Mandy,' he said, 'It's just a sensible business proposition. In the unlikely event that we ever split up, then we
would have to sell Gedding and Vence and split the money down
the middle. You'd get a ridiculous price for them. In a divorce,
it's always the buyers who gain because divorcees need the money
in a hurry. We'd lose a fortune. And I don't want to lose the
homes, do you?'

But they were not *our* homes. They were Bill's homes and
were destined to be so always. He never even gave me my own
key. I had always had to ring his office to make an appointment
to enter the flat or pop down to Gedding, to make sure that a
staff member was in attendance, ready to let me in. It was a
ridiculous state of affairs.

Feeling guilty now, Bill tried to cover his tracks. 'Look,
I have to let you know how our marriage is going to work
financially.'

I looked at him, still silent, wondering what incredible proposition was coming next. This was my lover, the man I had
shared six years of my life with, the man I would walk down
the aisle with in just a few days' time and here he was, coming
on like some bank manager with an errant customer who had
plunged deep into the red.

As he spoke on, I was, indeed, getting redder and redder,
with embarrassment. This whole situation was ludicrous,
humiliating.

'I will give you £250 a week allowance.'

Pocket money, is it, Bill? Still I said nothing.

'Er . . . all right then, and a percentage of the takings of Sticky
Fingers. And I'll get Karen to fix up a Barclays account and
arrange for the money to be paid into it once a month. How
does that suit you?'

Fine, boss. Sure thing, boss. Whatever you say, boss. After
all, I am only a humble worker and you are the breadwinner.
That was exactly how I felt by now. Bill was trying to fit me
into a working role in his life: wife, seven days a week, twenty-
four hours a day. Yours for £250. Take it or leave it.

I felt deeply depressed by this whole encounter. Bill knew
that I wasn't the slightest bit interested in his money, but he just
wanted to clarify this little issue before he said 'I do'.

I gathered up all the dignity I could muster and said, 'No,

Bill. I won't sign any such agreement. So far as I am concerned, this is a marriage of equals. You know full well I can earn a great deal of money from my modelling and singing. I've just done so for the past two years. If I choose to give all that up to be your wife, then that's because I love you. And if you don't love me enough to trust that I'm not after your money, after all this time together, then I suggest we call off the wedding. But it's your decision, not mine.'

Sheepishly, Bill backed down. He knew it was the truth and he was way out of line but, for Bill, money always came before love. Money and sex were his twin gods. This time, sex won the day. I never did sign the agreement.

Later, this scenario was to plague me in a recurring nightmare. When I was branded a gold-digger, I would recall how we sat down together that day and Bill laid down his financial law. I knew people had this image of me walking around Chelsea with a bag full of credit cards and a joint account with access to Bill's millions but nothing could be further from the truth. I was simply one of his employees, only I was paid less.

It should have been enough to make me turn on my heel and say, 'This is not a marriage that will work,' but I was too far down the line for that.

My health was really suffering now. The stress and pressure were mounting and the weight was dropping off me at an alarming rate. I felt faint and nauseous much of the time but there was still so much to be done and somebody had to do it. There was a panic when I went for a last fitting of my dress and it draped on me like an outsize frock on a wire frame. I had to have it hurriedly re-altered again, at the eleventh hour, to fit my rapidly diminishing figure.

My illness took the edge off my excitement, too. All the time I was thinking, 'I'm supposed to be feeling radiant, I'm going to be a bride,' but all I felt was sick and exhausted.

Problems rose to confront me around every corner. There was trouble with the guest list and trouble with the staff. Bill had refused to let his new Gedding housekeeper, Connie, or her husband, Carl the caretaker, come to the wedding. They had replaced Monique and Louis a year before, when they flew off to the South of France to be housekeepers at

Bill's house in Vence. They had lost no time in getting their feet under the table.

It seemed to me that Connie and Carl regarded Gedding as *their* home. I secretly felt that they regarded Bill as a bit of a nuisance, certainly more that than lord of the manor. However, Bill put a high price on staff loyalty and both paid, and treated, them well so Connie and Carl naturally assumed they would be guests at the wedding. When Bill nixed this possibility, they seemed furious and I felt they blamed me.

That was not the end of it. I think their expectations had been even higher than that. I think they wanted their daughter Becky, who was around eleven, to be a bridesmaid. Personally, I nixed that one. So the atmosphere at Gedding was icy.

Then Bill became even more ruthless. He said he did not want his mum and dad at the register office ceremony. It was to be quiet, informal and strictly restricted to the four of us – him and me, plus two witnesses. Not only was this deeply offensive to Bill Senior and Molly Perks, it was deeply upsetting for me. I wanted the parents of the bride and groom to be present. Let's face it, it's not every day you see your children married, is it? It was a momentous occasion for the Perks, seeing Bill finally wed again. Not least of all, it was an unrepeatable moment of great joy for my mum to see her younger daughter, whom she had raised single-handed, get married. These are moments in life that you want to share with those you love.

Bill was having none of it and I did not try to pressure him. What was the point? It would only have given rise to another argument and we certainly did not need any more of those. However, my disappointment was pretty obvious.

Finally, he relented a little. He said my mum could come after all, *if* she insisted. Mum, bless her, felt that it would be an impossible situation. How would that make his own parents feel when they had been excluded while she was invited, albeit under duress? So she told Bill that, truly, she would rather not be there.

It was not just Bill's stance over the guest list that was creating problems. I had plenty of trouble with my own family – mainly, my father.

He might have walked out on us all those years before, he had never contributed in any way to our family life, he had

222

Sticky Fingers opening in 1989 and for once Bill looked nice. I chose the outfit for him after he threatened to wear one of his old Farmer Joe jackets again.

Top left: Mum and Dad's wedding day on January 15 1966.

Middle left: What a cutie. Here I am aged 15 months.

Above left: This is Bill aged five or six – even then he looked like an old man!

Above right: ARGH! My real hair colour revealed. I'm only four here but look a lot older. I've often wondered if my life would have been any different if I'd stayed that colour.

Left: This one was taken a few weeks before I met Bill when I was 13.

Right: My first break into showbiz – Miss Lovely Legs competition in Birmingham in 1983. The contest was for over 18s only and everyone presumed I was old enough.

Top: The wedding. The look on my face speaks volumes.

Above: At the wedding reception in the Grosvenor House Hotel. It was a lovely day until Mick Jagger told my young relatives to f*** off when they asked for an autograph.

Me and my uncle Harold at Gedding Hall. Bill was away on tour so I raided his attic and dragged out all his old stage clothes. That guitar is probably worth thousands. Bill would have had a fit if he saw me playing tennis with it that day!

Top: My first ride in a stretch limo without Bill. My manager Maurice Boland hired the car after one of my early performances in 1987.

Above: Keith Daley and I at the airport in 1986 as we returned from Spain.

This was one of the first Hippodrome gigs where I sang Positive Reaction. I remember not feeling too well even then.

In the living room at Morant Place in 1985, getting ready for a night on the town.

Here I am with Paul Young in Stringfellows in 1986. He's a lovely guy and was always up for a good natter.

Top: With Kylie and Jason in Sydney, Australia. They're fun people and Kylie was a real help over the years. I turned down one of her songs, she recorded it a few weeks later and it went straight to No l. That's showbusiness!

Above: Backstage at the filming of Bryan Ferry video Kiss and Tell with my friend the model Denice Lewis in 1988.

Top: Performing with Bryan on the Roxy TV show.

Above: With Rick Astley at PWL. He was a tea boy when I started there and ended up a huge star. Rick was a great, great friend and a real shoulder to cry on.

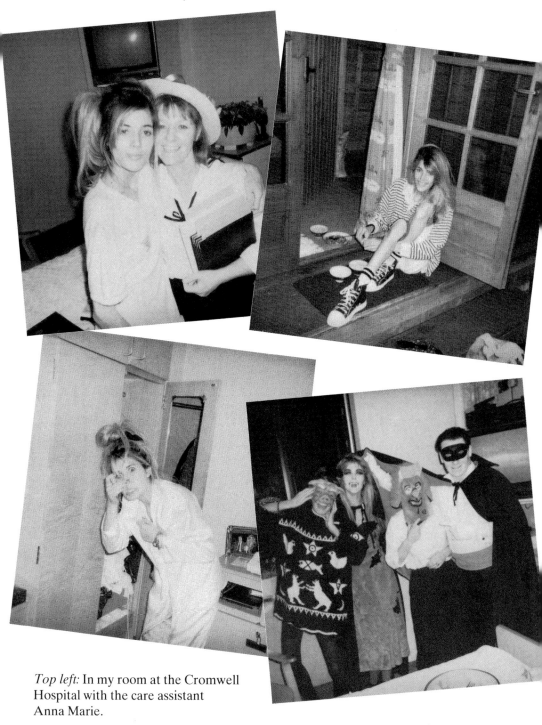

Top left: In my room at the Cromwell Hospital with the care assistant Anna Marie.

Top right: On the doorstep of my bungalow at the Springhill. I use this picture to remind myself just how thin I became.

Above left: Nic was at my side almost constantly when I was in the Cromwell. Here we are messing around in my room.

Above right: Halloween in October 1990. Nicola turned up with a load of masks and she sneaked me out to a party. That's me in the pig head. I could only manage half an hour at the party but it was great fun.

Outside the High Court in November 1992. The dark glasses came in very handy!

Shopping with Reggie in Hampstead in 1991.

Top left: Having fun with my husband-to-be. Reggie started a cake fight during a visit to a friend's house in Hampstead.

Middle left: Gazza getting down with my mum Patsy at a party we threw for the Spurs players at our house in 1991.

Above: My 21st birthday party at home. Bill tried to spoil things by sending me an orchid – the flower that used to be a love token between us.

Top right: At Bill's house in Vence with my cousin Julie. Bill let us use the house while he was away on business and we both dressed in his stage clothes – with a few added fruity extras.

Top: Mrs and Mrs Smith van den Hauwe. The happiest day of my life.
Above left and right: Stephen, Nic and Mum arriving for the big day.

dedicated himself to his gambling, his golf and his girlfriends, in that order. He had not been a father to either Nicola or me, nor a support to Mum but he was still my dad after all.

After years of acrimony, we had finally healed the rift. There was an uneasy truce between him and Mum, and sporadic contact with him for Nic and me.

Lately, however, we had begun to make contact with him on a weekly basis. We either saw him or he phoned, usually at the weekends. When I asked him to give me away at my wedding, he was thrilled.

To be honest, I was in two minds about the whole thing. I did not want to be a hypocrite, merely reaching out a hand in token friendship so that he could fulfil a function at my wedding. It had to be an emotional decision, from the heart. I had to *want* this man, who had walked away from me when I was three years old, to give me away.

When I looked into my heart, however, I knew what I truly felt for Dad was love. That was the bottom line. There were many mucky and mixed emotions layered over that love but, yes, it was there. We had been apart for most of my life but he was still my dad no matter how much water had flowed under the bridge. I was willing to forgive and forget.

Dad was overjoyed and we began to involve him in the preparations. Then, as always, a fly found its way into the ointment. Suddenly my name was splashed all over the papers again. 'Mandy Smith Has Love Cheat Dad. Read all about it.'

For years I had managed to keep my front door closed to the press. They had been camped on my doorstep day in, day out, but never really managed to dig up anything on me or any of my family. They had speculated, but they had no facts and that had really hacked them off. Now they had something to get their teeth into – my father.

With the wedding coming up, Fleet Street had naturally been hell-bent on finding out all they could about Bill and me and our wedding plans. Then they got wind that my long-lost dad was back in the fold and invited to the ceremony. They knew only too well they would never get any stories from either Bill or myself. Our love affair, our wedding and our lives were strictly our business. Unfortunately, there were those around us who did not feel the same way. With pound signs flashing in front of their eyes, they rushed off to the papers with any little titbits they could rake up about our lives.

None of my own family displayed such a lack of integrity but Dad's ex-girlfriends had no compunction about spilling the beans on Dad and on me.

Dad had not gone into hibernation in the sixteen years of his separation from Mum. There had been a girlfriend, then another, and another. Suddenly, all these stories about his ex-girlfriends started appearing in the papers.

It was desperately upsetting. I did not know who or what to believe. Dad said we should ignore it and that we just had to live with it. That was absolutely typical of him. He preferred to look the other way, just like he had always done. Well, I couldn't handle that. I wanted him to stand up for himself and us. He dug his heels in and refused. On top of all the tension over the wedding, this was like a fast-burning fuse attached to a keg of gunpowder.

We had some horrendous arguments over those stories. More than one culminated in Dad walking out without a word, non-confrontational as ever. That infuriated me more than anything. My fiery Irish temper got the better of me and finally I exploded.

'You can forget about the wedding,' I yelled at him as he disappeared out the door after one particularly heated exchange, 'Because you're not coming!'

I was as good as my word. I immediately got on the phone and asked my mum's brother, my Uncle Vivien, to give me away as I had always been close to him. There was no going back.

It sounds harsh but the way Dad chose to turn a blind eye to all the lies was a terrible reminder of the past and the reason why Mum and Nicola and I had learned from hard experience to stick up for ourselves.

The family feuds were far from over, however. There was also the delicate issue of my Nan and Grandad. Now it was their turn to dig their heels in. They refused to come if Dad was not coming; then some of the other uncles and aunts jumped on the bandwagon and it was everybody at each other's throats.

Enough was enough. I had had it up to the neck with all the family in-fighting by then. I said to the lot of them, 'OK, that's fine by me, don't come then.'

I wanted a simple wedding but nothing in life is that simple or straightforward, least of all my family...

* * * * *

At last the wedding day dawned. It was 2 June 1989 and it was finally going to happen – Bill and me, Mr and Mrs Wyman.

Bill had got his way as always. The register office ceremony was, indeed, to be very quiet and simple, with just Stephen as Bill's witness and Nicola as mine. It was the complete anti-thesis of the big blessing ceremony we had planned two days later at our beautiful church, St John the Baptist in Hyde Park. I had poured all my time, attention and energy into that. The register office ceremony was completely last-minute and pretty haphazard.

We had gone down to Gedding the night before. There had been no celebrations, no toasting our last night of independence. It was a night like any other except that Bill and I were both so shattered that we almost slept in and missed our own wedding!

Just as we were rushing out of the door, we realised we'd forgotten something. We hadn't arranged any flowers. Bill and Stephen had no buttonholes; I had no bouquet! Luckily, Mum, resourceful as ever, had a brainwave. She rushed out into the garden and picked some lovely old English roses. Hey presto, buttonholes for the boys, a sweet-scented corsage for me. The panic over, we shot off to Bury St Edmonds for the ceremony.

Curiously, I was not at all nervous, nor was Bill. My religious beliefs meant that I would not feel properly married until after our church blessing ceremony. As we said 'I do' and Bill slipped the ring on my finger, I had expected to feel different somehow.

I felt a warm glow of pleasure as Bill kissed me and Nic and Stephen looked on smiling, but it was all over so quickly. I remember thinking, 'Getting married is so important, it shouldn't be as speedy as this.' There was no depth or meaning to the few words the registrar spoke; it was simply a piece of paper, a token bow to officialdom.

To be real for me, getting married meant the hymns and prayers, the music and majesty of a religious ceremony. I did not feel properly married yet.

And Bill? He, I discovered, was also saving himself for something more momentous. He had lined us up for the Wogan show that night.

He sprang it on me like it was my first wedding present, just as we left the register office. 'Thought it might be fun, love,' he said. 'They booked me weeks ago but they haven't a clue we've just got married. Can't you just see Wogan's face when I turn up with you and tell him we've just got spliced?'

I didn't have time to be stunned because, as we stepped out into the summer sunshine, suddenly two *Sun* photographers leapt out of the bushes and showered us with confetti. 'Just had a tip-off, Mandy,' one said. 'You know us, we always like to be first with the exclusives. Come on, love, give us a smile for the camera.'

It would have been churlish not to grin at that moment, but a sneaking suspicion flitted through my mind that the little bird who had tipped off Fleet Street's finest might not be a million miles from where I was standing. I might even be holding his hand.

A smile, a twirl, a kiss for the camera and then it was straight into the car and off to the TV studios for the Wogan interview. We were, by now, being carried along on a buzz of excitement – all engineered publicity.

It was just too perfect timing. I knew Bill had planned all this to coincide with a nice plug for the Stones tour but, what the heck, so long as he was happy.

Wogan was happier still. It was quite a scoop for his show. Both the Irish blarny-merchant and Bill were on good form. Wogan reduced me to fits of giggles with some of his cheeky Irish banter and Bill was delighted that the whole thing went off so well – no fumbles, no faux pas.

He was still in a good mood when we set off back to his flat. I, however, was beginning to flag. It had been a long and exhausting day, full of events for which I had been totally unprepared. Bill, of course, with his prior knowledge of what was going to happen, had paced himself. Now he intended to round the day off with a good session in bed.

He couldn't wait. The minute we got in the door he turned to me with all the seduction technique of a housebrick and said, 'Well, Mrs Wyman. How about it?'

Drained and feeling light-headed from the pace and events of the day, I murmured, 'Can we leave it tonight, Bill?'

Throughout the course of the day, the candida problem that had arisen earlier had been increasingly playing up. I felt sore and tender. I was still affected by the *Chlamydia* infection that Bill had also passed on to me but I didn't want to have to spell it out word for word.

'Aw, Mandy,' moaned Bill and pulled his sulky little boy face.

Okay, I thought, I will spell it out. Patiently, I explained to him how I felt and, when he realised that I was still affected by problems *he'd* given to me, he agreed. OK, he'd had a busy day too. There was still the blessing ceremony to get through. We were both really excited about that; it was the really big event for both of us. So, with these dreams, we lay peacefully in each other's arms and instantly, happily, fell asleep.

My last thought as I drifted off was, 'This is wonderful. At last, things have changed. Bill is actually respecting my wishes – and on this night of all nights. Now I know he cares...'

Wrong again, Mandy. A few hours later, I was to wake up to a very different reality.

*   *   *   *   *

The day of our blessing ceremony, 5 June, the day I regarded as my real, true wedding day, was a beautiful sunny summer's day.

I was up at the crack of dawn at Mum's flat, with more butterflies in my tummy than there were embroidered on my dress. I was more excited than I had ever been in my life. All those weeks of planning and preparation and now, finally, it was all happening. There was so much still to do. Hair, face, nails, flowers, get into my dress, get into the car, get into the church...

'Oh my God,' I wailed as I tried to wrench an unruly hairpin into place, 'I've changed my mind! I can't go through with it!'

Mum, sitting a few feet away at her dressing table, and busy fiddling with her own hair, nearly fainted. She gawped at me, not really believing what she was hearing.

'Just a joke, Mum,' I squealed with laughter and had to duck hurriedly as she lobbed a handful of hair rollers at me.

'You're a horror, Mandy Smith. I'm going to be well shot of you!' she laughed.

It was a day filled with laughter and love. We were all carried away on a wave of emotion. As I was driven to the church, I thought of my lovely mum and all that I was leaving behind. Today was going to be the biggest turning point of my life. I was well and truly going to be Mrs Bill Wyman. No longer his child, his lover; now his bride, his other half – equals.

We pulled up outside the beautiful old church and I swear the air was filled with birdsong. As I entered and began the long walk along the aisle, I saw Bill standing before me at the altar.

I felt touched by the sight of him, his slender back in his silver-grey Tommy Nutter suit, the way his hair curled softly over his shirt collar. For a second, tears of tenderness pricked at my eyes and then I caught sight of the most bizarre couple, sitting in a pew to my right-hand side.

Draped from neck practically to ankle in long raincoats with the collars turned up, their faces nearly obscured by huge dark sunglasses, they looked like a pair of spoof spies from a Pink Panther film.

'My God,' I thought, 'Somebody's going to play a practical joke on me. At any minute now, they're going to jump on me and say, "Watch out, Mandy, Beadle's about!"'

I squinted harder, trying to concentrate at the same time on my supposedly dignified progress up the aisle to where Bill was patiently waiting. All eyes in the packed church were on me. The whole congregation was waiting with baited breath for this vision to take her place at the altar. You could have heard a pin drop.

I focused on this weirdest of apparitions and, to my sudden astonishment, realised it was my own Nan and Grandad in disguise! Laugh? I nearly wet myself. The penny dropped. They had been too proud to renege on their decision not to attend the wedding after Dad was banned but they couldn't resist seeing their grand-daughter wed so they had come in disguise and made themselves all the more noticeable for it!

Somehow, I managed to reach Bill's side without dissolving into hysterical laughter and the vicar's serious tones, as he began to read the blessing, brought me back down to earth but all the time I was praying, 'Please don't let that vision of Nan and Grandad pop into my head again. Please let me get through this with a straight face.' I swear I had to cross my legs beneath my dress and mentally pinch myself to get through it.

Of all the thoughts that run through a bride's head during her wedding ceremony, a prayer that you won't wet yourself laughing must surely be one of the rarest. It was sad really, though, because, immediately after the ceremony, Nan and Grandad disappeared. They had just wanted to see me wed, then slip away. I felt guilty about that, although it had been their very definite choice not to attend.

However, guilt and sadness should have no place on the happiest day of a bride's life so I swept my feelings under the carpet and tried to savour every moment of my wedding day. It was not too difficult. After all my years of practice with Bill, I had become a bit of an expert at sweeping my emotions to one side. That apart, I was on cloud nine throughout the blessing.

Outside, hundreds of wellwishers lined up with our families to throw confetti at us and wish us well as we took our place on the church steps for the photographs. We kissed for the crowds and a great cheer went up.

One silver-haired old boy stepped forward and shook Bill by the hand as we walked to our car. 'You're a lucky man, Mr Wyman,' he said with a big smile. 'Your young missus is the most beautiful bride I've ever seen and no mistake. What's your secret, eh?'

Bill just smiled. 'Dunno, you'll have to ask her that!'

I laughed. I wasn't too sure how I would answer that question myself. What exactly was it about Bill that still captivated me? I looked at him and he looked so lovely in his suit, with that big boyish grin that had stolen my heart all those years before. Funny old thing, love.

So off we sped, Mr and Mrs Bill Wyman, floating on air on our way down Park Lane to the Grosvenor House Hotel for our wedding reception.

They called it the wedding of the year and certainly the paparazzi and the press were out in force, flashbulbs popping like a November fifth fireworks display as we entered the hotel. Inside, it was an oasis of calm as the massed ranks of Stones bouncers kept out any would-be gatecrashers and newspaper infiltrators.

All the Stones were there, somewhat to my surprise, as I

knew relationships were strained, particularly between Bill and Jagger, but, no, there was Mick, Jerry clinging elegantly – but tenaciously – to his side. Both of them wearing sunny smiles, especially for the cameras. How silly of me. Of course all the Stones would be in attendance at the wedding of the year. Their world tour would kick off in just a few weeks' time. What perfect timing for a splashy and happy bit of worldwide publicity.

However, this was my day and nothing could spoil it, although Mick had a good crack at trying just that. The Stones might have graced our reception with their presence but it appeared that they would be damned if they were going to mingle with the *hoi-polloi*. While both my own and Bill's family mixed, chatted, ate, drank and danced with the others, the Stones formed an exclusive little clique at their own corner table.

There were all the Wymans and the Smiths table-hopping and bopping with each other, while the rest of the Stones were tucked away, huddled together like some summit meeting of heads of state.

They made it quite clear to all the assembled guests that it would be quite *infra dig* for them to mix with the general public. To everyone's credit, they respected the Stones' distance and simply left them to it. If they wanted to be miserable and élitist, that was their loss. It struck me, as it must have done many others, that if the price of fame was an ensuing superiority complex that prevented them from having some plain, straight-forward, down-home fun, then they could keep it.

The rest of us were having a ball. The champagne flowed like water. I wanted everyone to share the happiest day of my life with a bit of their own happiness too.

The problem was, children don't understand the power games that adults play. All my young nephews and nieces knew was that the Rolling Stones were here. They had seen them on the telly, heard them on the radio. They were rock stars. They gave autographs. Not these rock stars. They didn't.

In their innocence, one or two of my little cousins dared to breach the invisible wall that the Stones had erected around them. 'Excuse me, Mr Jagger,' they went, 'Can we have your autograph, please?'

I watched, transfixed, as Mick turned round very slowly to face these awestruck kids as they held out scraps of paper and a pen to their hero. Those enormous lips curved in a caricature of copulating slugs. 'Fuck awff!' said the world's number one rock star.

However, no one and nothing could ruin the wedding reception for us. As the day blurred round the edges and tumbled into night, Bill and I finally said our farewells and set off on the first, to me at least, true night of our married life.

Sensibly, Bill had taken the precaution of booking several rooms for guests who had travelled a long way for the wedding. Even more prudently, he had booked the honeymoon suite for us. Good thinking, Batman.

Bill, for one, was in no fit state to travel far. Copious amounts of champagne, wine and vodka had flowed down his throat throughout the course of the day. I held Bill's hand as he led me, swaying slightly, up the stairs. Giggling like . . . well, a couple of newlyweds, we careered along the corridor to our suite and Bill fumbled ineptly with the key in the lock.

'Bugger it, Mandy,' he muttered. 'Can't get in. I think we'll have to spend the night in the lift! How about it? Sex in a lift is great fun, y'know. Especially if you get caught . . .'

Just then, with a sudden lurch, the door swung open and Bill fell through the doorway and crashed on to the floor. 'Help me, Mandy,' he moaned in mock pain. 'I've crippled myself!'

No chance of me being carried over the threshold then. I helped him to his feet and, with a sudden yank, he dragged me over the floor and was rushing to the bedroom. 'No time to waste,' he panted. 'This is what we're here for.'

'Bill!' I squealed as he pushed the full force of his nine stone on to me and shoved me down on the kingsize bed. 'Watch the dress!'

He had gripped the neckline of my bodice and was poised to rip my £10,000 designer wedding dress to shreds. 'Oh my gawd,' he moaned. 'Take it off, take it off.'

Frenziedly, he threw off his jacket and was struggling, one leg on the floor, the other in the air, to get his trousers off as quickly as possible. In his customary Marks and Sparks white Y-fronts – Bill always wore the same sort of underpants, yes, even on his wedding day – he was a comical sight as he struggled to keep his one-legged balance. He failed. As I walked into the adjoining dressing room to strip off myself, I heard an almighty crash.

I turned round and tried desperately to suppress my laughter. There was Bill, spreadeagled on the floor, trousers round his ankles, Y-fronts round his knees – the bridegroom in all his limp and tipsy glory.

Five minutes later, when I emerged, all set for my first night of lawful wedded passion with my new husband, I found him already in bed. Strewn around the room were his jacket, waistcoat, trousers, tie and pants. Bill was in bed, sleeping like a baby and snoring loudly enough to awaken the dead.

'Oh well,' I thought. 'Welcome to married life, Mandy,' as I slipped between the crisp cotton sheets beside him. Gently I reached out to pull him to me, wanting to feel the warmth and comfort of his soft, smooth skin. As I slid my body against his, I suddenly got the shock of my life.

Instead of his warm flesh meeting mine, something cold, squidgy and slippery had pasted itself to my thigh. I leapt out of the bed in sheer terror and flung back the sheet to see what the heck it was. Bill, stark naked except for his socks, was curled up and sleeping in a bed full of squashed banana skins. Some joker had secreted a bunch of bananas in our bed as a just married prank but it had backfired. Oblivious to everything, Bill had thrown himself on them, squashed them and squelched them out of their skins.

There was no way I could wake him. Sighing, I stripped off the top sheet, rolled the disgusting sticky mass that had spread over the bottom sheet up to Bill's back – and prepared to sleep on the mattress cover.

'So this is marriage?' I thought wryly, as I slid into the abyss of sleep.

CHAPTER SEVENTEEN

The Honeymoon is Over

Bill woke with a thundering hangover.

'Tea,' was his first word to me on that first morning of our marriage. 'Mandy, get us some tea on room service. My mouth feels like a vulture's armpit.'

As he groped around to find his bearings, Bill found, instead, the squashed bananas he had slept in the night before. 'Aw, that's disgusting,' he groaned, smearing the blackened, speckled mash all over the counterpane in a bid to detach himself from it.

'Well, that'll be a surprise for the chambermaid,' I thought. 'Doubtless she's cleaned up many a stain from the honeymoon suite sheets before but this must surely be a first.'

Bill was not in the best of moods to appreciate a bit of humour so I adjourned to our adjoining lounge.

Wedding gifts lay stacked in neat piles all over the floor. More boxes were piled on the sofa and the chairs. I knelt by an enormous present. It was a walking frame that Spike Milligan had given to Bill with the hope that it would see him through his honeymoon!

The internal phone rang. It was Mum calling to say that she and Stephen, having breakfasted, were checking out of the hotel.

'Oh, come in and see this, Mum. There's a mountain of wedding gifts to open here. I could do with a hand if you and Stephen are not doing anything else.'

Mum was reticent. 'But what about Bill?' she queried. 'I don't want to pop up on your first day of married bliss, like the proverbial nosey mother-in-law.'

I explained Bill's prior appointment with a pint of Perrier and a couple of Nurofen and told her that for the next few hours he would be more married to the toilet than to me. So, a few minutes later, Mum and Stephen joined me in my Aladdin's cave.

Our laughter must have reached Bill's ears because it wasn't long before his head popped around the door. Bleary-eyed and unshaven, he looked like an old grandad in his hotel dressing-gown. 'What's going on?' he moaned. 'What's all the racket about? I've got a thumping migraine and wouldn't mind a bit of peace and quiet.'

Mum, Stephen and I exchanged wry glances. 'Come and help us open these,' I said. 'Here, someone's given us a pair of solid silver nut crackers in the shape of a stripper's legs!'

Bill was immediately cheered. There was nothing he loved more than getting presents. Several hours later, surrounded by a mountain of discarded wrapping paper and another empty champagne bottle, Mum and Stephen politely made their excuses and left.

Bill immediately got to his feet. 'Got to take another shower. Got some writing to do and if I don't get it out of the way now it will be hanging over me all through the honeymoon.'

'But Bill,' I countered, 'this *is* our honeymoon.'

'Mandy, you know I can't do anything now. I've got things to do first.'

Married or not, some things were obviously not going to change overnight. A kiss, a cuddle or anything else of that nature was still confined to night-time, behind bedroom doors.

'Okay, then,' I thought. 'If you can discard me on our first day of married life, then I'm not going to waste my time hanging about here for you to finish your work. I've got things to do too.' I banged on the shower door. 'Bill, I'm going back to Mum's to pack my suitcase for the honeymoon.'

He carried on singing.

'Bill, can you hear me? I'm going to pack my case for France.'

The torrent of water suddenly ceased. Bill's bedraggled head popped round the side of the shower enclosure door. 'You what?' he said. 'Did I hear right?'

'Yes,' I was slightly taken aback by his snarl. 'I have to pack for France.'

'You must be joking. Why haven't you done that already? You've had plenty of time to pack. What have you been doing for the last six weeks?'

'Organising a wedding,' I snipped. 'And let's face it, all you had to do was organise the honeymoon – and you couldn't even manage to do that properly.'

Maybe that was uncalled for but it was quite true. The honeymoon was the one thing I had left to Bill – at his own insistence. He wanted to go to Turkey, his choice, not mine. He wanted to get a good deal on the holiday booking. He didn't trust me to negotiate a cheaper price with the travel agent so he would sort it out. He didn't. At the last minute, he had informed me that Turkey was off but he didn't come clean and confess that he'd either: (a) Not done a damn thing about it; or (b) failed to get a cheap holiday even though he was Bill Wyman, Rolling Stone; or (c) simply come round to thinking that whatever it cost, it was too much. So he'd told me he couldn't face the thought of flying because the airports would be packed with press. It would be a nightmare. They would be tipped off about our honeymoon destination. They would be peering at us through the bushes with their zoom lenses. No way. Turkey was definitely off the menu. France was on. A honeymoon at his house in Vence. At least we could drive there.

It was the biggest load of nonsense I had ever heard. There were more likely to be press and paparazzi sniffing around his Vence house than some remote Turkish villa. The whole of Fleet Street knew the location of the house. Bill was just cutting corners and, more likely, cutting costs.

He was also avoiding the truth. The bottom line was Bill's phobia about flying. It was more than fear, it was an irrational terror. He would never fly if there was an alternative. He always travelled by car and ferry to France.

He reckoned he had flown so often with the Stones without incident that his number had to come up one day. He was so petrified, he had to take Valium to get through a flight. You could always tell when he'd been on Valium. His eyes were like saucers. Eventually, he had arranged to see a therapist about it but he kept missing the appointments. His sessions would have meant confronting his innermost fears and feelings and Bill was not equipped to deal with that. So he gave up the therapist as a bad job and dismissed him as useless and a complete waste of money. Naturally, there was nothing wrong with Bill's mind...

Even now, he could not admit to me, or even to himself, that he had an abject terror of flying.

Then there was the little matter of Mum and Stephen. Bill had already invited Stephen to Vence for the month that we had planned to be on honeymoon in Turkey. Stephen had happily agreed, with the provision that he could also enjoy his holiday in Vence with Mum. It had all been openly aired and agreed.

When Bill pulled out of the Turkish honeymoon, it meant we would all be sharing the Vence villa for the month of June. What a delightful surprise wedding present. I was to share my honeymoon with my own mother and my potential stepson and it was all Bill's doing.

So here we were, Bill stark naked and dripping wet, me with one foot out the door of the honeymoon suite, poised to have our first fight as a married couple. We had been married for less than twenty-four hours and were arguing over the honeymoon before we had even gone on it. It did not bode well.

'You'd better be back here later,' he warned me. 'No, I'll meet you back at the flat. Get there by 9 pm. We'll have dinner, then maybe go on to Tramp.'

Tramp? On the second night of our married life?

I looked him straight in the eye. Water trickled in a steady stream from his fringe over his eyebrows and down his cheek. Already, his white roots were beginning to show through. How dare he talk to me like that?

'I'll ring you as soon as I've packed,' I said and removed his dripping hand from my arm. 'You can organise a car to take the presents away.'

It was a show of some considerable strength on my part but it was merely a show.

In fact, I'd begun to feel strangely lightheaded as the day had progressed. It was a weird kind of other-wordly feeling, like floating on air, dizzy, faint, and yet, curiously, my feet felt like they were weighted down with lead. I felt very, very unwell.

Depleted, I sank into the vinyl seats of the black cab and let myself be driven back to Mum's place. She was shocked to see me but more shocked by my wan appearance. 'I could have dropped off your case, Mandy,' she said. 'But, judging by the look of you, I'm glad you came back for it. Sit down. I'll make you a cup of tea. You really don't look at all well...'

The next thing I knew, someone was kissing my eyelids. A rough, rasping kiss that reminded me of ... Minnie, my Yorkshire terrier! I opened my eyes and a tiny bundle of silky fur met my gaze. Nose to nose, she gave a great big doggie grin. I rubbed my eyes. It was 6 am. I lay, curled up in a little ball, on my mum's settee. A duvet was tucked into the cushions all around me and Minnie was loyally perched on my chest.

The pieces of the jigsaw fell slowly into place. I had come home for my suitcase, sat down and complained to Mum I was cold. She had ignited the roaring gas log fire and that was the last I remembered. I had obviously fallen asleep where I sat.

Fourteen hours ago! I knew I had been exhausted, but this... What would Bill think? I had promised to call him. It was 6 am. There was no way I could call him at that hour and yet he would be worried sick.

I heard someone stir in the bedroom above. Mum's slippers padded gently down the hallway. 'All right, love?' she smiled. 'I didn't want to leave you there but you were so shattered.' She came and sat beside me and stroked my arm.

'The wedding has really taken it out of you, hasn't it? I don't think you're one hundred per cent, Mandy,' she felt my forehead. 'You've got a temperature. You're run down. I think you need a good long rest.'

'Well, I'll get that, won't I? Tomorrow I'm off on my honeymoon with my own mum.'

'Well, I don't plan on seeing too much of you, my dear. Stephen and I will keep out of your way so you and Bill can enjoy yourselves. Oh, and don't worry about Bill. I called him last night. Told him what had happened. I knew he'd be worried if he didn't hear from you.'

'What did he say? Was he angry?'

'No, not at all,' she smiled. 'He said he knew you had pushed yourself too far lately.'

I looked into her eyes. She was a very bad liar, my mum. But I let it pass. I didn't have the energy to tell her I knew the truth. She was protecting me from Bill's fury – for now. I'd catch the full force of it later, no doubt about that.

I snuggled up in the duvet. 'I'll just sleep a little longer, Mum.'

So it was that, out for the count, feverish and shivering, I passed the next day, the second of my new life as Mrs Bill Wyman, at my mum's.

It was not just exhaustion. It was not simply the aftermath

of throwing myself into organising a big wedding. Nor was it merely the backlash of emotion that went along with finally achieving my dream and marrying the man I had loved from the age of thirteen. It was all of those complicated factors and more but the end result was straightforward enough. I was becoming very, very sick indeed.

While I drifted in and out of a fevered sleep, Mum fended off calls from Bill, with a mounting fear. She alone recognised my symptoms. Nerves, stress, strain and a hormone system in uproar. She had been through it all herself, years before, but she had been a grown woman and was gradually able to control her condition. I was eighteeen.

When I woke again, my case was packed. My new life was waiting.

A cup of tea and a piece of dry toast and I took a taxi to Bill's flat. Despite my forty-eight hours' rest, I still felt light-headed and dizzy. Over the last three days, I had lost four pounds in weight.

Bill was waiting with a look of black fury on his face but there was no time for recriminations. 'Just get in the car, Mandy and let's get on the way.'

The long drive to Paris was wordless, bleak and black with a silence that hung over us like some seething cloud of bitterness.

Bill had been married for several days and had had no sex for several nights. Whenever he threw a mood like that, you knew all about it. He would go into a terrific sulk and chainsmoke a hundred cigarettes with a ferocious, sour look on his face. No one would dare go near him.

Trapped together in the car, Bill maintained his distance and his rage in silence.

I was left alone with my thoughts and it was then, speeding through the French countryside, that the anti-climax of the wedding really hit me. I knew then that the fairytale I'd dreamed about so long just wasn't going to happen.

I watched Bill as, white-knuckled, he gripped the steering wheel of his beloved Mercedes and ripped down the French motorway. I could see, written all over him, the look of furious concentration that meant he was plotting. Bill was waiting for his moment to get back at me. It was only a matter of time. However, for now, at least, I was grateful for the lack of inquisition. All I wanted to do was sleep.

So too did Bill when we finally arrived at our hotel on the Champs Elysee.

Arriving in the late evening, Paris seemed eerily silent, despite the pavement cafés dotted on every street, their lights blinking away to attract the late-night clientele.

For me, Paris was haunted by the ghosts of our early years there together. The scenes of our energetic first lovemaking loomed like spectres round every street corner – the ghosts of a love that lay long buried.

We booked into a lovely hotel but could only get a small room with twin beds. I did not demur over Bill's weary suggestion that we share a bed. I very much wanted the tension to be resolved between us. I wanted to be held and cuddled, reassured that our relationship was not simply purely sexual. To my immense relief, Bill agreed. For once, he seemed to understand, but I knew, too, that the effort of controlling his rage, and driving all those miles while still seething, had drained his own reserves of energy.

He was, after all, a man in his fifties. He no longer had the limitless staying power and stamina of youth. His greatest mortification was being unable to feel a hundred per cent of his manhood and, equally as bad, being unable to sustain it for long enough. I knew all this but Bill was much too macho to admit that, simply, he needed to sleep too.

Our lack of sex that night would be stored in his emotional armoury and later used as a weapon against me. He was chalking up notches in his head – another night Mandy did not want to have sex.

Lying next to him that night, I wondered if we could ever recapture that precious first love. Being married was not what I had led myself to expect for all these years. Everything – and nothing – had changed.

We fell asleep, untouching, unloving, Bill's anger lay like a blanket of rage over us; my illness was the pillow on which I laid my head.

The following day, with nothing yet resolved between us, again in silence, we drove to Vence. It was 9 June, exactly a week to the day since our blessing ceremony.

The tension was almost tangible by now. Bill was always in

a foul mood the next day if we hadn't had sex. He'd be whistling away if we had. There was no whistling on this nine-hour drive.

I used the journey to plan ahead. I'd decided that this tension between us was unbearable. I would capitulate. I would try to be as cheerful and normal as I possibly could. I would abandon my rigid diet and risk eating all the things, like sugar and oil and fat products, that I'd long had to abandon because they aggravated my hormonal problems. Perhaps, now I was married, my health problems would disappear. Wishful thinking.

Dirty, sticky, tense and irritable after the silent journey, we dragged ourselves into the house and knew that, yet again, for the eighth night in succession following our marriage, we would not make love.

There was no love. There was no understanding, no compassion. Even in my frail and weak state – by now I was several pounds under seven stone – I knew that what Bill wanted from me was sex, his marital rights.

That night, if I would not give them to him, then he had decided he would take them.

After dinner we sat and watched TV and I could feel myself getting more uptight and apprehensive as bedtime approached. Bill, too, sat stiffly on the other end of the sofa. I sat there thinking: 'If only he would be nice to me. That's all I want.' He had absolutely no idea how to woo me. Already, I knew what was coming but I was unprepared for the ferocity of it.

As we got ready for bed that night, Bill's pent-up fury and frustration exploded and I was right in the firing line.

He did not try to seduce, cuddle, coax or cajole me. Unable to contain the resentment any longer, he said bluntly, brusquely, that he wanted sex and he wanted it there and then. Despite my exhaustion, I refused. I could not, would not give in to this same tawdry game that he had played so often during our years together – and apart. I was his wife, and I wanted more than to be his sexual plaything.

We had argued often, long into the night, in just this way but now the goalposts had been moved. He was my husband, he had a right to sex with me. I was his wife, I had a right to affection and respect from him. I could not, and would not, be used, now more than ever.

That was it. He blew his stack and started ranting, 'We've

been married over a week, and I haven't had it yet. I got more sex before I was married.'

I retaliated, 'Consummating our marriage is not an act of love for you, Bill. It's just a function to relieve your aching sex glands. It's just part of a rota to you, Bill, like writing up your diary every morning. That's how you live your life, isn't it? Bound by routine. There's no feeling, no emotion in you at all, is there?'

It was true. The next morning and on all the following days throughout our honeymoon, Bill would spend most of his time working at his computer. There were no romantic strolls through the beautiful French countryside, no evening excursions to candlelit restaurants for hands-held-over-the-table meals. This was our honeymoon but Bill was married to his damned computer. He went straight to his desk in his office down in the cellars, slamming the door behind him.

Every morning was the same. I was on my own, feeling increasingly more lonely, unloved and bored. It was hardly surprising that, when it came to bedtime and Bill extended, not an arm of love and friendship round my shoulder, but another part of his anatomy in my direction, I rebuffed him. Sometimes, he would storm off out of bed and go straight back to his computer.

On 16 June, precisely two weeks to the day since we married at Bury St Edmonds register office, we made love for the first time in our marriage. It was not a moment born of great love and passion. I simply gave in. Bill's anger behind the bedroom doors was mounting, so I ceased to resist. Bill had worn me down.

I was frightened for many reasons – frightened of the implications of having sex without the attendant love and affection. Most of all, I was petrified of the pain. I still carried a legacy of Bill's repeated infidelity before our marriage. Painful cystitis meant that any sexual contact left me in searing agony for days afterwards.

In fact it wasn't as bad as I expected. The act itself was not overlong – Bill could hardly contain his excitement after a fortnight of anticipation and frustration. I, too, actually enjoyed it. As Bill put his arms round me at the moment of ultimate pleasure, I felt, briefly, that we were as one together. We slept like babies in each other's arms. Bill woke whistling away happily to himself, a huge grin all over his face.

I was doubled over in pain. The cystitis had sprung back into life with a vengeance. I gritted my teeth and told myself to bear it. I thought maybe our honeymoon would improve from that point. I had made Bill happy. He had left me in pain. No change there, then.

Perhaps, I felt, Bill would now relax but no sooner had he breakfasted than he took himself off down to his office and the tap-tap-tapping of the keyboard informed me that he was back at his computer again. The deadline on his book was drawing nearer. He had to get the manuscript out of the way before he embarked on the Stones' world tour the following month. The book. The tour. The honeymoon and the bride came a poor third and fourth in Bill's priorities. It was with great relief that I greeted my mum and Stephen when they flew in to join us at the villa. Bill, too, was more than happy that they were coming. They would provide a distraction for me and keep me out of his way so that he could work on his magnum opus. Also, if I was happy and had some company during the day, worked his reasoning, then I would perform in bed at night. At the thought of this, his magnanimity knew no bounds. Keep Mandy happy, keep her occupied all day – the more company, the merrier the bride.

He extended the invitation to his secretary, Karen Kearne, with whom I had long enjoyed a good girlie friendship. Karen had just had a baby. No problem, said Bill. Bring the baby too, plus the baby's nanny. To make the gang complete, he also invited my sister Nicola, along with her boyfriend, Lino. He would even – a sign of his great generosity, or perhaps more a way of getting me out of his hair during daylight hours – pay for their tickets as a birthday present to Nic.

So, out they all came. My compatriots and cohorts on my honeymoon, all at Bill's invitation and at Bill's insistence. There we were, a house full of people in the South of France, accompaniments to a honeymoon with Bill Wyman.

In fact, it was a clever ploy on Bill's part. I was reassured by the mixed company of Bill's workforce and my own family, yet the atmosphere was awful because of Bill's foul moods. Despite the extended company, he made that honeymoon into a complete misery. He wanted a group of people around him to distract me, yet he bitterly resented the fact that he then had to share me with mixed company. As usual, Bill knew what he wanted and, simultaneously, did not know what he wanted.

I was further distracted by the fact that, as soon as Karen, Mum and Nic arrived, they realised there was something seriously wrong with me. Mum knew best. She had no sooner landed than she spotted the signs of an illness that she knew only too well. She immediately contacted my doctor back in London, who sent out some medication.

In foreign climes, with a husband who did not want to know me until bedtime, the stress on my nervous system was stretched to snapping point. I took my extra pills and potions without demur and felt the better for them but each day was the same. I spent my time either sunbathing or going into town with Karen, Nic and Mum. Bill holed himself up in his cellar-study and didn't get involved at all.

I began to liken his study to a dungeon. It was deep, dark and buried in the bowels of the villa, a most unprepossessing place to visit, never mind work in, but Bill felt totally at home there. It was his sanctuary. Every now and then he would stick his head outside and say: 'Bleedin' hot out 'ere, innit?' and then disappear again into the cellar.

He was the typical Englishman abroad. Despite the luxury outdoor swimming pool and the balmy heat, he wouldn't even come and have a paddle. I realised with considerable chagrin that here was something else I had never known about Bill, despite our many years together. He could not swim and would go to any lengths to avoid water, all the while denying admission of the mortifying fact that he was scared of it.

It all fitted the much broader picture. Bill was a closet xenophobe. He never went abroad without his English Typhoo tea bags, his chocolate digestives and Branston Pickle. He had no time for foreigners, unless they happened to be French and female.

It became increasingly apparent to all the assembled company that, not only were we at the behest of Bill's moods, but that, every day, they depended on whether we had had sex the night before. It was not only I who was privy to that knowledge. Bill would let everyone in the house know if we had or hadn't.

243

He talked about it quite openly to anyone who would listen, even strangers – to everyone, in fact, except me.

One memorable day, Bill was ensconced by the poolside – a rare event in itself – apparently deeply engrossed in conversation with Lino. It later transpired that he was having a 'man's heart-to-heart', revealing to Lino, whom he had only briefly met once prior to this holiday, how I'd refused to have sex and how it was wrong because we were married now.

Lino, who felt – and quite rightly so – that he hardly knew Bill at all, was deeply embarrassed but, in Bill's book, Lino was a man so it was OK for him to hear about and comment on his sex life with his wife.

Lino ended up giving Bill some astute advice. He told him to spend more time with me during the day instead of sitting at the computer. This was *not* what Bill wanted to hear.

It was not long after this astonishing revelation, which came to me via Nicola, in whom the disconcerted Lino had confided, that I began making an effort to keep out of Bill's way. There were two routes to the swimming pool and I always took the longer one round the entire villa, which kept me away from the door to the cellar where Bill was working. He had banished me to the company he had assembled for me during the day and I began to feel more comfortable with them than with him.

In the evenings it was the same. We would sit down together in front of the TV but I would pull away from any physical contact with Bill. He seemed oblivious to the shifting sands that he himself had put in front of me.

Immediately we were alone together, the pressure to have sex would start again. There would be a sudden groping hand on my thigh, a whisper in my ear but I wasn't prepared to be ignored all day and then be a sex object in the evening.

The biggest problem was that I had relented a few nights earlier. Bill had taken that as a tacit agreement to his superiority as my husband. I had given in once. I would do so again, preferably on a nightly basis.

The bedroom rapidly became a battleground. Every night was the same. Bill would approach me with his demands. I would rebuff him. Bill would press on. I would recoil. Bill would lose his temper and shout and yell.

This was new. This was married life in the bedroom. He had

never been abusive like this before. I would lie there thinking: 'Maybe he's showing his true colours now.' Sex – not love, not affection, not emotional intimacy – was always on Bill's mind.

One night we climbed into the jacuzzi together. Within seconds Bill's hand was cupping my breast and he was breathing heavily into my ear. We could do nothing together, it seemed, that Bill did not construe as a prelude to sex. It became an obsession with him. He developed an uncanny ability to turn situations that could be romantic into bestial animal acts. It got to a stage where I was frightened even to hold his hand because I knew he'd take it as a signal to drag me into the bedroom.

He, too, was unnerved by this turn of events since our wedding. He began bemoaning the fact that I had changed. He wanted back the girl that I was before. In other words he wanted a healthy fourteen-year-old who was prepared to have sex with him. But that girl was gone. In her place there now stood a woman and a wife, confused, yes, but more sure than ever that she was not to be dismissed as a sex toy.

I did give in to him on a few more occasions, particularly when I was feeling weak with my illness. I could never recall exactly how many times. They were a blur of half-feeling and later half-remembered memories. However, Bill knew exactly how often those fleeting bouts of one-way passion occurred. He itemised them with cold, unfeeling detail next day in his diary.

The end result was impossible to ignore. Bill had made me feel that sex was a chore and if that chore was not fulfilled to his satisfaction, there was hell to pay.

It was only a couple of weeks into the honeymoon when Bill's attitude to sex took a distinctly sinister tone. I had felt it brewing for a while. I had managed to keep it at bay by relenting when necessary.

Then Bill's tack changed. If I was his wife, I had to do his bidding in bed, which I had done. Taking that submission as his lead in a new direction, he dictated new terms. Now, if I did not give him his marital rights, I had to be made to pay for my failure as a wife.

One night, as I turned over to go to sleep, Bill suddenly went berserk. Like a manaic, he began ranting and raving, shouting at the walls. 'You're my bloody wife, we are supposed to be bloody married. Well if you won't do it, I'll do it for you.'

I half-turned, rigid with fear. He clambered on top of me, squatting directly over my face and began masturbating, but not in a normal way – he was really fierce and demented, like a madman. I was petrified. This was not a normal nor a natural act. It was maniacal.

I felt the sickening fear in the pit of my stomach turn to nausea as, wide-eyed, I watched him perform this bestial act only inches above me. Then my horror turned to disgust. I lay there, sobbing silently, praying for it all to be over, for this madman to finish, this nightmare to end. He slumped, his seed and his bile spent, and fell into a heavy snoring sleep beside me.

Then I knew that Bill wanted to demean me, to exert total power over me, to make me feel soiled. He did not really love me, perhaps he never had. He had loved and lusted after a fourteen-year-old child because she had been totally under his sway. He could get her to do anything he wanted. He had married me in pursuit of that child but she was long gone.

Yet, even though I saw this truth with a blinding clarity, I still could not walk away from Bill. We were newly married. He was the only man I had believed in since my father had left me as a child. Those ties that bound were still unbreakable.

Those demeaning, violent scenes of humiliation and masturbation were ones I had to live through time and again before I could break free.

Sometimes I asked Bill what had driven him to do these things to me? Why had he married me, only to abuse me? He gave me no answer. He had no answers for himself, so how could he explain it to me, or to anyone else? He revealed only that, for him, marriage had been a massive step.

He had been married only once before – thirty years ago. Sometimes, in his mellower, more communicative moods, usually after sex, he would speak of his ex-wife, Diane, but, again, only in the context of sex. He said that she, too, refused to let him have it. He was so furious that he used to smash up their home in violent retaliation.

I would think, 'But it works two ways, Bill.' Why didn't he try giving his first wife some overt affection and care, not just demanding sex all the time? No wonder she pulled away. Couldn't he talk to her? Love her in a different way? The answer was, no he couldn't, and here he was, not having learnt anything from experience, still unloving, still ungiving, repeating the pattern with me. Bill would never learn from his mistakes. If he did not get his own way, in bed or anywhere else, that was it. End of story. He would switch off. There was no compromise.

The honeymoon became my own private hell. There was only one night on which I felt a release from the mounting pressure and ever-widening chasm between Bill and me. That was the night when Ronnie and Jo Wood arrived for the evening.

They, too, were holidaying in France, not far from Vence. Bill invited them to join the merry throng of the Happy Honeymooners and Co.

We all went out to a restaurant together. Ronnie was on great form and we had a real laugh. It was the first time in months that I had felt so free and at ease in Bill's company.

I had always got on well with Jo, although she was never someone I could confide in. Giggling girlishly over some shared joke, she and I adjourned to the Ladies loo while Bill and Woody swopped drunken Stones reminiscences.

As we stooped over the washbasins to wash our hands and repair the mascara damp with the tears of laughter, Jo looked at me quizzically. Taking in my skinny frame in the mini-skirt and T-shirt top, she said pointedly, 'You've lost an awful lot of weight, haven't you, Mandy?'

I stopped reapplying my make-up, bracing myself for her next question.

'You're anorexic, aren't you?' she said.

I laughed. A genuine, honest-to-goodness laugh that would have been a pleasure if it had not been so poignant. 'If only, Jo,' I said, 'If only it was that simple.'

Anorexia, I knew, could be cured, likewise Bulimia. I had never, nor would I ever, stick my fingers down my throat in a bid to lose weight. I was as far away at the opposite end of the spectrum as it was possible to imagine. I wanted to put *on* weight, to be normal, not to drop pounds day by day, week by week but no one else could see this.

Jo had just voiced the common opinion that I was sure Bill and the rest of the Stones held – that I was just a silly girl who made herself sick.

Maybe it was at that moment that all my dreams truly crumbled to dust. Not just for Bill and me, but for the Stones and me, too. I had spent a month with a new husband who neither truly loved nor understood me, nor, apparently had any desire to. Bill and the rest of the Stones lived in a world of their own making and their own money. They had no grasp of love or emotion, of pain or anything real. I was sick of them all. I wanted to go home. The honeymoon was over.

CHAPTER EIGHTEEN

You Can't Always Get What You Want

On 8 July, Bill and I parted company. While I flew from Nice to London with Mum and Stephen, Bill drove to Paris to pick up a flight to New York for the start of the Stones' US tour. The strain of flying long-distance proved too much for him, however, and he had a massive anxiety attack just days later in New York. He let me know all about it in every last intimate detail because it happened to coincide with my nineteenth birthday party.

Bill had kindly given me permission to hold a small celebration for my family and a few friends at Gedding Hall but he did not do it lightly. There were strict restictions on certain no-go areas of the house and a very tight rein on the budget.

When we arrived for the weekend, the fridge and freezers were empty. I felt Carl and Connie had obviously not forgiven me for my transgression over not inviting them to the wedding. They made it quite clear that Bill might be master of Gedding, but I was certainly not mistress, and especially not in his absence.

Bill expected the staff to run Gedding. I felt I was treated as an unwelcome visitor. It was a ridiculous set of circumstances for a new bride whose husband was away on long-term business but I refused to let it spoil my birthday.

There were double celebrations that month because I passed my driving test just days later. Bill offered to buy me a car as a combined birthday present, wedding present and congratulations. I was thrilled by this generous offer and, four days later, bought a sweet little VW Beetle for £10,000, which I paid for with my own money because Bill seemed to keep forgetting to authorise a cheque for me. (In fact, he 'forgot' for almost two years. Even then, he only paid up on the advice of his divorce solicitor.)

When I told him of my impulse buy, Bill was pleased with my choice. I secretly suspected he had spent those days in abject terror, wondering if I might rush out and buy an Aston Martin.

In fact, one day I did test-drive a beautiful automatic Mercedes 190. I did not feel it was the right car for me, but I tried one out, just to see what it was like.

God knows how he found out – he must have had spies cruising the streets of north London – but the next thing I knew, Bill rang me and demanded to know what the heck I was doing test-driving a Mercedes. 'A car like that is far too flash for you. Don't be ridiculous, Mandy.'

It was typical, vintage Bill. I hadn't even thought about signing on the dotted line but he was scared stiff that I might blow some of his money on an expensive motor. He wanted to keep me well and truly in my place.

The tenor of some of those long-distance phone calls was often rather strained – sometimes more than that. The bottom line was that Bill was not happy about being on the road on his own. He wanted me to be with him. All the other Stones had their wives and girlfriends with them, he wheedled. Why wasn't I there?

The reason was that I was so ill I had had to move back into Mum's flat.

I'd come back from honeymoon and gone straight to see my doctor.

Bill was constantly on the phone, badgering me to join him on the US tour. I told him that, quite simply, I could not. I could not travel all that distance on a plane and life on the road was too erratic and unhealthy. There is no regular routine, no healthy food. I knew I could not handle it in my condition. I was well under seven stone by that time and my weight was continuing to drop alarmingly.

My doctor ran a battery of tests on me but they revealed nothing. Then she rang Karen to suggest that I was perfectly all right and should join Bill on tour. If, for a second, my doctor felt that being with my husband might alleviate my nerves, she could not have been more wrong.

It stepped up the pressure immensely. Not only did Bill believe there was nothing wrong with me but now here was my own doctor telling him, 'Mandy is fine. She should be out there with you.'

I did not know it then, but Bill immediately got in touch with his solicitor, Paddy Grafton Greene, to discuss the possibility of divorce. He was already thinking, 'OK, Mandy won't join me? Fine. I'm going for a legal separation.'

It was blackmail of the most invidious kind but, as yet, he said absolutely nothing about it to me at all.

From what I know now about the legal process of divorce and of Bill's situation, it seems that he was advised to play it very carefully. He was a man of considerable fortune, much of it dependent on his high public profile but that income-generating image would be considerably damaged if he was seen to be divorcing his schoolgirl bride of a few weeks in such an indecently short space of time.

He had been lucky once before, when he got off scot-free after having sex with me while I was under-age. That had now been made right when he was seen to be so deeply in love with me that he married me, but all the good that had been done could be undone. His career and his reputation would once again be in the limelight – and in jeopardy. He would have to be extremely cautious about ditching me this way. He had to make it look like I was the one at fault.

While all this subterfuge and plotting was going on behind my back, my head was in the clouds. I was so sick that all I could concentrate on was trying to find out the cause of my illness and get from day to day.

Bill stepped up the pressure. His phone calls were hugely accusatory and full of self-pity. He was out there all on his own. He had married me. I was his wife. Why couldn't I be with him? Everyone else had their wives out there. Why couldn't I go?

I simply could not get it through to him that I was wasting away. I now weighed six and a half stone. I was sick. That did not matter. He had heard from the doctors – both my own and Bill's, Dr Kaye. They said I was fit enough to travel. Bill was dismissive of my opinion. 'They're the experts.' Just as though I was a silly little girl who knew no better.

But, excuse me, it was my body and I was the one who knew what it felt like, not the so-called experts who could not yet come up with a diagnosis, never mind treatment. How it felt to me was that I was dying a bit more every day.

Bill would not give up. He carried on, recruiting more members to his team, including the Rolling Stones.

One cold, bleak November day, out of the blue I got a call from Mick Jagger. You could have knocked me down with a feather – probably literally, as it happens. Mick had never had any time for me before. Now here he was on the phone, all concerned, it seemed, but it was not me he was concerned about.

'Ma–andy, come on over,' he said, in that unmistakable nasal Jagger twang. 'Bill's really miserable. He's all on his own.'

Bill was miserable? Did he think I was swanning around London, partying every night? Did he not realise that at six and a half stone and fading fast, with no hope of a cure, I was pretty miserable myself? No, he didn't.

'Look, Mandy,' ordered Mick, 'either get out here with your husband or leave him.'

I nearly dropped the phone, I was so shocked and upset at this astonishing and unsolicited ultimatum. However, I had no time to remonstrate because, just then, Mick handed over to Jerry and she drawled, 'Look, honey, why don't you just get over here and get yourself a shot? My mother has allergies, too. But she just gets herself a shot and gets on up and out.'

A shot? A *shot*? I felt like doing a bit of shooting myself at that moment. I was shaking with rage. How dare Mick ring me up and talk to me like that? How dare Jerry Hall be so patronising when she knew and cared nothing about me?

I slammed the phone down in fury, picked it right up again and immediately dialled Bill's number. He did not sound surprised to hear from me. He admitted straight out that he had put them up to it. He whinged, 'But I'm so lonely out here, Mandy. They were only feeling sorry for me.'

But who the heck felt sorry for me? I was the one who was sick. I certainly was not looking for pity or sympathy but I did want someone – anyone – to recognise that I was ill, not some crackpot little girl who simply did not want to go on a Rolling Stones tour of America.

No one was listening and, increasingly, it seemed to me that Bill was the one who was turning people away from me.

My doctor had run a battery of allergy tests on me which proved conclusively that I suffered from a huge range of violent reactive allergies. I had asthmatic tendencies and I was allergic to dogs, cats, fumes, cigarette smoke, dust and mildew. Alongside that, I had many dietary allergies to fats, sugars and dairy products. The list went on and on. But no one believed there was an underlying cause that was making me susceptible to these allergies – no one but my mum, because, of course, she had suffered from the same thing most of her adult life and no one had listened to her either.

I felt constantly nauseous and the condition was much worse in the week preceding my period when the slightest thing could make me violently ill.

At first, my doctor had believed I had anorexia but, gradually, as she got to know me, she came to believe it was something quite different. She prescribed antibiotic cream for the candida and began investigating my other illnesses.

She was a practitioner of alternative medicine. Accordingly, ours was an alternative relationship to the normal doctor-patient role model.

We had become very good friends. We would go shopping in Hampstead and out for afternoon tea together. She came to look on me as the daughter she never had. So it was all the more shattering when, behind my back, she suddenly started talking to Bill.

Who did I turn to now? Just a few pounds over six stone and still the scales were dropping. Then I remembered something. I had read about a woman in Ohio who had been critically ill for years, rejected by the medical profession who conceded that she was seriously ill but could find no reason for her illness and no cure.

They finally diagnosed her as allergic to the twentieth century and she was forced to live encapsulated in a sterile glass bubble in order to prolong her sad life. In the end, out of sheer desperation, she devised her own medication, eating and exercise lifeplan, and cured herself.

Her symptoms sounded so familiar to my own that I had to get in touch with her. I thought perhaps she was my last chance.

Amazingly enough, this time Bill agreed. 'Fine,' he said. 'Get her over to London.' He even agreed to split the bill with me. If I treated the whole experiment as a business proposition and retained receipts for every single item of financial outlay for this woman, he might be able to recoup it against his tax. I would pay for her flight, living expenses and medical bills and Bill would reimburse me at some later stage. (Much, much later, again, under legal duress.)

Her name was Vicki Glasburn.

We arranged for Vicki to fly over that December and she stayed with us for a couple of weeks. She was fantastic, blooming with health and vitality. You would never have imagined she had once totally wasted away through her allergies.

She put me on an incredibly strict health regime. It was so arduous that Mum, Nic and my aunt Pauline joined in to lend me some moral support.

Our day started at 5 am, when a woman's hormone level is at its peak. Then, without even a life-sustaining cuppa, it was out on to the dark pre-dawn streets of London, pounding the pavements for two solid hours to raise the cardio-vascular rate.

On our return home, we would breakfast on the dubious delights of a huge bowl of rice, beans and vegetables with loads of garlic tablets, kelp and rice cakes.

All this happened thrice daily. It was, as it sounds, an abject nightmare for the first few days, principally because I was so weak, but, by the end of the fortnight, all of us we were positively radiant. I had masses of energy for the first time in months.

I even found the strength to go out for the first time in weeks. Kylie Minogue, an old friend from my PWL days, was throwing a party after the premiere of her latest film and she invited me along.

Mum and Nic, worried sick at how ill I had been, encouraged me to go. They thought it would be a tonic. Encouraged by my new surge of energy, I thought, OK, we will go to the premiere and see how I am after that.

I had felt so low for so long, however, that I thought for this, my first foray into a social life since my wedding six months earlier, I might like to change my appearance. Mum had borrowed a dark, bobbed wig for a dressing up party. I tried it on and, for a laugh, I decided to wear it.

There was another reason for altering my appearance, though. I really did not want to attract the attention of the press who would be milling around. There had been enough speculation in the papers recently about Bill and me. Fleet Street, in their inimitable fashion, had put two and two together and made six, surmising that if Bill and I were not together on the Stones tour, then we were not together at all.

They were not far wrong and I knew that any pictures of me in a social environment would enrage Bill, after all my protestations about illness. So I donned my wig and off I went.

Up to a point, my disguise worked, probably due more to the fact that I had lost so much weight that even some of my old friends did not recognise me. I stood right next to the DJ Gary Davies, whom I had known for years and he did not bat an eyelid. To him, I was just another gawky, skinny kid, though a whole heap skinnier than most.

Others, like Pete Waterman and his wife Denise, did spot me. They were aghast at how thin I was and lost no time in telling me so. However, I had learned from experience not to blather on about my allergies. No one understood. You could see their eyes glaze over the minute you mentioned it. Also, I did not want to be the centre of attention at Kylie's do, so I made to leave. Unfortunately, just as I was heading for a side exit, some lesser-known film producer spotted me and came haring after me. In true, clichéd Hollywood tradition, he breathlessly demanded to know my name.

I smiled. 'Holly,' I said, which was the first thing that came into my mind. Then this would-be Spielberg asked me if I was a model or an actress because, y'know, honey, I should be and well, with the right make-up and lighting, he could help make that happen for me . . . yawn.

I was keen to escape, not just from his clutches but from the eyes of anyone who might be watching this little scenario, so I told him thanks, but no thanks, and turned to go. Persistent little devil that he was, he held my arm and asked for my surname.

I looked back over my shoulder at him, smiled serenely and said, 'Wood'.

The look on his face when he realised he had been had was a moment I shall treasure forever. I was unable to stop a big grin from breaking out on my own, with spectacularly bad timing.

Some nearby newspaper snappers had suddenly twigged what was going on and who I really was. Flash, bang, wallop! There I was, captured on camera. Sure enough, next day, I was splashed all over the papers, silly wig on, great big grin all over my face.

Bill was *not* happy. He rang up in high dudgeon, demanding to know why, if I could not fly to the States, I could go to a film premiere? I did try to explain that an hour or two in the cinema was a bit different to a month or two on a tour bus in the States but he would have none of it.

He was really hacked off and wasted no time in letting me know all about it. He couldn't believe a word I said. I was always on about being sick, yet I was well enough to hit the town. He couldn't trust me. Condemnation and accusations. That was what my marriage was built on.

'OK, Bill,' I pitched back, in total exasperation. 'If you don't feel you can trust me, why don't you divorce me, then?'

All I wanted to hear him say was, 'Mandy, I love you. Please look after yourself until I get home. It won't be long now and we'll get you well soon.'

Just a bit of care and compassion would have done me the world of good. Instead, we slammed the phone down simultaneously on one another.

Next morning I woke up to a letter from Bill's solicitor. It said, in unemotional and unequivocal legalese, that the marriage was over and therefore I should consider that Mr Wyman and I were officially separated pending a divorce.

Nothing had been mentioned to me about this. We had never even discussed the possibility of separation. Now here it was in black and white. Those words from a complete stranger, some official I had never met, telling me that my marriage was at an end before it had even begun.

It was the last straw. I curled up in a corner, clutching this cold, hard letter and sobbed my heart out.

* * * * *

256

If anything was responsible for tipping me over the edge into the abyss of near-death, it was that letter. It was an indictment of me as a person. It listed my failings as a wife. It was the most brutal, undermining letter I have ever seen. I was devastated by it.

Couldn't Bill see that I had mentioned divorce in a fit of pique? It was one of those vicious things you throw at one another when you are suffused by rage in a no-win situation. We all say things we don't mean to the ones we love when we are trading insults with them.

I did not want a divorce. I wanted Bill. I needed him to be by my side. I was sick. He was my husband. Instead, he had been demanding I be at *his* side because he was bored and lonely. All the time I had fought to bring him closer to me. Now this.

It revealed the indisputable and insurmountable abyss between us that Bill could use a throwaway insult used in an argument as the basis of an official petition for divorce. Worse. And this was the fact I really did not want to face – it showed how cold and calculating he had been all along, waiting for an opportunity to make it look like I was the one at fault, the guilty party.

All the time I had been crying out for his help and he had taken my vulnerability and was using it against me.

Mum was furious. She found me sitting there, crying, with the letter in my hands. She knew how low I was and that this letter had really tipped me over the edge.

I did not feel like fighting any more. I just wanted to give up. Bill had turned his back on me. Worse, he had turned against me in the most vicious way possible.

Up until that moment I had always fought my illness but that letter was the turning point. What was the point of going on?

Mum got straight on the phone to Bill, demanding to know what the hell was going on. Did he realise how dangerously ill I was? Did he have the slightest inkling that what he had done could have killed me?

All he said was, simply, 'Well, Mandy said she wanted a divorce.'

I could almost see the steam coming out of Mum's ears. She exploded 'You stupid man, what is wrong with your brain? Can't

257

you use your head and see what she's doing? She's sick and she wants *you* to be here for her.'

I spoke to Bill myself then but all he could do was reiterate, 'You wanted it, Mandy.'

I was in tears of exasperation. Why could I not make him see I needed him? Why did he always put himself first and never consider anyone else? Above all, the unanswerable question, why on earth did I still love a man like that? Yet, I did. The lethal, emotional wires of my dependency on Bill were choking me, strangling me, but I could no sooner sever them than take my own life. Ever since I was thirteen, he had woven his web around me like a black widow spider and I was still trapped.

There were many things I did not understand about my love and dependency on Bill. Many things I could not bear to look at for fear they would destroy that love. Now here I was being forced to confront the most destructive suspicion of them all. The possibility that the man I loved had been plotting this all along. That he had married me to enhance his own reputation and to engender worldwide publicity for the Stones tour, his restaurant and his book. That he had intended to divorce me with indecent haste, as soon as he could find some evidence that would pin the irretrievable breakdown of the marriage on me.

My intuition was screaming at me to examine this possibility. My love for Bill made me turn a blind eye to it. I was trapped between those two extremes of my own feelings and I was ripping myself apart.

What I did not know, what I could never have dreamed, was that Bill had, indeed, coldly, calculatedly been planning to discard me. The previous month, he had hired a team of private detectives to put a round-the-clock watch on me. He was looking for a reason to divorce me but he would find nothing there – no dirt to dish, no secret lover hiding like a skeleton in my wardrobe. There was, there had only ever been, one man in my life and that was Bill.

Then he backed down. He conceded, 'Look, I don't want a divorce any more than you do, Mandy. This is just a case of the lawyers being officious. The letter is merely a formality. I'll be home in a couple of weeks and we'll patch things up then.'

I believed him. I listened to him, I trusted him, I needed him and he was lying through his teeth to me.

I spoke to him once more on the phone a week later. He reassured me that things would be all right at Christmas when he came home. We would have a lovely family Christmas at Gedding Hall. Everything would be fine again. We could be together and finally start our married life properly. As it happened, nothing could have been further from the truth.

On 21 December, Bill flew back from New York, arriving at his flat around 8 pm at night. I waited, restless and excited, for the phone call that would say, 'Hi, honey, I'm home.'

But the phone did not ring.

Lying in bed, drained of energy, fighting the symptoms of PMS – even through the heat of my migraine, I could feel the searing pain of disappointment.

I called him first thing the next morning. His voice, still furred by jetlag and lack of sleep, still blurred by the Valium intake he had needed to get through the long flight, mumbled, 'Mandy, can you call back later? I'm still in bed.'

I did not call. I went round to see him, my husband of six months, in his own flat.

It was a very strained and tense reunion, as might be expected under the circumstances. Bill looked older, tired, thinner.

What did I look like? I was certainly not the glowing bride he had left five months before. I could see he was shocked by how thin I was but an admission of this would have meant a denial of all the accusations he had thrown at me over the phone for months and his utter disbelief over my condition.

Bill could not meet my gaze. His conversation was stilted. I began to wonder if there was more than straightforward guilt over the way I looked. There was guilt there all right. Did he have more to feel guilty about? Had there, let's say, been other women on tour? I knew his sex drive could never sustain a five-month abstinence and yet he had vowed he would be faithful. I really wanted to cling on to that belief. I dismissed all my suspicions. There was no point in being paranoid right now. I had Bill home. That was all I wanted.

I suggested we go out and do some Christmas shopping but, as we trudged along the streets of South Kensington, the festive spirit was only in evidence above and around us, in the shops festooned with glitter, the street lights draped with tinsel. We were further apart than ever. We talked small-talk, trivia, like a couple of strangers – the price of this gift, the prettiness of that, anything to fill the silence that said we are avoiding the issue of the state of our marriage.

The embers of too many hurtful things we had spat at each other over the past few months lay like smouldering coals, just waiting for another remark to fan them into a raging conflagration.

I wanted desperately to resolve the tension and awkwardness of the day. I thought that if, perhaps, we stayed in that night and had a nice quiet meal together, then we would begin to relax again in each other's company.

Bill had other plans. He was going to a party. On his own. He told me his staff had laid on a huge welcome home party for him that night at Sticky Fingers. Naturally, he said, if I really wanted to, I could go along and join him later.

I was flabbergasted but I knew nothing would budge Bill from his plan. He had to have his fix of London life again, knock back some bottles of bubbly with his chums, be the centre of attention, fêted and fawned over. That was far more vital to Bill's wellbeing than his marriage.

Piqued and wounded, I refused to let him see how this demonstration of his priorities had hurt me. I declined the offer and said I would rather pack our stuff and get ready for our trip down to Gedding next day.

There, at least, we would be together. Then maybe we could start to work on this relationship, maybe we could begin the marriage. Fool's paradise, Mandy.

*　　*　　*　　*　　*

The minute we walked in the door at Gedding Hall, I knew Christmas was going to be a disaster.

On Christmas Eve, Mum, Nicola and I drove down together, along with Nicola's friend Ross. Bill did not come to the door to greet us; only Carl and Connie, who were their usual cheerless selves.

They hated me. They saw Bill as their boss and ignored the fact that he had a wife. They had made no effort to decorate the house.

The previous housekeepers, Monique and Louis, had been so wonderful, so helpful and caring. They had always decorated the house with exquisite French flair, with beautiful table decorations, a huge tree with masses of fairy lights, scented candles everywhere, and always free-range chicken for Christmas dinner.

This year, there was a piddling little tree in the corner of one room. The place looked so bare that Mum and I decided to cheer it up a bit with some more decorations. Connie went mad. 'I suppose our decorations aren't up to your standards,' she snapped bitchily.

Mum said, quite kindly, 'Look, we're only trying to make the place look a bit brighter.'

Whereupon Connie retorted: 'So what's it got to do with you then? It's not your house.'

That was it in a nutshell. I believed they looked on Gedding as their own place. They had their own staff quarters but rarely ate in their own dining room it seemed, preferring the kitchen in the big house.

You could have cut the atmosphere with a knife.

When Bill wandered down from his room to investigate the raised voices, I discreetly took him to one side and spoke to him about it but his reaction was the same as ever. He shrugged it off. 'What can I do about it? The place looks all right to me.'

Dinner that evening was stilted, with an all-pervading atmosphere of Scrooge-like misery. There was no fun or laughter at the table. Frankly, no one felt like eating.

I ascended the stairs to Bill's bedroom with a heavy heart. I could never think of it as 'our' bedroom while the bachelor-style decor remained unchanged, just as I could never think of Gedding as 'our' home, when Bill would not give me a key nor even let me visit it without permission.

We shared a bed that night but nothing more. The unspoken tension between us was unbearable. I don't think either of us slept a wink. What we needed was to get our feelings out in the open and clear the air but I was scared of rowing with Bill after the way our last argument had been twisted and used against me.

We stumbled into Christmas Day, bleary with tiredness, reluctant even to bid one another good morning, never mind

Merry Christmas. It was not an auspicious start. Things only got worse when we exchanged presents. Bill's gift to me was a beautiful gold and diamond bracelet.

I could not fault his generosity until I discovered the spirit of meanness in which it had been given. Bill had not even bothered to look for a gift for me himself. He had delegated this boring duty to Nicola.

I felt deeply hurt by this. It was another reflection of how little he cared. Had he bothered to stop and think of what I actually liked and enjoyed, it would have meant more to me. I would have settled for a pair of fluffy bedsocks sooner than an anonymous Cartier bracelet, because a gift like that would have meant he had actually thought about me.

I said nothing but Bill knew I was offended. There was no point in explaining. So far as he was concerned, he had spent a bit of money on me so what was the problem? I was conscious of him giving me dirty looks all the time. Somehow he had managed to turn the entire situation around again so that it appeared to be me who was culpable, me who had created this atmosphere.

I wanted nothing more than to link my arm through his and snuggle up against him to watch TV, simply to share some moments of pure affection to break the ice, but I was terrified to do so, because I knew any move like that would be misconstrued by Bill. He saw any little tender touch as a pointer to only one thing, sex.

All those years of having my every physical gesture of affection interpreted as a precursor to a sex act had left me deeply scarred, unable to show any sign of warmth, even to those I care about. It is a scar that has stayed with me to this day.

Bill was my husband but I had spent only two days with him since our honeymoon. I had not had sex with him since our honeymoon.

I knew what was coming. Bad vibes or not, I dreaded the rapid approach of nightfall. I was scared of getting into bed with him. Petrified that if I refused sex, he would turn into the maniac who ranted and raved and masturbated all over me.

On that Christmas Day, however, the bad feeling that hung around all day was enough for Bill. That night, he made no attempt to make love to me. We slept, back to back, miles apart in every way. Then, in that miraculous way that sleep has, in the morning we woke as lovers do, all entwined round each other. That naked togetherness made us both feel a bit better. The ice started to melt and we both felt more optimistic on Boxing Day before I returned to London. Bill stayed behind in Gedding to do some work and we arranged to meet on his return to London on New Year's Eve.

1990 loomed. A new year, a new decade. Hopefully, a new start to my life as Mrs Wyman. Ever the romantic, I dreamt that Bill and I could toast our future together as we toasted ourselves in front of a cosy fire at his flat. In the background, Big Ben would peal out our hopes for the future as we kissed and fell into each other's arms. Some hopes.

Instead of a romantic night that would have helped to heal the rift between us, Bill insisted we go to Tramp where there would be a big party in full swing, with everybody throwing back champagne like there was no tomorrow. He wanted to avoid me, to run away from the situation. I refused to go.

So it was that we saw the New Year in apart. Bill knew where I was but there was no midnight phone call to wish me a Happy New Year. It was to be an omen for the future.

Bill was partying with a bevvy of girls around him. I later learned that he had picked one and taken her home to his bed.

I was at Mum's, sitting round the kitchen table toasting the new year with a cup of tea and the people who cared about me. Not my husband, but my family and a few friends. This was a marriage in name only.

In the end, as always, Bill won. It was I who gave in. I was desperate not to lose my marriage or Bill. He said sex was the root of our problem. I knew it was not but I figured that things had become so bad between us that if sex would help to sort them out, then we would have sex.

In my heart, I knew it was nonsense. Not wanting to have sex with Bill was only a symptom of what was wrong between us; it was certainly not the cause.

So I joined him once more at Gedding on a freezing winter weekend in January and we made love for the last time but it was not love. For Bill it was satiating his sexual desire. For me, it was an act in which I had my need for his arms around me fulfilled.

The next day Bill drove to France to prepare for the second, European leg of the Stones' world tour. We were to be apart for months yet again, and nothing had been resolved between us.

Given no access to 'our' homes, I would carry on living at home with Mum, looking for a cure for the illness that had now brought my weight down to just six stone.

Bill would carry on being a Rolling Stone, rocking and rolling and bedding other women, but he could no longer pull the wool over my eyes. This time, I was to find out that the man I had married was still, at heart, the playboy who had bedded a thousand women – and was hell-bent on bumping up the score.

CHAPTER NINETEEN

Nineteenth Nervous Breakdown

My weight and health continued to deteriorate in the weeks after Bill went back on tour. I was now hovering a few pounds under six stone.

I had turned into a virtual recluse. Lacking the strength or stamina to do more than walk painfully from bedroom to living-room, I was, in effect, housebound, if not rapidly becoming bedridden.

My only contact with the outside world was the sporadic phone calls to Bill as he embarked on the Stones tour of Japan. Of couse, Mum and Nic were always there, even though they were themelves being worn away to shadows in their concern for me.

We had finally managed to find a new home for Mum, a small, but pretty, three-bedroom detached home in Muswell Hill, north London, and had moved there in the spring. Because of my illness, I couldn't help much with the move but I was greatly cheered to see Mum happy and ensconced, finally, in a home she could call her own.

For years, she had been hounded by the press who camped on her doorstep day and night in their endless quest for a quote from her, or any member of my family. We would never give in but still they had kept banging on Mum's door.

Bill and I had one of our happier moments together just before Mum's move, when Bill flew back from Amsterdam to have a wisdom tooth extracted. He visited me for a couple of hours and we spent the time pelting a pack of newshounds with egg and flour bombs from Mum's first-floor windows.

However, that was the only moment of levity. For many months life had been no laughing matter for Mum, as the neighbours had persistently complained to the housing association. Ultimately, she had been edged out. At least now she had her very own doorstep on which the pack could park themselves.

Meanwhile, I was being bounced from one medical expert to another. They were all baffled by my symptoms and incessant decline in weight. Many plumped for the all-too-obvious diagnosis of anorexia. PMS did not figure in their diagnosis.

Others, the psychiatrists and psychologists whom Bill had called in to check on my mental health, said I was of extremely, sound mind, if not of body.

The one thing they all had in common was that none of them was willing to declare that my marriage was a contributory factor to my declining health.

It was far easier to plump for the obvious targets. 'A dependency problem on her mother,' said one damning indictment.

'An unhealthy and incestuous family relationship with mother and sister,' spat another, doubtless influenced by the public perception of the Smith family.

All I could do was thank God that I *did* have Mum and Nic to tend to me in my hour of need. Without them, I would have died.

I had made it clear that I didn't want to go into a hospital to be poked, prodded and subjected to infinite, and inconclusive, tests. I had tried that before. I was now five and a half stone and I'd had enough.

It looked for a while as if there was no way out of this mess. Then, out of the blue, I received a letter from a young man called Frank Lamprill. In it, he explained that he had read about my physical problems and was wondering if his mother, Dr Nadya Coates, could be of some assistance.

Dr Coates, he revealed, owned and ran the Springhill Centre in Aylesbury, where a highly qualified team specialised in looking after people with long-term illnesses, and especially – and this was what caught my eye – allergies.

He enclosed some colour brochures of the place, detailing the services on offer. I read all the brochures and immediately felt that it might be a good place for me, so I called them. After speaking to Frank on the phone a few times, I made up my mind to go down there in search of a cure. As it turned out, that was one of the worst decisions of my life.

It was 22 May 1990 when Mum, Nic and I drive to Springhill Centre. The journey down was a nightmare. I laid on the back seat, wrapped in blankets, feeling the agony of every bump.

The main house, where Dr Coates lived, was only a short walk away from the patient's chalets and the entire place was buried deep in the heart of the English countryside. It was spring, all the trees were in bud and, as soon as I set eyes on this tranquil place, I thought, 'Please God, let me find a cure here.'

Mum and I set about making the chalet as homely as possible. There was only one double bedroom and a set of bunkbeds. They were really uncomfortable, with hard, slatted wooden bases, particularly for me, because I was now so thin that all my bones protruded. Mum and I decided to sleep together in the double bed.

Whether it was the atmosphere of the place or the fact that I was sleeping like a little girl again, safe in the same bed as my mum, I felt an overwhelming sense of relief. Finally, I felt prepared to give in and let these people find out what was wrong with me. I stopped trying to fight. But something went terribly wrong.

Dr Coates visited me every day on her rounds and a specialist visited me once a week. They decided to put me on a specific gluten-free, fat-free, sugar-free diet but they warned me that, at first, I might get far worse before I got better.

They were right. Within weeks, I had dropped another half stone. I now weighed under five and a half stone and looked like a concentration camp victim. Those were truly desperate weeks. I was getting thinner and thinner by the day. There was no flesh left on me at all.

I'd look at myself in the mirror and break down in tears – great racking sobs that shook my bony frame to its very core.

Something as simple as having a bath became a nightmare, an exruciatingly painful experience. I was too weak to bath myself. Sitting there, looking at my bony body as Mum gently splashed me with water and washed me down, I became convinced I'd die.

On better days I might manage a stroll in the grounds with Mum. Once or twice I managed to venture up the road to the shops, but then I caught sight of myself in a shop window and the image of my full-length reflection in the glass made me stop short with shock.

Suddenly, my past life flashed before me. Those happy days

267

when Nicola and I would stroll down Wood Green High Street, cheeky little pre-teen nymphs in cut-off shorts and T-shirts, checking our hair in shop windows and laughing as all the office workers leaned out to wolf-whistle at us. Happy days, before I met Bill.

Now I was ugly. There was no denying the truth. All that was left of Mandy Smith was hair, elbows and kneecaps.

I felt that my heart, as well as my spirit, was broken. Back in the chalet I would sit brushing my hair and know that the end of the road could not be far off.

In the mirror I could see the faint outline of a gaunt, angular face that once used to be mine. And I'd think, 'How am I ever going to get better?'

I could barely even cry any more. I was all cried out.

The humiliations kept coming. As I grew weaker I couldn't even get up to go to the toilet. I had to use a bedpan and, even then, needed the help of Mum or Nic to slide myself on to it. It was a deeply degrading experience but, by then, I was almost past caring.

Frank was always around trying to help me but, in the end, he became a pain. It was like having a fan running around all the time. 'Can I do this for you, Mandy? Can I do that? Here, let me help you.'

In fact, his interfering often made me even more ill. He'd come over to the chalet and insist on cooking me food. I'd tell him exactly what I wanted because I knew what I could and couldn't have but he'd slip in extra ingredients behind my back.

Then, minutes later, when I'd start to react by coming up in a virulent rash or having palpitations, he'd panic and confess what he'd done. He'd be deeply apologetic, wringing his hands and pleading, 'I was only trying to help, Mandy. Sometimes we're not allergic to things we think we are. I just wanted to see if you would notice.'

I would lie there, perspiration forming in beads all over my brow, hives appearing all over my hands and feet, and think, 'Is this for real? His intentions may have been honest but it was bloody dangerous.

When I informed Nadya what Frank had done, she, too, was deeply apologetic and vowed it would never happen again. She confessed that, even in my emaciated state, Frank was still a bit in love with me.

She seemed very understanding and I decided to trust her, although, during those early weeks, she tried out various treatments on me.

She pumped me full of vitamins, simply to see what would happen. Any healthy person would have spent a week on the toilet after that, but not me. My body was so messed up by that stage that it actually had the reverse effect and I became horrifically constipated. My stomach distended so far that I looked like an African famine victim. My temperature shot through the roof as all the toxins in my intestines increased and blocked up.

I spent a whole night sitting up in bed shivering, shaking, on the verge of delirium. Next day I had to have a strong enema and, in the event, it took three full days before the vitamins were flushed out of my system.

The experiments went on and on, my weight fell off and off, and, with what few resources I had left, I began to think to myself that I should get out of Springhill.

The following day, however, Dr Coates came up with a diagnosis. 'Mandy,' she said, grasping the stethoscope around her neck and looking very grave indeed. 'I'm afraid you have Addison's Disease. 'But at least', she added, before I fainted, 'we know how to treat you. It is a treatable condition.'

She went on to explain that Addison's affected the adrenal gland and caused a malfunction that was the single cause of all my many and varied problems. If we could control the Addison's, we could whack the lot.

The most immense relief swept through me. At last someone had come up with a diagnosis other than anorexia. At last I knew I wasn't crazy.

Dr Coates immediately commenced an intensive course of treatment by putting me on a wholefood diet and prescribing a heavy-duty course of steroids. Within days the pounds were beginning to pile back on. There was a farm shop at the centre and soon I was their best customer, sending Mum off to pick up lots of goodies and tucking in daily to their fresh free-range eggs and home-baked bread.

It took a few weeks for me to regain the half stone I had

lost when I first entered Springhill but, finally, I reached the wonderful target of six stone. To celebrate, I decided to venture out of the chalet for the first time and walk over to the main house where the other patients met up during the day for therapy sessions.

That, in itself, was a massive step for me and I was scared stiff. I dressed, slowly and painfully, for I was still stiff after several weeks of bedridden inactivity. Then, with Nic's help, I walked out of the chalet, over to the house and stood looking at the fields that stretched before me as far as the eye could see.

'Oh God, Nic,' I said, close to tears, 'I'm so happy to be alive.'

It was a fantastic feeling to be out in the real world again. I didn't enjoy the walk, I was absolutely shattered by the sustained effort of taking a few steps but it was a real break-through. I felt triumphant.

After that momentous occasion, things seemed to get better and better. I started to go swimming every day and even managed to use the exercise trampoline in the gym.

There seemed to be no doubt about it, the steroids were working and my state of mind improved a hundredfold with each daily advance. I truly believed I was on the road to recovery.

One glorious day, I ventured out in my car for the first time in months and drove to the shops. Life was very definitely on the up. With one exception, my marriage to Bill.

I had been at the centre for almost two months and it was even longer since I had seen Bill. The week prior to my admission, Stephen had taken me to visit Bill at his Evelyn Gardens flat. Bill had driven over from Paris, where the Stones were rehearsing for their European tour, to spend a couple of days prior to the start of the tour in Rotterdam.

I wanted to wish him well on the tour but he was too busy to come and visit me. I had to go to him.

Stephen, deeply embarrassed by his father's gross insensitivity, had helped me into the car and driven me down to Evelyn Gardens. By the time we got there, I was feeling desperately car-sick from the traffic fumes. I knew I could not make it up the steep stairs to Bill's flat so Stephen had gone up to drag Bill downstairs to see me.

I sat in the car, grey, ashen and near-to-fainting but Bill was less than sympathetic. Turning to Stephen, and oblivious of me, Mum and Nicola sitting in the car, he said, 'Christ, she looks like she's got cancer.'

Stephen was so incensed that he got in the car, slammed the door and we drove off.

That had been my last contact with Bill while I lay at death's door for over two months.

He knew I had checked in there. He had handed Stephen his mobile phone so that I could call him on it as there was no phone line in the chalet. On my first call, however, we had argued violently and I told him not to contact me until I was better.

He took me at my word. Not only did he not call, he even ignored our first wedding anniversary on 5 June. Neither a card, nor flowers arrived.

Although I was very sick at that stage, I could not let a date like our anniversary slip by. The Stones were in Europe so I had sent a bouquet and a card to Bill's hotel in Holland.

Even then, he could not be bothered to call. He tried to tell me later that he could not find the phone number but it was *his* mobile phone . . .

I was terribly hurt, but Mum, living off her nerves and prayer, while trying to steer me through this crisis, was livid. She rang Stephen and got a number for Bill. Then she rang him and really let rip.

He must have had some pang of remorse because, a few days later, a bunch of flowers arrived for me but, by then, it was too late. Once again, the damage, had been done.

However, Bill did use this initial contact to his advantage. He began to have regular contact with Dr Coates, checking up on my condition. When she told him that she had confirmed Addison's Disease, he called Dr Kaye and had the disease checked out.

Dr Kaye immediately told him that there was no way I could have anything remotely like Addison's. He had treated me before and was one hundred per cent certain that there had been a misdiagnosis.

The situation was dangerous. Bill did not hang about. It was time he paid me a visit and, at the beginning of July, he came to see me for the first time in months.

He rolled through the entrance gates in his Mercedes, along with Stephen and a couple of minders, which was somewhat superfluous as no one was likely to mob him in the middle of nowhere in the English countryside, but Bill always liked to put on a good show.

I can't say I was thrilled to see him because I truly wasn't. I was hurt and angry at his total lack of concern and communication. He asked me how I was, a rather gratuitous question in the circumstances, as I weighed under six stone and looked it.

I felt he was only asking out of politeness. There seemed to be no genuine concern in his voice or his demeanour. Throughout it all, he never once removed his Raybans – Mr Cool, with all the bedside manner of a bedpan.

Mum tried to make things easier by suggesting to Stephen that they go for a walk together, leaving Bill and me alone.

We sat down and made polite chit-chat for a while. There was something I had to ask, something I had to know.

A few weeks earlier, a friend of ours had gone out to Germany to deliver a package sent from his office to Bill at his hotel. She got as far as his hotel bedroom when one of the Stones minders stopped her from going into his room. She knew Bill was in, because when she checked with reception they had told her to go on up and his key was not on the board. However, the minder was insistent that Bill was 'otherwise occupied' and could receive no visitors. She left the package and returned home, feeling I should know about this.

I decided to confront Bill. It was now or never.

Looking him straight in the eye, I said, 'Please don't lie to me, Bill. Were you seeing another woman in Germany?'

He met my unsteady gaze with his own. 'Yeah,' he said, unflinching. 'And I'll tell you why, Mandy. I did it because I don't feel married.'

I erupted. 'What a lame, pathetic excuse. You're my husband, for God's sake. What happened to all your promises of being faithful? I know we've had a hard time, but I can promise you I have never even entertained the notion of being unfaithful to you while you've been off all around the world.'

He did not even have the good grace to look guilty. He just looked at me and shrugged his shoulders. 'I don't consider myself married,' is all he could say. There was no apology.

Just an icy coldness in his eyes. I felt completely numb.

We sat there quietly for a while. I couldn't bring myself even to look at him. Then, silently, he got up and left. That visit was something less than a morale booster.

During the following week, we spoke on the phone a couple of times but the conversations always ended in rows. Try as I might, I could not get the vision of Bill in bed with another woman out of my mind.

Then, on 11 July he turned up again, without any prior warning.

It was obvious that this was an uncomfortable position for him to be in. It was a chore. He was restless and ill at ease. So, why then, had he come back? Possibly because the press had now discovered my hiding place and, more to the point, noted Bill's lack of visits.

We went out for a walk but talked very little. When we returned, we had a cup of tea and off he went again. Personally, although the feeling was obviously not reciprocated, by now I was glad to see him.

There was so much that I wanted to say to him but I was so weak and my head was so mixed up that I just kept it all bottled up inside. Any true husband would have noticed my confusion and my dilemma. Yet all Bill could do was contribute to my unhappiness by informing me that he was sleeping around and then leaving me to think about it.

He visited me on one more occasion: 17 July, my twentieth birthday.

I'd decided to make an extra-special effort for that day and Mum helped me to have a bath. I even shaved under my arms, which was a pretty difficult exercise, because I was so thin, my armpits had almost disappeared.

I dressed in some nice clothes rather than the shapeless sweat-shirts and baggy leggings I had lived in for months and, for the first time in ages, put on some make-up.

When Bill finally arrived, Mum looked at me proudly and said, 'Doesn't she look well, Bill?'

Bill's response was to turn to her and retort, 'No, she doesn't,' as if I wasn't even there.

In some way, perhaps, I wasn't all there. Because I was so fazed out with all the effort of getting ready, the comment just washed over me. I didn't react to it at all.

Bill presented me with three cards and a bracelet that looked astonishingly familiar, as well it might, as it was identical to the one he had already bought me for Christmas. Fair enough, it was a lovely bracelet but the thought struck me, 'Why has he bought me two? Has he forgotten what he bought me before? Did he get a discount on a job lot?'

I was wasting my energy. The simple truth was that he didn't care. He just knew that he had to get me something. However, I certainly was not going to be so ungracious as not to thank him. Then we set off for the big house where Nadya, in preparation for Bill's arrival, and by way of a birthday treat for me, had organised a celebratory lunch.

Bill sauntered by my side, looking nonchalant and still wearing his rock star shades. He strolled into the house, completely ignoring all the assembled guests, the staff and the other patients.

Nadya directed him to his seat and he turned round petulantly, saying, 'I don't want to sit there. I want to sit over there, on that other seat.'

To everyone's amazement, here was this Rolling Stone behaving like a spoilt child. He then turned to Stephen and I heard him mutter, 'I can't stand all this. I've got to get out of here.' I couldn't believe what I was hearing. Impulsively, I told him, straight out, to shut up and sit down. Amazingly, he did.

For the next half-hour, Bill didn't say a single word. He just sat there, sulking and picking at his food. After a while I'd had enough. Folding my napkin, I rose from the table, excused myself and left the house.

There, on the grass outside, I sat down and started to cry. I'd made an effort, God knows why after the other two visits, and so had Nadya and all the other guests, yet here was Bill playing Mr Rolling Stones with his superior air, dark glasses and selfish moods.

I sat there sobbing quietly for a while, thinking, 'He's going to come in a second. He's sure to come out.'

He didn't. Eventually Nicola came out and put her arm around me. She comforted me and told me to pull myself together. As I walked back into the house, Bill looked at me and said, 'You all right then?'

I sat down and wiped the tears from my face. There was a really tense atmosphere in the room by this stage but suddenly Bill's mood changed. He started cracking jokes, being the life and soul of the party. It was a complete turn-around. Perhaps, for once, he actually felt guilty.

Everyone started to laugh at his jokes and his antics and, in the end, I was smiling too. I should have told him to get lost but I was just desperate to smile.

As we left the house, Bill took me conspiratorily to one side and told me to stuff a balloon up my top. Outside, in practically every tree top within spitting distance, there were photographers with long lenses looking down into the centre, desperate to capture a picture of me. Bill knew, as I did, that they were keenest to snatch a picture of Bill and me together.

He said, 'Let's give them a real one to think about. I arrive and five minutes later you emerge looking six months pregnant!'

He was on fine form by then and we fell about laughing at the thought of this unprintable picture.

Still, when Bill left, I felt a curious sense of relief. We'd laughed together but that was superficial. He had still done nothing to repair the damage. When I look back on it all now, I often wonder if Bill was only coming to visit me because his lawyers told him to. He was certainly talking to his lawyer, Paddy Grafton Green, long before I went into Springhill. Bill obviously had divorce on his mind then and was protecting himself. Those three visits gave the impression that he was a dutiful husband when, in fact, they did me more harm than good.

However, the important thing was that Fleet Street snapped those precious moments on camera and duly reported them to the world. Enter Bill Wyman, Mr Clean, visiting his poor sick wife. That would do nicely, thank you.

* * * * *

My life at Springhill continued as usual. I kept taking the steroids until, one day, I noticed that my legs had swollen up. My ankles were the size of an elephant's and ached terribly.

The next morning my feet had swollen, too. I called for Nadya and she told me it was simply the heat. This was a long, hot summer, after all, and if I were to go for a walk, my circulation would get going again and everything would be fine.

When she left, I looked at my bottle of steroid pills and, for some reason, I decided not to take another.

Even at the very moment I was thinking I could not put one more pill in my mouth, my mother was up at the big house where Dr Coates lived. Unbeknown to me, a farce had developed beyond anything that Brian Rix could ever have dreamed up.

Nadya had fallen down the stairs and managed to do herself some quite serious damage. She gashed herself rather badly and the end result was that an ambulance had been summoned and was already on its way, sirens blaring.

Stumbling in on this incredible scene, Mum had done her duty as guardian angel and minded Dr Coates until help arrived.

When Nadya had been reassured and made comfortable by her own nurses, Mum had rushed back down to the chalet to inform me of these incredible goings on – and found me gone. I had left her a note on the kitchen table, I'd scribbled down something along the lines of: 'I can't go on. The steroids are killing me and I know I'm going to die. Please help me, Mum.' Then I had walked up the hill to die.

Completely unaware of what was happening over at the house, I had staggered across the grass to sit under a tree. I was more depressed than I had ever been in my entire life. I felt, in my heart of hearts, ready to shuffle off this mortal coil.

For some inexplicable and bizarre reason, I had taken a bar of chocolate – something I was absolutely banned from eating – with me on my journey to death.

I think I saw it as some kind of ridiculous suicide weapon. Some people use guns, some ropes and others poison but I was always different. I was going for death by chocolate.

As I lay in the long grass, gazing at the sky and thinking that very, very soon I was going to breathe my last, an apparition suddenly appeared, hovering over me. It was Mum. She immediately knelt down, linked elbows with me and helped me to my feet before leading me back down to the chalet. It's a funny old thing, fate, because, just as she struggled in the door, half-dragging, half-carrying me, the phone rang. It was Bill, calling from Rome where the Stones were now on tour. Mum told him straight, 'Bill, Mandy is dying. Get an ambulance over now.' Then she slammed the phone down and hurriedly began to pack a few essentials for me – pills, potions, nightshirt, toothbrush – but before she had even finished we heard the wail of sirens in the distance and knew that an ambulance was on its way.

I was slumped on the bed, gasping for breath. My chest felt like it was being compressed by an iron band and I was gasping for air. Mum sat me up and I tried to concentrate on breathing. Then an ambulance roared up and, to Mum's astonishment, pulled up outside the big house. Within seconds, Nadya was being stretchered out by two burly medics and gently placed in the ambulance. She had a large surgical collar round her neck.

The whole situation would have been hilarious if it hadn't been so serious.

Minutes later *my* ambulance from the Cromwell arrived. By this time, my feet had swollen up to the size and texture of sandbags and were rapidly turning blue.

The ambulancemen strapped me into a wheelchair, loaded me on board and Mum jumped in the back with me. Then the never-ending journey to London began.

I truly never thought I would make it. My breathing started to falter and one of the medics, his hand on my pulse, decided the only course of action was oxygen – and quickly.

He hurriedly placed a mask over my nose and mouth and told me to breathe deeply. I felt myself slipping into unconsciousness and the last thing I remember was his big kindly face looking down on me and the mask being strapped over my ears.

CHAPTER TWENTY

Crackin' Up

As soon as the ambulance arrived at the Cromwell, they rushed me straight up to the renal unit on a stretcher. They took me to a little room by the nurses' station and lifted me into bed. I couldn't move by myself. I was in a daze, drifting in and out of consciousness. A nurse took my temperature and blood pressure, then Dr Kaye came to see me.

I was so glad to see him. I was sobbing, repeating over and over, 'What's wrong with me? Please tell me what's wrong with me. Please, please help me.'

I could see he was shocked at my appearance. I was wearing cotton dungarees and a T-shirt and they were hanging off me.

He said very calmly, 'Well, we've got to do something, haven't we, Mandy? We'll start by doing some tests.' Then he took Mum to one side and, just out of my earshot, told her I was at death's door. He was very solemn as he said, 'Patsy, two more days and she would have gone. Please God she doesn't catch anything. If she gets a virus now, a cold – anything – she'll be blown away.'

To me, he said nothing of this. Simply, 'We've all got to work very hard to get you well, Mandy. And we're starting right now. Tomorrow, you have to decide if you can eat, or else we will have to feed you intravenously. The choice is yours.'

I weighed seventy-two pounds. Every bone in my body stuck out. Every nerve ending in me ached. My arms and legs felt like they weighed half a ton. My feet and ankles were swollen like barrage balloons.

Yet I could not eat. I simply couldn't get my throat to swallow. The thought of food made me feel ill, but I desperately did not want to be wired up to drips and I desperately wanted to live.

I promised Dr Kaye I would eat. That night and next day, they ran every conceivable medical test on me. They discovered I had circulation problems, breathing problems, my blood was not clotting and I had toxins in my blood from steroid poisoning. My immunity was at rock bottom.

Only Dr Kaye could take blood from me. The nurses were too scared to stick a needle in me. There was no flesh on me at all. I was like a rag doll with holes all over my arms because I had had so many tests.

Suddenly, I developed a terrible allergic reaction. My skin flared up and itched furiously. It was as if every inch of me was on fire. I was sensitive to the starch in the hospital sheets. They rushed me to another bed and changed the bedding from the white cotton covers to soft pink ones.

There were several panics like that. I flared up at the slightest thing, even a slight change in room temperature.

The most important thing, however, was for me to eat. I couldn't manage a single morsel the first day, so they spoon-fed me a build-up drink, full of protein. After that, I managed to force down a few spoonfuls of cereal, then some rice. I had made the breakthrough.

Dr Kaye devised a massively high-calorie, high-protein drink for me. He would not tell me what was in it. He said only: 'If you want to stay alive, you will drink it.' He warned me that there would be horrific side effects and there were. Everytime something touched my skin, it left a huge and deep indentation in it. It was quite astounding. I was like a cushion. However, the magic potion worked. I had to drink it three times a day, plus eating regular meals.

Although it was a complete shock to my system, I worked very hard at eating. I tried to cram in as much food as possible. I so much wanted to get well.

For breakfast I would have three slices of toast, two eggs, fruit juice and prunes. The nurses got terribly concerned because I was actually eating too much and my digestive system was overloading. I did not care. If I could eat, I would live.

It worked. I put on weight rapidly but I could hardly move. I was stuffing in so much food that I was weighed down. All I could do was eat and lie in bed all day.

I knew everyone was convinced I had anorexia. I knew nothing I could say would dissuade them but I did not care any more. All I wanted was to get well. Let them think what they wanted.

They would watch my every move. I had a bathroom and toilet adjoining my bedroom and there was a mirror on the wall so that, when the door of the bathroom was left open, I could see the nurses' station.

It did not take me long to fathom that this also meant they could see me. There was to be no privacy, no hiding place. If I ever closed the door to go to the toilet, they were out there, banging on the door, saying, 'Mandy are you all right in there?'

Obviously they wanted to know if I was sticking my fingers down my throat, which I most certainly was not. I was not, nor had I ever been, bulimic, anorexic or suffering from any eating disorder. I knew plenty about these afflictions because I had been labelled with each and every one of them on many occasions.

The experts differed, swinging from one diagnosis to another, but largely coming down in favour of anorexia, probably with bulimic tendencies, just to be on the safe side.

I had long lost count of the occasions I had cried myself to sleep, screaming inside my head, 'Why won't they believe I am not anorexic?' I had long since given that up as a futile exercise. I knew that what I had was food sensitivities, not eating disorders. Mine was a physical, not a psychological reaction. Let them believe what they wanted. If they couldn't help me anyway, what did it matter?

Here in the Cromwell, however, it was different. I felt comfortable here. I liked the staff. I felt secure and on the road to recovery. I did not want to bang my head against a brick wall to persuade them I was neither anorexic nor bulimic. They were living alongside me, keeping me under a twenty-four hour guard, watching my every move. They could see it for themselves, provided I kept the toilet door open.

I became the fastest pee-er in the west. I used to be in and out of that toilet like a shot.

They did not need convincing for long, though. They could see I was improving daily and, as they got to know me, they understood that I was not trying to make myself ill.

I genuinely wanted to be strong, healthy and normal again. I had been knocking on death's door and I didn't want to be there ever again, thank you. Not until I was ninety years old, anyway.

Despite the rules and regulations, far from being a prison-like environment, the hospital was a very friendly place. There was a genuine warmth between staff and patients, with everyone concerned for everyone else's welfare. I became especially close to two nurses, Chris and Marion. We would spend hours talking about our lives and they were full of constructive advice on how to handle relationships.

Even the cleaning staff were part of the team. One of the domestics in particular, Ann-Marie, was a real laugh. At meal times, she would wheel me up and down the ward on the front of the food trolley, doling out lunch trays to the patients, all served up with double helpings of raucous laughter.

She was entranced by my wardrobe. Spending all day in a frumpy bri-nylon uniform, she said, made her want to transform herself into a butterfly when she was off-duty. My clothes, young, bright and glittery, fitted the bill perfectly.

She was forever asking to try on my clothes. She always wore stockings and suspenders and, when she came into my room, she would doff her overall and dive into my clothes like they were her last meal on earth. Then she would hoik up one of my already short skirts right up over her thighs, flash her suspenders and mimic, ''Ere, Bill, what do you want an ugly bird like Mandy for when you could have gorgeous me?'

She had us all in fits. It became a regular routine, Ann-Marie queening it in my clothes, sashaying up and down the corridors... until, one day, she was doing her tarty act when Bill actually walked round the corner. She nearly died.

Bill, of course, was nonplussed, but the rest of us did have a laugh. It was so lovely to be able to laugh again. I had been so unhappy, so despondent and so sick for so long, I had honestly believed I would never smile again.

Bill's first visit came as a complete surprise, not just to Ann-Marie, but also to me. He had made no prior mention of it. He just turned up. He made me feel as if he was doing me a big favour, simply being there.

His first words to me were: 'I was actually thinking of having a holiday, but I suppose that's out of the window now, with you in here.'

In all my months in hospital, Bill never once enquired about, nor discussed, my condition. I used to wonder if it was simply that he did not want to know about things he could not understand.

Bill's insensitivity and ignorance could not have been more clearly displayed than during one of his evening visits not long after I'd been admitted.

We were lying on the bed watching TV. I was under the covers and Bill was propped up next to me.

It had been a lovely night, just the two of us alone, chatting and cuddling.

Suddenly Bill jumped off the bed, kicked off his boots and dived under the covers, sniggering, 'Come on Mandy, let's have a proper cuddle then.'

He pushed himself up against me and started to touch and stroke me in a way that I recognised all too well.

My body froze and after a few seconds Bill realised that I just wasn't interested. Even if I had been interested I wouldn't have been capable. I was still riddled with infections and I weighed six stone. Neither fact, of course, had occurred to my husband.

Luckily, the doctors were more sympathetic. Dr Kaye came to see me every day. I felt he had become a personal friend over the years I had spent with Bill. He would sit down by my bedside for about an hour and ask me how I felt, not just physically, but emotionally too.

I poured my heart out and let him in on everything about my life: how things were between Bill and me; how my family were the only ones who had ever been there for me; how I felt deceived, rejected and abandoned by the man who was supposed to be my loving husband – all the things I had kept bottled up over all my years with Bill, all the feelings I had never had the vocabulary for, nor the grasp of, until now.

Dr Kaye listened sympathetically and made silent notes but he never passed judgement. He was a counsellor, not a lecturer.

In talking to him, in letting it all out, I could feel myself growing in strength, mentally and emotionally. Coupled with the vast improvement in my physical condition, I felt that, finally, I was going from strength to strength.

Many of my friends rallied round and came to visit me.

Bros star Matt Goss was especially kind. He rang me all the

time and was a great shoulder to cry on. Cliff Richard, too, was a source of great solace. When he sent me two books that he personally recommended and which had got him through times of crisis, I broke down and wept at his generosity of spirit, his love and kindness.

Then there was dear, sweet Terence Trent d'Arby, who had gained a reputation as standoffish and arrogant. Terence sent me notes which touched my heart and gave me strength.

Even Mark Shaw, whose advances I had rejected all those years before, sent huge bouquets of flowers and get well cards. All their love and friendship helped me through those black days and nights.

Bill, however, was not given to kindly gestures. He was unhappy about me being in the Cromwell, right from the off. On the first day he rang me in a raging fury, ranting on about some insurance forms. It seemed that his private medical insurance did not cover me. He had discovered that while I was at Springhill and had asked me to fill in the appropriate forms so that I would be covered in future. Karen had sent them to me, I filled them in and sent them back to him but it seemed that they had gone missing. He had then sent me another lot but I never got them. So it transpired that I was not covered by his medical insurance and Bill was having to foot the bill.

I could not believe his attitude. I had been pulled back from the brink of death by treatment at this hospital. The specialist himself had confirmed that I would otherwise have died within days. And my husband was quibbling over medical forms.

When he came to see me, it was a duty, not a gesture of love or care. He had made it obvious by now that I was a burden to him and not just a financial one. I found that out over some scones and a loaf of bread.

The whole episode arose one Sunday, when I was seized by an overwhelming craving for scones and jam. It may sound bizarre but when you have been unable to face food for months, then suddenly realise you can eat again, a whole world of pleasure is opened up to you. When the urge for a certain taste strikes, there is no quelling it.

I imagine it is akin to being pregnant and having insatiable desires for lumps of coal or bits of chalk. You have to have this thing you crave, and you have to have it *now* – bit like Bill and sex, really. . .

So there I was one afternoon when a vision of scones and jam implanted itself in my brain. I could not budge it. I could see them on a plate in front of me – soft, crumbly, powdery scones that melted in the mouth, topped with lashings of home-made jam. Yum.

Where on earth was I going to get them on a Sunday in hospital? Then I had a stroke of genius. Bill was staying at the Savoy Hotel at the time and was due to visit me later in the afternoon. Hotels always serve afternoon teas. We could ring Bill and ask him to bring a couple of scones for me.

So Mum did just that, expecting Bill to say sure, no prob- lem. How silly of us. He went berserk. He was furious. He screeched at Mum, 'Where do you think I am going to get f****** scones from?'

Very calmly and collectedly, Mum said, 'From room service, Bill. Or try the restauraunt, or the tearoom. Bill, all hotels have scones for tea.'

Yet Bill was enraged that he should have to do something for someone else. Anyone who cared about a patient who was ill in hospital would not have minded doing that for them. It was a very minor request and so easy for Bill, currently a resident in a top hotel. But that was typical Bill. You could never, ever ask him to do anything for you. You were always expected to wait hand and foot on him, not the other way round.

However, in the end he gave in, with extremely bad grace. He arrived, as late as possible, well after visiting time, with a face like thunder and a paper bag in his hand. He threw it across the room at me and snarled, 'Here's your bloody scones.'

Inside were two worse-for-wear scones, a tiny room service pot of jam and a plastic knife. You would have thought I had asked for the moon.

It was a salutary lesson and one for which I should not have been unprepared, given that I had spent long enough with Bill to know how he operated on a 'me first, last and only' axis.

I only ever made one more request of him. I was allergic to the preservatives in ordinary bread but a friend had found an organic wholemeal loaf in Harrods that I could eat without having a violent allergic reaction. It was lovely, like manna from heaven. Immediately I rang Bill's office and asked Karen, who shopped in Harrods every day, to pick me up a loaf when she next popped in there.

She refused point blank, saying she was just too busy, as did her assistant, Sally Ann. So did Bill, naturally enough. I was left in no doubt that they thought I had a bloody cheek. As Karen put it to me, 'What's wrong with hospital bread. Why can't you eat that?'

I didn't bother explaining. The point was, none of them could be bothered doing anything for me.

In my whole time in hospital, seven months in all, not one of Bill's staff ever sent me a card, a letter, a bunch of flowers or came to visit me. There was just one occasion, when Karen was forced to come to the Cromwell to pick up Bill en route to a party at Sticky Fingers. Bill would not normally have put a damper on one of his fun nights out by visiting me on the same day, but this was a special occasion – his birthday, his party. He wanted to look his best, so he stopped off at the hospital so that I could do his hair for him.

The scene was farcical, like an emblem of our marriage. There he was, all dressed up for his fifty-fourth birthday party and I was in my bed, wearing a regulation gown, confined to four blank walls, doing his hair.

I did not object to that, nor did I think Bill was being a cheapskate in avoiding a hairstylist's fee. He had always liked me to do his hair; he felt I had a flair for it. Also, I knew all his most intimate secrets about hair dye and balding spots.

Then in breezed Karen, whom I had not seen for months. She sauntered into the room, said airily, 'Hi, how are you? You do look better. Come on then Bill, we'd better be on our way,' then wafted out again with a sheepish Bill in tow.

I was dumbstruck. I looked better than what? She had not seen me for six months. How did she know what I looked like at death's door?

Being in hospital really made the scales fall from my eyes. I saw everyone around Bill in their true colours. Nobody was in the least bit interested in me or, I now came to realise, Bill, for that matter.

However, I was steadily improving, there was no doubt about that, and, oddly enough, so was the relationship between Bill and me. Or so it seemed, because suddenly, on one visit, he suggested that we live together on my discharge from hospital.

This really was a surprise. He had adamantly retained his bachelor status while I had been ill – for over a year now. I was immediately and immensely cheered by the suggestion. Married life at last! As always, however, there were strings attached.

He added: 'If you ever go back to stay with your mother, I don't care how long it's for, a day, a week, a month, then we're through. The marriage is over.'

This posed a small problem. Where else was I supposed to go? Bill had made it clear that his Evelyn Gardens flat was his bachelor pad. I did not even have a key to it. Gedding Hall was his country house, not his home. Where exactly did I fit in?

'Are you suggesting we actually buy a house and make a home for ourselves, as Mr and Mrs?' I queried, still in some state of shock and confusion.

'More or less,' he said non-commitally.

It was good enough for me. So I said, 'OK, well we had better start looking then.'

I wanted to live in north London, which I knew well, although I did not mind if Bill wanted to stick nearer the West End, which was his favourite stamping ground. Bill agreed. He said we would look at properties in both north and west London. If we found the right house, then we would buy it, whichever of those locations it was in.

A few days later, I rang round some London-based estate agents and asked to be sent house details. It was the magic shot in the arm that I needed. I really began to look forward to coming out of hospital and having a home of our own at last. Mum, Nicola and I spent a couple of afternoons visiting some lovely houses in Hampstead. We even went to Bishop's Avenue, the north London equivalent of millionaires' row – and thereby walked into yet another massive marital dispute.

We had simply visited Bishop's Avenue to have a look. I never for a second dreamt we would move there – but I reckoned, what the heck, I'd never get another chance to take a look at houses in a street like that.

That was my big mistake. Some newspapers got wind of the

fact that I had been to Bishop's Avenue and printed a story on it. Naturally, this did not go past Bill with his eagle eye for cutting out every newspaper clipping that had anything remotely to do with him.

He hit the proverbial roof. He read me the riot act, demanding to know what I thought I was doing, what I thought he was made of, gold-dust or something? And he generally accused me of being a spoilt cow.

Nothing I could say made any difference. Again, I was the one who was culpable, I was the bad girl, wicked child, in need of a smack. I took the only possible course of action in such circumstances with Bill, and left him to calm down.

Bill's method of revenge in a situation like that was to exert his supreme power. A few days later, he informed me that he had found a fabulous place in the West End and insisted I should come and see it with him immediately.

He came to the hospital, picked me up and we drove over to view a gorgeous penthouse in Chelsea. It was the top-floor conversion of a magnificent home; it really was stunning and the views over central London were breathtaking. It was lovely but I was not sure if it would ever make a family home. It was more like the London base of a high-flying business executive.

I arranged to have a second viewing a few days later, with Mum and Nic, and, at the same time, we took a peek at the rest of the house, which had been converted into showhouse flats.

Ten days later Bill told me the decision had been made. He had bought it. I was stunned to say the least. He had not bothered to consult me at all. Then I realised the truth. It was obvious he never intended it to be our family home at all.

He then informed me of the house rules: 'You can have one room. You can decorate it as you want. The rest is staying just the way it is and I am moving my own furniture into it.'

Basically, it was to be Bill's bachelor pad mark two and I had no place in it. At that moment I knew I was no longer part of Bill's life. He could not even be bothered with the charade any more.

From those foundations, Bill began building the bridge that would take him across the troubled waters of our marriage and away from me, preferably without a backward glance.

I knew it in my heart, I could see it happening, every inch and brick of the way, but I could not bring myself to admit it, nor to discuss it with him. It was too painful by far.

He took the next step along the way when he informed me that he would be bringing his computer into the hospital so that he could sit and work while he visited me, rather than just sit there doing nothing. It was only a matter of time before he pulled the plug on me altogether. All I could do was watch and wait and build up my strength for the inevitable parting of the ways.

A few weeks later, as soon as my weight had gone up to a respectable seven stone and I was officially off the danger list and on the path to health, it happened.

Because he was incorrigibly unconfrontational, Bill, as usual, got someone else to help him. This time, it was the man I had come to love and trust, not only as the person who had saved my life, but as a friend and confidante, Dr Georges Kaye.

It was early in October and I had been resident in the Cromwell Hospital for over two months. I weighed around seven stone, enough for Bill to want me discharged. Every time he looked at me, I could see the pound signs flashing in front of his eyes. He was footing the bill. It was making him a very sick man indeed.

The medical staff and I all knew I was not physically fit enough to leave yet, but Bill had made up his mind.

Mum was the most vociferous campaigner for me to stay in the hospital until I had fully recuperated. She, alone, had nursed me through the bleakest, blackest hours of my illness. She, more than anyone, knew how easy it might be for me to slip back down that road unless I had full-time medical supervision for as long as it took.

Bill saw Mum as the great threat to his bank balance. He had to get rid of her. She was still spending most of her time in helping to nurse me at the hospital. She was still sleeping in a separate bed in my room at night when she occasionally went home, Nick or Aunt Pauline stayed with me.

Bill decided that, in order for me to leave the hospital, I must first be separated from the influence of my mum. He didn't hang about. He phoned Dr Kaye and told him he wanted Mum out of the Cromwell.

Dr Kaye came into my room to talk to Mum and me. It must have been a pretty unpleasant task that Bill had apportioned to him, because he went all round the houses before he got to the point. He first used some spurious excuse about Mum having a rash on her hands. It would not do for Mandy, poor allergic little soul, to catch that nasty condition. I tried to explain that Mum had suffered from the problem for years but it had never affected me because, in fact, it was nervous excema and wholly non-contagious.

He just shrugged his shoulders and said, 'I really think it would be better if your mum left.'

I was enraged. He was right about one thing, however. Mum *was* my main support in life and there was a very good reason for that, because my husband had never been a husband in anything more than name. He had never been there for me to lean on, confide in, care about or share with.

I rang Bill that night and told him what Dr Kaye had suggested. I added that I had, naturally, declined the suggestion. Mum was staying put. As usual, Bill feigned total disinterest, as if he had had no prior knowledge of it whatsoever and the conversation deteriorated from then on. Round One to Mandy.

However, I lost the next battle. About a week later, Bill came to see me at about 10 pm, way beyond visiting time. We sat together in my room amid the peculiar silence that only a hospital asleep at night possesses, and the talk was of divorce.

Still stung by his underhand method of trying to evict my mother, who had nursed me through my blackest hours. I told him unequivocally that our marriage was not working in the way that a proper marriage should. There were problems that we had to sort out if it was ever to work properly.

Instead of trying to find a solution, to air his grievances and to take a look at those problems, Bill's immediate rejoinder was: 'So you want a divorce then. Fine. No problem.' And he got up and walked out. Leaving me aghast with the realisation that he had managed to turn the situation on its head yet again and construe it as: 'Mandy asked for a divorce'.

That was precisely how he was later to use it in court.

Over the next couple of days, we spoke only on the phone. He'd upset me so much that I couldn't cope with seeing him in person. Then he dropped his next bombshell. He had arranged

290

for me to see a psychiatrist, Dr Jeannie Speirs.

However, Bill knew I would never agree to be labelled as in need of a shrink, not without a bit of co-operation from him. So he, too, would sit in on the sessions. It would be like marital counselling. The psychiatrist would assess both of us simultaneously; help us along the road to a better understanding of one another.

I would buy that. I had long wanted to know why, when I loved him so much, he treated me like dirt under his shoe by exerting the most manipulative and destructive kind of emotional blackmail over me.

We arranged an appointment. Dr Speirs asked us both a lot of questions about how we felt for one another and whether we thought we could live together once I left hospital.

Bill was first into the breach, confessing how much he was suffering, how my behaviour had ruined his life. His life? Excuse me. I just sat there thinking, 'You selfish sod.'

Dr Speirs was very understanding and made some suggestions about us spending more time together, discussing our differences with honesty and openness, which I was happy to go through with. Bill grudgingly agreed but I could see that his heart wasn't in it.

That session clarified at least one issue for me. It proved to me that, despite everything he'd done, I still wanted to be with Bill, I wanted to be his wife. So maybe I *was* nuts after all.

I still carried around a pronounced insecurity, deepseated in me from my early childhood. Being with Bill had not alleviated that. It had exacerbated it.

Instead of saying, 'I can't wait until you're out of hospital' he would say, 'If you don't come to live with me when you leave I'm divorcing you.'

He was blackmailing me. I, in turn, had made myself easy prey for blackmail because I loved him. I hated myself for it. I hated him for it. I gave him a hard time over it, but at the end of the day I had fallen in love with him at the age of 13.

After seeing Dr Speirs, we decided that we would give it another go but, deep down, I knew that it was all over. We were both carrying much too much emotional baggage and scar tissue from old war wounds that we had inflicted on one another.

It was early in November when Dr Kaye came to see me in my room, on a special visit outside his normal rounds. He seemed very concerned and chatted about my general health first of all. He explained that I was still some way from a full recovery. Then he asked me how the situation was with Bill. I told him about the recent rows and how devastated I felt when they were not resolved.

Dr Kaye gently touched my hand and said: 'Mandy, you'll never be well until you leave Bill.'

Sorry? Was I hearing right? Were doctors supposed to make comments on the prognosis of your marriage? Surely, if you're ill you need the support of your partner. The last thing you want is the pressure of a divorce.

Dr Kaye did not pause. Quietly, but firmly, he continued to explain how certain relationships were destructive. I sat open-mouthed, listening to this monologue.

He finished by recommending a solicitor to me.

On 9 November Bill rang to tell me that he was sick and tired of paying the hospital bills and that I couldn't expect him to foot the cost for much longer. He informed me he would continue paying my £1,000 a month 'marriage allowance' (a.k.a wife's pay packet) but that was it. Anything else was down to me.

After he'd finished dictating these terms to me, the phone went down. No regrets, no emotion, just finances. Bill didn't want to discuss us or our future. He didn't even want to know how I was. After that body blow, I picked myself up and rang him, again and again. He did not want to know. It was over as far as he was concerned. I had to get out of the hospital. Each call was the same. Those were the last times I ever spoke to Bill outside a courtroom.

*   *   *   *   *

On 20 November the confirmation of Bill's plans arrived in a letter handed to me by Dr Kaye.

Looking extremely embarrassed by the whole situation, he passed me an envelope with 'Mrs Wyman' scrawled on the front. I opened it and slowly read it through. It was a formal notification of the divorce.

Reading the words in black and white, I felt numb, unreal, as if I was the central figure in a play. This was happening to someone else, not me. I had never envisaged things this way. I'd always thought that there would be some prior discussion, consultation... not just being handed a letter out of the blue by my own doctor.

Later that day, the solicitor who had been recommended to me arrived to talk to me. He decided that I should turn the tables on Bill and divorce him. I told him that Bill had admitted being unfaithful and he therefore advised me to divorce on the grounds of adultery. As he talked me through the paperwork, I merely nodded at all his suggestions. I was in a daze as the enormity of it finally hit me.

A few days later Dr Kaye suggested that I should leave the Cromwell before Christmas. He admitted to Mum that he still didn't know what was wrong with me (although he would later diagnose that I was anorexic) and he said there wasn't a doctor in London who could treat me. He added that my health would most likely deteriorate again, as I was sensitive and susceptible to the kind of pain and pressure that a protracted divorce case would bring but there was nothing more he could do.

I appreciated his honesty in the face of all the lies I had been spun. I mustered what remained of my dignity and said, 'Don't worry. I'm off anyway.' I packed my bags and, on 13 December, I was discharged.

I had survived an illness that reduced me to five stone. I had survived a marriage that reduced me to a quivering emotional wreck. I had proved to myself and all the experts that, against stacked odds, I was a survivor.

However, the worst was yet to come.

CHAPTER TWENTY-ONE

Hey, You, Get off my Cloud

I was granted my decree nisi, on the grounds of Bill's adultery, at the High Court in London on 8 May 1991.

I did not attend the court hearing myself, but a letter from Bill's laywers, proclaiming the divorce, was delivered by hand to my house later that day. Paradoxically enough, it was addressed to Mrs M. Wyman.

Seeing that name scrawled on the envelope in barely legible handwriting, my reaction was one of intense pleasure. I thought, 'No one will ever call me Mrs Wyman again. Now I am free to be me, Mandy Smith.'

However, I was not free yet. The ties that bound me to Bill were to carry on strangling me for months to come.

The letter also informed me that there would be a settlement hearing and that Bill would fight for everything. I knew Bill only too well. He would begrudge me every single penny. Things were ever thus, even during our marriage. After all I'd been through, my toughest year still lay ahead.

From that point until the hearing – for which no date had yet been fixed – my life was consumed by a round of doctors' and lawyers' appointments.

It would be a lie to say I felt no emotion over my divorce. I cried long into the night, but these were no longer tears of grief and sadness over the loss of my love for Bill. They were, invariably, tears of frustration over the waiting and the power he still held over me; sometimes they were tears of total exhaustion.

I was still not well, my weight hovering around six and a half stone. My legs, like sticks, sometimes seemed too spindly and fragile to carry me to the garden gate, never mind out into the real world again. However, my faith in God helped me through once again. I prayed every night for my health and, also, for Bill. I bore him no bitterness, not even over the acrimonious

295

divorce. I simply left that to the lawyers to sort out. For Bill, I felt only pity. I had finally come to realise that although he might be rich in wealth, he was very poor in spirit.

In the beginning I had thought we might actually get back together again. He had been the biggest influence and the biggest part of my life for eight years. As time went by and there was not a word from him, I knew, this time, it was irreversible.

I still missed him at times. That was inevitable. He had been much too big a part of my life for too long for there not to be a gaping hole. There were occasions when the pang of remembrance became too much to bear and I would reach for the phone, already hearing the reassuring tones of his voice, admonishing me, criticising me, yelling abuse at me. I knew this was ridiculous but I could not deny that, inside me, I heard a still, quiet voice saying, 'Bill is gone. Walk back to him.' From somewhere, thank God, I always found the strength to resist that overwhelming urge.

Time dragged on and on and on. There had recently been a High Court ruling that families with children were to receive priority in settlement hearings, so we simply had to wait for a date to come up. Not until 16 November 1992, would the case of Wyman *v*. Wyman finally come to court. Eighteen months, lost in a morass.

It was an interminable wait, a living nightmare hanging over all of us and it was not made any easier by the knowledge that there were private detectives on our tail.

Bill had put them on to us prior to the divorce, in a desperate bid to find some dirt he could sling at me and thereby countersue for divorce on the grounds of my adultery.

There would be snow in Hell before he found any such evidence. I had not even looked at a man, never mind dallied with one, in all our years together. The emotional scars Bill had inflicted on me meant that I was certainly not going to start now that I was nearly a divorcee.

The private dicks, as we nicknamed them – well, you have to try to laugh when there are men in dark overcoats shadowing your every move – were intrusive and annoying but there was nothing we could do about it.

Mum was still involved with Stephen, even though he was under constant threat from Bill who had warned him to stay away from us and never to go near our house. Their love was too strong then for that. In defiance of his father, Mum and Stephen used to meet secretly every week.

Being in daily contact with Bill and running his business affairs, Stephen kept us informed about what was going on. He said Bill was adamant that I would not get a penny out of him. It had become the most important issue in his life. This is why the detectives, had not been called off after the decree nisi. They were out to paint me in as bad a light as possible, so that Bill would not have to pay out any settlement.

However, for all his years' experience of me, Bill did not act very wisely here. He still had not learned the maxim by which I live my life, 'What goes around, comes around.' Keen to save himself money on a settlement, he now shot himself in the foot, because the detectives cost him an absolute fortune!

Bill's paranoia over money had breached the boundary of simple neurosis and somehow become warped into spite. He would use anything and anyone to try to get at me, even his only son. Bill had now begun to exploit Stephen ruthlessly.

When he wanted to know what was going on with us, he would send Stephen as his go-between. Unfortunately for Bill, Stephen loved Mum and actually cared about the rest of us. He would never double-cross us. Instead, he threw in his lot with us and told us precisely what Bill was up to.

Bill had dispatched Stephen to find out exactly how much money I wanted from him. I told Stephen to tell him I wanted nothing. I had a roof over my head, that was enough for me. However, I also had a backlog of bills, mostly medical, amounting to around £20,000. I told Stephen to inform Bill that if he would pick up the medical bills for the treatment that had saved my life – as he had always promised – then we could call it a day.

So it was agreed. Bill would pay the medical bills and we would be quits. Then he changed his mind. If he had to pay out for those, he decided, then he was going to refuse to pay the legal fees for the divorce and settlement, which came to a whopping £60,000.

In effect, he might have to part with £20,000 but, at the end of the day, he would be £40,000 up on the original deal.

He dug his heels in and insisted. He was foolish really,

because, in the end, he had to pay out far more than that, but that was Bill, through and through.

At one point, during these fraught negotiations over the legal fees between the two camps of lawyers, I almost gave in and called him. I thought we could resolve the issue far quicker and easier if we talked head to head rather than through the legal middle-men. But Stephen warned me not to. He said that Bill's final word on the subject was: 'I hope, when all this business is all over, I can pick up the phone and speak to Mandy at any time.'

I went wild when Stephen told me that. What a bloody cheek. He assumed I would be there for him, the sweet, forgiving child I used to be, at his beck and call as ever, even after he had put me and my family through all that pain. As if I could put it all behind me.

He was not far wrong. He knew me well enough to know that I would never bear grudges. Already my resolve to stay away from him had weakened considerably. However, that one comment changed everything. It made the decision for me. There was no way I was going to offer an olive branch when that was his attitude.

However, Bill still had one, last, vicious trick left up his sleeve. On my twenty-first birthday in July, he sent me a single orchid. One flawless orchid had always been a symbol of our love. It was our very special flower, the one that, above all, we sent to one another on extra-special occasions.

He knew how much that would hurt me. It was a sign and a symbol of all I had lost. Along with it, there was a card: 'Wishing you every happiness for your future. Bill.'

It was a spiteful, malicious and devious action, but his ploy misfired. I was not devastated. I was outraged. I thought it was despicable to sour my twenty-first birthday with a pretence of showing he still cared.

At times like that the pain and pressure simply got too much to cope with alone. I felt that the church was the only place I could turn to. I spent a lot of time there, silent, my head bowed in prayer. The Bible became a good and trusted friend.

The strain was beginning to show on Mum and Nicola, too, though, naturally, they tried to hide it from me. For my part, I did not want to burden them any more with worries about my health, so, for the first time, I went to see a counsellor. I had so many mental and emotional scars from those years with Bill, which I knew would never heal without help. The counselling helped but. I knew I still had a long way to go.

All these things, and more, combined to help me face the day when it finally dawned, on 16 November, the beginning of the very end of my relationship with Bill Wyman.

On the first day of the court case, I was ill with tension. I had slept erratically, tossing and turning and being torn apart by nightmares.

I rose at dawn, unrested and fearful, and steeled myself to get through the day, the week, however long this ordeal would take. At that point, I truly did not think I could go through with it. It was only the knowledge, the certainty, that, once it was all over I could start a new life, that kept me going.

Mum and Nic were by my side, as I walked into the courtroom and came face to face with Bill for the first time since I had left the Cromwell Hospital nearly two years before.

I had promised myself I would show no giveaway emotion when I first set eyes on him after all this time. Every nerve and muscle in my body was tense as I turned to look at him where he sat with his bank of legal advisors.

He looked smaller than before, slight and old in his smart Savile Row suit. I was surprised that I did not feel a pang of love for him. I felt nothing, but I was not prepared for his reaction. Coolly, and completely at ease, he beamed me a great big grin and gave me a cheery wave, like we had just bumped into each other and were off to have a picnic. I realised later that it was the easy grin of a man who believed he was victorious.

Stunned, I mumbled, 'Hi,' and sat down. I could feel his eyes on me constantly. We were only a few feet apart, separated by my solicitor next to me, then his assistant next to Bill.

I tried to blank Bill from my mind but it was impossible when, out of the corner of my eye, I could see him, so relaxed, very calm, constantly massaging his rheumatic hands.

Then it was my turn to go into the witness box. I was so apprehensive that I could barely speak. My voice was not much more than a whisper.

Bill went for me in typical, underhand fashion. He kept

turning to his lawyer and, pulling an uneasy face, saying, 'I can't hear what she's saying.'

His ploy worked. His lawyers reported this problem to the judge and the judge asked Bill to move forward. Firstly, it disrupted my testimony; secondly, I found it deeply unnerving. There I was in the witness box, frightened to death, with Bill sitting a few feet in front of me, staring at me.

I realised he was trying to intimidate me, so I called on all my reserves of strength and vowed, 'I am not letting him get away with that. I will be strong. I will not let him break me now.'

I put both feet firmly on the ground, stood tall and started to speak out very clearly. Hidden from sight beneath the witness stand, I cluched my Bible.

As I looked at Bill sitting there, sneering, confident that he had already won and that all this was a mere formality, I knew that all my previous fears were unfounded. I could not walk back down the road into his web of promises ever again. Bill's arrogant, patronising behaviour in court was the final nail in the coffin.

By this time, I had become very close to Pat van den Hauwe, the Spurs footballer. Although there was no romantic or sexual involvement between us, it was the strongest platonic relationship I had ever felt in my life.

Pat was there for me, every inch of the way, during the court case. While Mum, Nic and I were being bled dry at the hearing every day, Pat would sweep into our home and prepare a warm welcome for us.

When we arrived back, late in the evening, totally drained and tearful, we discovered that Pat had cleaned the house, made dinner and lit the fire. It was a real homecoming. I realised that, no matter what I had gone through with Bill, I was lucky to have a wonderful friend in a man like Pat.

If I had thought that day one of the court hearing would be the worst, I was sadly mistaken. The following days were even worse. I felt ashen, exhausted, drained of all emotion.

Each day I brought my own lunch to court with me because I could not eat any of the processed food on offer. I had recently started to follow a strict regime of a three-hourly starch intake to conquer the PMS that had crippled me for so long. In court, it was patently impossible to maintain that discipline. I began, literally, to wilt.

I had sworn I would not break down in court. I wouldn't give Bill the satisfaction of seeing how deeply all this had hurt me, but, when they got Mum on the stand, it was all too much to bear.

Bill's lawyers really went for her. They tore into her in such a cruel, savage way that it took my breath away.

Basically, they were saying that everything was Mum's fault. She had neglected me as a child. She was irresponsible and had not looked after me, so I had gone off the rails. She should have prevented me from getting involved with an older man. She had made me ill . . . it went on and on and on.

Poor Mum was not able to say anything in her own defence. All she could do was answer yes or no to these heavily loaded accusations. It was too much. I could feel the tears welling up and suddenly I lost it. I sobbed my heart out. Very patronisingly, Bill's lawyer made some sneering reference to me and the judge, who was quite kindly, really, put him in his place very smartly.

Then I saw Bill, sitting back, arms folded, with a look on his face that said it all. He was loving every second of the pain this was causing Mum and me. He was positively gloating.

I cried tears of anger then, mixed with tears for Mum. I wanted to see Bill get that sort of treatment, be torn limb from limb by accusations of under-age sex, manipulating a minor, perpetrating sexual, emotional and psychological abuse on a child, but, of course, he never would.

I felt that the odds were stacked against us.

My lawyer had warned me that they would go for Mum in a major way. He encouraged me not to stay to watch the blood-bath. He knew it would destroy me, but I had to do it. I wanted to face every second of it. I wanted to endure the pain, I wanted to see Bill's reaction. Yes, it was awful, watching the mother I loved so much being grilled like that, so unjustly, but it served a purpose. We all came through it a little bit tougher, and we knew that we had been right in everything we did. It just put everything into perspective.

I knew we had lost but, in a way, we had also won. I had to settle out of court for £580,000, but that included the house, expenses to my benefit, the legal fees and tax.

At the end of the day, I came out of the court, and out of the marriage, with £20,000. At a conservative estimate, Bill Wyman was reported in *The Sunday Times* to be worth £24 million.

Then the man who had taken my youth, my innocence, my virginity and my entire life from the age of thirteen to twenty-one approached me.

'I hope we can put all this behind us, Mandy,' he said and even he, master of disguises, could not conceal the smirk on his face.

I looked at him with total contempt. Then I pulled myself together, wiped away my tears, mustered my dignity and walked away.

As I went, leaving Bill, the past and the court behind, I knew, in fact, that I had won. I had been awarded the greatest gift of all – freedom.

CHAPTER TWENTY TWO

Happy

February 1991 had been a bad month for me. The final divorce loomed ahead and Bill and I had had no contact since I was discharged from the Cromwell three months earlier. It was as if, for Bill, I never existed. To be honest, I felt a bit that way about myself too.

My health was terrible. I constantly felt ill and my weight was still under seven stone. I was at my lowest ebb. I holed up at home with Mum and Nic in our house at Creighton Avenue and tried to shut out the world. I was absolutely despondent over the death of the marriage. I felt as if eight years of my life had gone down the drain.

From the age of thirteen onwards, my life had revolved around Bill. Now it had all ended in bitterness and acrimony. I had nothing to show for it except scars, both emotional and psychological. My entire teens had been thrown away. I was still only twenty but felt like my life was over.

I would lie in bed for hours on end, too depressed to get up, just wishing I could sleep for a very, very long time. Then, maybe, when I woke up, everything that had happened would be just a distant memory, a bad dream.

However, I had reckoned without Mum and Nic. They were still desperately worried about me and they were going to make sure I did not give up now, after all we had been through. Towards the end of February, they decided to throw a dinner party.

Mum knew she could not get me out of the house, so she would bring the world to me.

She invited a few friends, including my Uncle Harold, who is the world's biggest Tottenham Hotspur fan, and Harold had brought along Pat van den Hauwe.

This tall, tanned man walked in the door and I did a double take. He looked absolutely amazing, like some Greek

god in a beautifully cut brown suit. I was not sure that I fancied
him – it had been so long since I even looked at a man and,
after what I had been through with Bill, I wanted a new man
in my life like I needed a hole in the head, but he was drop-
dead gorgeous, there was no getting away from that.

Harold brought him forward to introduce us and suddenly
I was overcome with a wave of nausea. Pat was plastered in
Armani aftershave, you could have smelled him halfway down
the road.

Now, Armani is a beautiful smell but one of my most violent
allergy reactions is to strong perfume. As this gorgeous hunk
shyly held out his hand for me to shake, I nearly threw up!

I smiled 'Hi' at him, made some excuse and turned away
abruptly before rushing out into the garden for some fresh air.
The poor guy must have thought he had leprosy. I simply couldn't
bear to be near him but how do you tell someone you've just
met that their aftershave turns your stomach?

It was not the most auspicious of beginnings to a new relationship. True to form, there were to be quite a few stumbling blocks
along the way.

Pat and I had two serious problems – his crippling shyness
and my total reluctance to let myself fall for anyone again. We
skirted round each other warily all evening, but both of us knew
there was a powerful chemistry going on between us, although
neither of us wanted it.

Pat stood shyly in the hall for most of the evening, just
watching what was going on – and getting progressively more
and more drunk. He was throwing back gin and tonics like they
were going out of style. I did notice he was a heavy drinker but
I just thought, well, it is a party after all. Everyone else seemed
to be getting fairly loaded too.

At one stage, Uncle Harold, who had also had a few too
many, grabbed me and tried to do the lambada with me. He
was being fairly energetic, spinning me round and round, when
suddenly Pat stepped in and pulled Harold away from me.

'Don't do that,' he hissed at poor Harold, who looked a bit
taken aback at the intrusion from this hulking great footballer.
'You're being too rough. She's fragile,' he said.

Duly warned, Uncle Harold sheepishly calmed down and
moderated his lambada to a more sedate pace.

I was pretty taken aback myself at this chivalrous intervention, but my knight in shining armour had gone. He just faded into the background and made no further advance towards me all night. Yet, everywhere I turned, for the rest of the evening, I felt Pat's eyes on me, just watching.

There was something there all right but neither of us was prepared to do anything about it. It was just too much, too soon, for both of us.

After that night, it was to be several weeks before I came into contact with Pat van den Hauwe again. Once more, Uncle Harold played the unwitting Cupid.

After a big Spurs game, he turned up on our doorstep early one evening, with half the team in tow. There was Paul Walsh, who is married to my cousin Bev, Paul Gascoigne, Gary Mabbutt and, hanging back in the shadow of the others, Pat.

Casually dressed in a tracksuit this time, he was still as breathtakingly handsome as I remembered and twice as shy.

The others were in great spirits as they had just won a match. Soon the booze was flowing like water as they all celebrated.

Being the only person there who did not drink, I was well placed to find out just what Pat was all about as he began to unwind with his team-mates.

It was incredible to watch. This sweet, shy, tongue-tied bloke gradually transformed into another person entirely. As the level of gin in his personal bottle gradually dipped lower and lower, he went through more changes than Dr Jeykll did when turning into Mr Hyde.

First he loosened up and began smiling, then he laughed as Gazza began clowning around in his usual manner. Then, wonder of wonders, he got up and started dancing to the music that was playing out in the hall. Obviously this was a guy with big-time inhibitions who used booze to break down his barriers.

However, it did not stop there. There was more to come. I was to discover that, as Pat drank progressively more, his upbeat mood swings would, at some point, take a serious nosedive. He began to get a bit silly, trying to get me to come and sit down and talk to him.

I'm not a fan of booze and have never been a drinker myself, so there was little point in him trying to talk to me at that stage. I knew I couldn't have a conversation with a guy who was drunk – a few more glugs of gin and Pat would have been dribbling.

I went to bed and left the lads to it. Let them dribble together – none of them was going to dribble over me, that was for sure.

The next morning, when I got up, Mum revealed that the boys had sat up, joking and clowning around, until 3 am, then all crashed out on our living room floor.

God knows how they managed it, but they all succeeded in getting up at 7.30 am and headed off for a training session. There is no doubt about it: Spurs footballers need to have premier league fitness, espcially when it comes to working off premier league hangovers!

I had dismissed Pat as definitely 'not for me'.

Number one, I did not want another man in my life for a very, very long time. Number two, I did not want one who came with a whole load of first division problems, not least of which was an obvious battle with the bottle.

Then fate – or, more accurately, Uncle Harold – stepped in the way again.

The following week, Harold and some of the Spurs gang popped in to say hello again and, sure enough, Pat was among them. This time things were different. It was not a party situation, so Pat was stone cold sober.

For the first time since we had met, a month earlier, we actually sat down and chatted. I discovered that, contrary to the impression he gave when he was drinking, Pat was that rare creature, a genuinely lovely, honest, sincere fella.

He told me all about himself. How his Belgian dad and English mum had moved from Belgium to Britain when he was a young boy. How he had left home at sixteen and gone into digs – which he hated with a passion – as his footballing career had rocketed.

He told me about his marriage, which was very sad, as he and his wife had obviously come to the end of the road together, although they were both making a go of it for their little daughter Gemma's sake.

It was a situation I could relate to only too well. Mum and Dad had gone through the same farce when Nic and I were tiny.

I liked him very much, especially his sensitivity, which was a million miles from anything that Bill had ever manifested, but no way was I looking at him as a prospective boyfriend. A married man with a mountain of problems? No thanks.

However, Pat definitely had designs on me. He told me he had fallen for me when he saw me on TV with Bill. He thought I was so beautiful and fragile and vulnerable and did not know what I was doing with a man like Bill.

That, I was to discover, was typical of Pat. Unlike so many others, he had not – wrongly – assumed that I was with Bill for his fame and fortune.

Automatically he had thought I deserved better than that. He recognised that I needed protecting.

I knew we were getting on to dangerous ground here, so I made my excuses and went into the kitchen for a glass of water. Pat followed me in. Mum, Harold, Nic and a couple of the other guys were in there, all having a cuppa, when suddenly Pat came towards me, put his hands on my shoulders and pressed me gently to the wall. I looked up at him in sheer astonishment. Then he leaned down and, very gently, but very positively, planted his lips on mine in the most magical, lingering kiss, right in front of the astounded, assembled company.

That kiss took everyone's breath away – not least of all mine!

Then Pat just smiled and some sort of automatic reflex in both of us led us out into the garden where we sat, saying nothing.

There was nothing to say. Whatever we were going to get ourselves into would surely be a mess. Pat was stuck in a dead marriage; I was trying to extricate myself from the same.

When he left later, nothing had been said about meeting again. We never fixed up a date, we never swapped phone numbers. In our heart of hearts, however, we both knew that the inevitable would happen. We would meet up again, no matter what, but neither of us was going to press it.

I did a lot of thinking over the next few days. I had decided that we would be friends, no more. Pat needed a friend. In many ways, he was a very lost and lonely man.

And me? Well, my years with Bill had taught me many things, not least of which was that, because of my background and my genetic make up, I was on a quest to find a caring, responsible man. I had always craved a male soulmate, ever since I lost Dad, twenty years before. Now, here he was, my guardian angel, telling me that all he wanted to do was look after me.

I had bought that line once before, from Bill, and paid a heavy price for my naivety. So what was I doing, walking into the same trap again? No, as long as I kept it on a platonic basis, I knew Pat and I could enhance each other's lives.

For a long time, that was exactly what it was between Pat and me.

He shipped into our home with increasing regularity and practically became part of the fixtures and fittings. He was a friend – and no more than a friend – to us all. He adored Mum and Nic, who, in turn, thought the sun shone out of his shorts!

Pat was everything that Bill had never been, nor could ever be. He was a man who understood – and liked – women, not as sex objects, not as domestic slaves, simply as women.

The very next time he came to my house after that kiss, I realised just how special Pat was.

Mum, who recognised that having a friend like Pat would help me in my fight to get well again, asked him round to join us for supper.

As he arrived, however, Mum conveniently remembered that she had a pressing appointment that she simply could not break. At that point she was still looking after me full-time. I was too weak to be left on my own, so she insisted that, if she could not be with me herself, someone else had to 'babysit' me. How handy, here was Pat!

Cunning old Mum had well and truly set us up. As was often the case, however, Mum knew best. My mum is one of the most intuitive people I have ever met. She has a kind of antenna that can sense the good and bad in people. She is rarely wrong. She was certainly dead right about Bill and Keith Daley. Unlike Keith Daley – the only other boyfriend I had ever had in my life apart from Bill – she knew that Pat was good news.

So off she went, knowing I was in good hands. I was not so sure. I was terrified he would head for the booze cabinet and spend the night nursing a bottle, not me.

I was wrong. Pat sat down by the fire and began talking to a bronze statue that sits by the fireplace. He was cracking jokes at it and I thought, 'Blimey, he's completely off his trolley.'

It turned out that he was thinking exactly the same about me, that I must be a bit loopy if, at the age of twenty, I had to be left with a babysitter, so he had decided to keep me amused with this little comedy routine.

There we were, both thinking each other was barking mad, when I had a brainwave.

Pat really was incredibly handsome – perfect, even features and the most astonishingly beautiful eyes. Ever intrigued by make-up, I had a sudden urge to see those eyes with mascara and liner on them. Mischieviously I said, 'Have you ever thought of having a facial, Pat?' Not surprisingly, he had not. I said, 'Well, now's your chance...'

Largely to humour this mad woman whom he had been left to babysit, Pat played right into my hands.

I don't know what Mum expected to find when she got back three hours later, after leaving the two of us alone for the first time, but it was certainly not the sight that greeted her.

There, in all his previously unseen glory, sat Pat van den Hauwe, alias 'Psycho', Spurs' brutal and aggressive defender, much loved on the terraces as a psychopath with the ball at his feet, father of one, with probably more male hormones than the rest of the team put together – in full make-up.

The now gorgeous, pouting Pat sported eyeshadow, eyebrow pencil, three coats of Ultralash mascara and a rather fetching shade of rust eyeshadow that really brought those great big brown eyes into their own.

Bronze highlighter gleamed on delicate cheekbones that, up until then, had never sported more than a pulsating purple bruise acquired from rebuffing a glancing blow.

Peach foundation blended in beautifully with his own tanned skintones and the whole lot was offset, to great effect, by glimmering coral lipstick.

I had not stopped there, though. His expensively cut brown hair had been rollered, tousled and teased into a rather sexy, swept-up style, a bit reminiscent of the blonde in Bananarama, even if I say so myself.

To complete the transformation, I had painted his fingernails and toenails with a complementary polish in Rich Russet.

Mum's mouth literally fell open when she came through the door and saw Pat.

Virtually speechless, she could only mutter, 'Mandy, what have you done *now*?'

I just fell apart with laughter. I was creased up at the sight of Pat, the long-suffering and unwitting artist's model, and at Mum's reaction.

'Just having a bit of fun, Mum,' I chortled, while Pat just sat there, an ever-increasing redness creeping through the inch-thick make-up on his cheeks.

My view was that if Pat had not really wanted me to make him up, he would have put his foot down. Humouring me was one thing – secretly, I reckon he rather enjoyed the whole experience.

He has occasionally asked me to repeat the process – but, I hasten to add, for purely party purposes. We have gone to the odd dressing-up do where Pat has been required to squeeze himself into a frock and go in drag. He's become quite an expert on what does and does not suit him in the way of frocks and make-up.

It was never going to be a conventional boyfriend-girlfriend relationship!

However, what Pat has always done for me, since day one, is look after me. He was as good as his promise. He is the older man I could only ever dream of. At thirty-three, he is ten years older than me, although you would never think it. With his help, and the help of the first doctor I have ever found who could actually diagnose and understand my health problems – Dr Katarina Dalton – my health has gone from strength to strength.

I am in no doubt now that the psychological torture that Bill put me through contributed hugely to my illness and helped to reduce me to a five-stone skeleton. I believe too, that all those troubles began when he put me on the pill at fifteen.

That being the case, when the divorce and settlement went through I was at my most vulnerable ever. Had I not had Pat, my family and Dr Dalton the world's leading PMS expert, I believe that the stress, combined with my illness, could have brought me to a point of no return.

Thank God, however, Pat held my hand every step of the way through the divorce proceedings and the following agonis-ing settlement situation. It was a desperately unnerving experi-ence – all the more so because Pat was going through exactly the same legal processes at the same time.

But Pat handled everything so differently to Bill. When his wife asked for their massive family home, he simply handed it over to her. When she asked for £1,200 a week in maintenance, he said fine. Whereas Bill spent hundreds of thousands fighting just to prevent me getting anything. That's okay, that's just Bill. I have come to accept that.

To get back a £300 video that he gave me, he actually engaged in a legal battle that cost him many, many times its actual value in legal fees.

Every nasty, petty thing that Bill did to me in his courtroom battle had a result. They reinforced my horror about the kind of man he was, and showed me, by contrast, how very, very special Pat was.

Pat was so supportive that I do not know how I could have got through it without him. He was always there for me, always ready to put an arm round my shoulders and offer his own shoulder to cry on – even though he had so many troubles himself. He never accused me of anything, he never pried, he never condemned me. He simply accepted that I had had many bad, bad years with Bill.

Pat's attitude was 'walk away from it'. He did not want to ask me anything about the past. He wanted me to be able to put it all behind me and forget so he never dug up any old skeletons. Unlike Bill, who was the ultimate sceptic, with all the sympathy and bedside manner of a housebrick, Pat never questioned me about my health. He never once doubted that my physical problems were real and that my psychological problems were genuine too.

They continued to blight my life. Bill left me unable to give myself to any man. He had ruined my trust in men. Even though Pat was gradually building that up again, I could not sleep with him. Bill's sexual abuse had left me with a fear and horror of sex.

It was to be a very long time before Pat and I could sleep together in the same bed and even longer before I had built up enough confidence to make our relationship physical. For many months after we first got together as a couple, Pat was relegated to the spare room.

I was still sleeping in a double bed with my mum, a legacy from the black months in hospital when I lay beside her, a bag of bones weighing five stone, thinking I would die in the night.

Pat accepted this totally. Often, late at night, he would come into my bedroom where I was lying next to Mum, just reading, and pass an hour chatting to the pair of us.

He saw nothing unnatural in the fact that I was still so insecure that I needed to sleep next to my mum. He had always recognised that frailty in me. Sometimes we would all fall asleep – me and Mum in bed, Pat on the floor. I would wake up and find my arm dangling off the bed and, at the end of it, a snoring Pat's big strong hand in mine.

He was just so unbelievably sweet and patient, I knew I was gradually falling in love with him.

To his eternal credit, he never tried to blackmail me into sleeping with him. Unlike Bill, he was prepared to wait until I was ready. Naturally, this was very frustrating for him, but, when the pressure got too much, unlike Bill, he did not take it out on me and force me into acts that turned my stomach.

Pat had his own solution. He took it out on himself by going on a bender.

He would just disappear and not come home after training. Then, a few hours later, I would get a phone call from one of his mates – sometimes as far away as Liverpool.

Pat was ashamed of his occasional drinking binges and wanted to get as far away as possible. Once the drink got hold of him, he would plunge deeper and deeper into depression – and then he needed me there.

Sometimes he would call himself, sobbing about how he loved me, adored me and that I was the only woman he ever wanted in his life. They were all the things he found it so hard to say when he was sober.

Sometimes he would get nasty and, when I refused to let him come home in that condition, he would tell me to go back to my dirty old man – meaning Bill.

These were deeply hurtful phonecalls, but it was the drink talking, not Pat. Next day, Pat would be back home, totally contrite, bearing flowers and begging me to forgive him.

I knew we could not go on if he carried on drinking – it brought out a terrible side to him that was buried very deeply. He had to deal with that and he could only do it sober.

I gave him an ultimatum. He had helped me throughout my recovery, now Mum, Nic and I would help him in his battle with the booze. He agreed, but it was a bumpy ride. He went on the wagon that very day but slipped off a couple of times over the months ahead. On one spectacular occasion, he disappeared for two days. No one knew where he had gone, not the club, no one. Then I had a phone call in the early hours of the morning.

A strong Liverpudlian accent, that I could barely decipher, came ringing out of the other end of the phone.

'Mandy,' this peculiar voice said, 'Mandy, it's Barry.'

I struggled to get my sleepy brain into gear. I knew no one called Barry. Certainly no one with a Liverpool accent that you could have cut glass on.

The phantom caller continued, 'Mandy, it's *Barry!*'

I was just about to slam the phone down, thinking it was a crank when he said, 'Mandy, it's Barry and I've got Pat here.'

The penny dropped. Pat, even though legless, had somehow got himself to his old mates in Liverpool and, sloshed and maudlin, was probably bemoaning the loss of his best girl.

Barry was most perplexed. He had never seen Pat in that state. Somehow, he had managed to get my number from him before he collapsed in a stupor. Now he was looking to me to drive three hundred miles to pick up my plastered beloved.

I'm afraid I told Barry in no uncertain terms what he could do with Pat. I think it involved a large sack, a few bricks and the Mersey.

Needless to say, Pat was back next day, but he heralded his homecoming in the most spectacular way. I had popped out at lunchtime to get some food for my dogs, Minnie and Moochie. When I got back, twenty minutes later, I was met by a sight I shall never forget.

I opened my bedroom door to hang up my coat and the scent of a tropical garden filled the air. The entire room was chock-a-block with flowers. The dressing table, the bed, the ensuite bathroom were overflowing with blooms of every size, colour and description.

Every square inch of floor space was covered. I could not walk across the carpet and the bath was full to the brim with bouquets. What would you do with a man like that?

Sheepish and vowing never to stray again, Pat came home.

He was – and remains – an incurable romantic. I am now well used to spontaneous love letters being left all over the house. His favourite is to write on the dressing table mirror or on the bedsheets and pillows.

Sometimes he uses indelible felt-tip pens for his missives of love. I should be cross but, every time I change the beds, I see the faint trace of his scrawled messages and can't help but smile at the reminder of his love.

Pat is a very special man. After all we have been through and shared together, I just feel so lucky to have found someone so extraordinarily sensitive. He recognised that what we had between us was special long before I could believe my luck. He asked me to marry him even while I was going through my divorce.

I thought he was simply being supportive and that it was far too soon for either of us to know what we really wanted. I was so fearful of a rebound romance that I backed off completely and kept him at arm's length.

However, Pat found a way round that. He wanted to show his commitment to me, even if I was having none of it. As soon as his own divorce was through – unbeknown to me or anyone else – he arranged to have a ring made for me as a token of his love.

He pinched one of my other rings to guage my finger size and had it sent to a friend of his who is a jewellery designer. Together, they made up an exquisite ring of diamonds and gold.

I knew nothing of what was going on. Then, one evening, after my own divorce was through, Pat took me out for a mystery drive in the car. He said simply that he had bought me a present and now we were going to collect it.

We arrived at his friend's studio in east London and Pat got out of the car and went indoors alone. When he came out, he was like a little boy. He was so excited that he was grinning from ear to ear. Without a word, he drove off but by now I was curious. I demanded to know what he was up to. He pulled up at a garage and took a little package out of his pocket. He handed it to me and, when I opened it, I practically had to turn my eyes away from the gleaming band of jewels. It was the most blindingly, breathtaking ring I had ever seen.

I would have smothered him with kisses but, typically, Pat

had done a runner. Embarrassed by the thought of what he had done, and fearful of my reaction, he had hopped out of the car and was on the garage forecourt, pretending to fill the car with petrol. That was Pat all over. Whatever he did, he did out of genuine feelings, not out of ulterior motives. I think at that moment I knew I would never love anyone more in my life.

However, I could still not accept his proposal. Yes, we would become engaged – but marriage? Marriage was too deep a wound yet. We had committed ourselves to each other, that was enough for the moment.

It was not until several months later, when the settlement was finally over, that I truly began to feel I could put Bill behind me.

Pat and I had a blissful Christmas together – our first – without the malevolent shadow of Christmas Past looming over us. We saw in the New Year together and toasted each other in boring old mineral water, knowing that our future really was beginning to look brighter and better than we had ever dreamed.

In February, when, out of the blue Pat suggested that we finally, formally announce our engagement and make it official, I was only too happy to say yes. After years of saying yes to Bill, against my better judgement, against my will and sometimes even against nature, this time, suddenly, it all felt right.

We became engaged on 14 February, Valentine's Day, and Pat sent me a hundred long-stemmed red roses, just in case I'd got cold feet again! No chance. We planned our perfect summer wedding in June, leaving a decent gap between Bill's April wedding to Suzanne Accosta, and our own.

I wish Bill all the best in his third marriage. I bear no bitterness. I think I am the luckiest girl in the world to have survived my years with him and come out of it alive and well and with a man I really truly love and, best of all, who loves me.

Pat and I plan to have a baby as soon as possible. Contrary to some spurious reports in the *Daily Mirror*, there is absolutely no problem with my reproductive system. I can – and hopefully will – have a baby when I choose, but, for now, I am completely happy practising for the event with the man I love.

Let's face it, I have a decade of lost time to make up for.